DAVID LIVINGSTONE

from the portrait by T. and R. Annan and Sons, Glasgow

Some Letters from
LIVINGSTONE
1840—1872

Edited by
DAVID CHAMBERLIN

With an Introduction by
R. COUPLAND
*Beit Professor of Colonial History
in the University of Oxford*

NEGRO UNIVERSITIES PRESS
NEW YORK

OXFORD UNIVERSITY PRESS
AMEN HOUSE, E.C. 4
London Edinburgh Glasgow New York
Toronto Melbourne Capetown Bombay
Calcutta Madras
HUMPHREY MILFORD
PUBLISHER TO THE UNIVERSITY

Originally published in 1940
by Oxford University Press, London

Reprinted 1969 by
Negro Universities Press
A DIVISION OF GREENWOOD PUBLISHING CORP.
NEW YORK

SBN 8371-2057-8

PRINTED IN UNITED STATES OF AMERICA

PREFACE

'I can only remember him as always writing letters.'

THAT is the recollection of Livingstone's youngest daughter, Anna Mary, who was five years old when her father came to Britain for the last time. They had not met before and were soon to be separated. But in that brief glimpse of her father the child saw him absorbed in a characteristic work which to him was hardly less important than his long toils among the people of Africa.

Livingstone's purpose, or that part of it expressed in his words, 'I beg to draw your attention to Africa', was fulfilled in several ways. His achievements and death not only drew attention, they compelled it, and called forth a new kind of interest in the people of Africa. But his letters had a needed part to play and they did great service to his purpose.

Hundreds of them still exist. Government departments, the Public Record Office, learned societies, and the children of his personal friends hold many of them; the Scottish National Memorial at Blantyre and the Rhodes-Livingstone Institute in Northern Rhodesia have their cherished collections which have been drawn upon for this volume.

The longest series, however, is in the hands of the London Missionary Society, of which Society Livingstone was an agent during the first half of his life in Africa. Those letters occupy most of this book. Letters which come from other holders make new and important contributions to our understanding of the writer and his work. The ownership is duly acknowledged where such letters appear, and the courtesy which permits their inclusion is now warmly and gratefully acknowledged.

The editing of the letters has been almost limited to the removal of repetitions and the addition of a few explanatory notes. Livingstone, when writing to his personal friends, frequently described the same events to several correspondents and did it in language which was so nearly common to them

Preface

all as to suggest that he transcribed them from his journals. In some of the letters which follow there are manifest gaps which may usually be attributed to the omission of such redundant material.

Many letters and dispatches from Livingstone, written in his later years in Africa, appear in H. M. Stanley's book, *How I found Livingstone*, and in the *Parliamentary Paper* (C. 598) 1872, while the two volumes of the *Last Journals* edited by Horace Waller continue the revealing narrative to the last day on that memorable Road of Suffering from which he had so often refused to turn back.

The spelling is often erratic, especially in the cases of names of persons and places, but all such deviations are given (without '*sic*') as they appear in the original documents.

It will be noticed that before September 27, 1855, Livingstone used the termination 'ton' to his signature, though he wrote 'Mrs. Livingstone' in his letter of March 17, 1852. He probably thought the matter of little importance, as a change of spelling had sufficient warrant in custom.

Mrs. Livingstone was the first of the family to use the fuller spelling in a signature. It occurs in a letter written from Hamilton, where Neil Livingstone, the father, lived. It is dated November 18, 1852. Neil himself added the 'e' to his signature, and David followed his example for the first time in a letter written from Africa on October 12, 1855. He lapsed into 'ton' once or twice afterwards, evidently from habit rather than intention.

The reason for the change must be a matter for conjecture. The name—in whatever variation—occurs prominently in Scottish history for at least eight hundred years, as may be seen in *The Livingstons of Callandar*, by E. B. Livingston (1920). In the long genealogy there printed will be found eminent statesmen, soldiers, and governors bearing the name, not only in Britain, but in France, Holland, and America. There was a Robert Livingston, of New York, on the Committee which drafted the Declaration of Independence, and a Philip Living-

Preface

ston among those who signed it in 1776. In Westminster Abbey there is a monument to Thomas Livingston, Viscount Teviot (d. 1711), Commander-in-Chief of the Army in Scotland. It is about thirty yards north-east of the world-famous slab on the floor over the grave of David Livingstone, whose desire was to be known as one of a humble Highland family and a son of poor and honest parents.

The most famous bearer of the name would have made no claim to be related to any of these. Tradition holds that his ancestors in the Western Highlands were the Mac-an-Leighs (Sons of the Physician) whose name was Anglicized into Livingstone.

D. C.

CONTENTS

INTRODUCTION	xi
LIST OF LETTERS	xxi
LIST OF ILLUSTRATIONS	xxiii
A BIOGRAPHY IN DATES	xxv
ABBREVIATIONS IN FOOTNOTES	xxvi
BOOKS ON LIVINGSTONE AND THE ARAB SLAVE-TRADE	xxvii
LETTERS 1–68	1–274
INDEX	275

INTRODUCTION

From the day he landed at Capetown in the early spring of 1841 to the May morning in 1873 when he died near Lake Bangweolo David Livingstone's life was given to Africa in body as well as in spirit. He only came home twice—each time only for some twelve or fifteen months. The rest of those thirty-two years he spent in Africa. But whereas all other great missionaries have been identified more or less with one place or one people—the place they made their 'station' for most of their working lives, the people they learned to know and understand by long and patient intercourse—it might almost be said of Livingstone that his field was not a country, but a continent. At the outset, it is true, in the days of his apprenticeship, he was working in one country, Bechuanaland, but he made three successive moves from his first head-quarters, each of them northwards towards the unknown heart of Africa; and presently he broke the bounds of Bechuanaland. In 1851 he was on the upper Zambesi, in 1854 on the coast of Angola, in 1856 on the coast of Mozambique, in 1859 and 1861 on Lake Nyasa, in 1862 on the Rovuma, in 1866 at Lake Nyasa again, at intervals between 1867 and 1872 at Lake Tanganyika, and in 1871 on the upper Congo. On most of those long and exhausting journeys he was without a companion of his own race and beyond the reach of communications or instructions from home. Enveloped in African darkness, he was often quite lost to the outer world for long periods of time. More than once he was believed to be dead.

All that movement, so continuous and so far afield, is enough in itself to distinguish Livingstone from a Martyn or a Selwyn, a Moffat or a Mackenzie. After 1853, in fact, Livingstone ceased to be a missionary in the ordinary meaning of the word. He still had a mission. His ultimate aim was still the spread of Christianity. But the immediate task to which he felt himself called was not so much to preach and teach his faith as to remove the obstacles which made preaching and teaching in

Introduction

Central Africa impossible or ineffective. And so from a propagandist he grew into an explorer and from an explorer into a statesman in the sense that he inspired the policy of Britain on the most vital issue affecting the fate of Africa in his day. Had he lived and died as a sedentary missionary of the normal type, he would still, it is safe to say, have made a name. As it was, he made a name as famous all over the world as that of any of his great contemporaries, a name that will be remembered in Africa when those other names are forgotten.

The letters printed in this volume belong to the first half of Livingstone's African career, and besides the glimpses they give, as only letters or diaries can, of his character and personality—the burning faith, the humility which has nothing to do with diffidence, the common sense, the Scottish humour, the inexhaustible patience, the courage that 'did not know what fear was'—they have a peculiar interest and value in that they reveal the thoughts and describe the experiences which brought about that development from a missionary into something more than a missionary and so determined the course of the rest of his life.

The first task, as it happened, which the London Missionary Society set him was not a sedentary task. He was sent to Robert Moffat's station at Kuruman with instructions to prospect for a new station farther north. 'I shall proceed to the northward', he writes in one of his earliest letters (No. 8), 'and live excluded from all European society'; and before long he was journeying through the tribes that lived along the fringes of the Kalahari desert (No. 11). The result was the foundation of Mabotsa, and Livingstone records the 'inexpressible delight' with which he hailed the Directors' decision 'that we go forward to the dark Interior' (No. 14). But Mabotsa was little more than a halting-place. Before long he had moved farther north to Chonuane (No. 25), and not long after farther north again to Kolobeng (No. 28). From there he writes (No. 30): 'All my desires tend forwards to the North. . . . We have a world before us here. We have no missionary beyond this—all is dark. . . .

Introduction

They live without God and die without hope.' A year after that was written Livingstone started on his first important journey of exploration—the crossing of the Kalahari and the discovery of Lake Ngami—but, apart from its geographical importance, it was a disappointing journey. A land of drought and fever was no place for the missionary outpost Livingstone was dreaming of. But he was not easily discouraged. 'A more salubrious climate must exist farther up to the North', he writes (Blaikie's *Life*, 87–8), and since the route from the Cape is so long and difficult, 'we must have a passage to the sea on either the eastern or western coast'. There first appears the idea of the great adventure which at one stroke was to bring the obscure young Scot, unknown beyond the circle of his family and friends and colleagues, to the front of the public stage throughout the western world; and he had not long to wait before the idea was realized. In 1851 he pushed on beyond Lake Ngami to the River Chobe, a branch of the upper Zambesi (Nos. 37–8); and two years later, having sent his wife and children home, he started from Linyanti, with only twenty-seven Makololo porters, to make his way through utterly unknown country to the Atlantic. How he reached S. Paolo de Loanda after six months of toil and danger and suffering and incredible endurance, how he made his way back to Linyanti in the course of 1855 with his faithful little party of porters intact, how he then pursued the eastward course of the Zambesi till in May, 1856, he reached the Indian Ocean at Quilimane—all that is a familiar story and need not be repeated here. But it is worth while, perhaps, to point out what an extraordinary feat it was. Few of those who acclaimed him as the hero of the day can have realized how truly heroic his crossing of Africa from sea to sea had been. Other great explorers were to emulate his example, but most of them ventured into the unknown with the backing of scientific societies or newspapers or governments, with careful preparation and costly equipment, with caravans of porters one hundred or even two hundred strong, and an adequate stock of food and beads and wire to buy their way through greedy or hostile tribes.

Introduction

But nobody financed Livingstone's enterprise. He did it 'on his own'. The African chief at Linyanti, whom he had made his friend, provided him with a handful of porters and an ox or so for riding. His store of 'trade goods' was pitifully inadequate. And he himself was alone with his Africans, often utterly exhausted, sometimes desperately ill. Consider the distance covered and the time spent under these conditions, and there is clearly no comparison, either in the difficulties and dangers of the enterprise or in the courage and endurance needed to surmount them, between this journey of Livingstone's and any, say, of Stanley's journeys.

Livingstone's decision to devote himself to the task of opening up a highway into the heart of Africa had involved an immense personal sacrifice; and the most poignant passages in this volume are those which deplore and justify the inevitable breakdown of his family life. In 1843 he had married Mary Moffat, and by 1852, when he started north for Linyanti and the crossing of Africa, she had borne him five children, three sons and two daughters. One of them had died when she was six years old. Another had been very near death on the expedition to Lake Ngami. The mother, too, had been dangerously ill. Quite obviously Livingstone could not take his wife, still less his children, with him on this difficult and dangerous adventure. He must either abandon his great design and settle down to the relatively safe life of a sedentary missionary, or part with them and send them home. What it cost him to make the choice his letters show. 'Nothing but a strong conviction that the step will tend to the glory of Christ would make me orphanize my children. Even now my bowels yearn over them —they will forget me.' (No. 39.) In the spring of 1852 Mary Livingstone and the four children sailed from the Cape for England. They did not see husband and father again till he came home from Quilimane at the end of 1856. A hint at what that long separation meant to him may be gleaned from a letter from Linyanti (No. 57) half-way on his return march across

Introduction

the continent. He had just received a packet of letters which had been waiting for him for a year. 'Such a rush of thoughts and trembling sensations when I opened letters from my family you may imagine if you can, taking it into consideration that I have been without information for nearly three years. Thank God, I had no reason to sorrow!' Did he realize, then, one wonders, that he was never to live a family life again for any length of time? In fact he was never to be so long with his wife and children as he had been with them at Kolobeng. He was only at home for fourteen months in 1856-8, and for twelve months in 1864-5. In 1862, in the course of the long and dreary Zambesi expedition, it seemed possible to break the rule of separation. Mary Livingstone came out to share her husband's life. Within three months she was dead.

An explorer's life meant more for Livingstone than the break-up of the family. For two of his three great periods of African travel he had no white companion. He was quite alone in that sense on his march to the Atlantic and back to the Indian Ocean, and, except for a few months after Stanley had 'found' him, quite alone throughout the seven years of his last long wanderings. But that did not affect him like the parting from wife and children. He was by nature a solitary man. Outside his home—if it can be said he ever had a home—he was usually happiest when he was alone. 'I am never low-spirited', he writes from far-away Linyanti (No. 52). 'It might be different', he adds, 'if I had a crusty companion.' And he, to be frank, could be crusty too. He was never quite as much at ease with white men as he was with black. Self-confident and self-reliant, he could not easily co-operate with others, he could not work smoothly in harness. Unquestionably he was happier on the first of his major expeditions and even on the third, despite his failing health and the growing sense of frustration, than on the second, the Zambesi expedition, on which, alone of the three, he had companions of his own race.

The course of Livingstone's career was determined, it has

Introduction

been said, by certain ideas and experiences in this first period of his life in Africa. The ideas have been mentioned—that the Gospel should be carried into the interior of Africa, that for that purpose a mission station should be founded in the relatively high and healthy country he expected to find somewhere north of Bechuanaland, and that a route from the sea to such a station should be explored and mapped which would be shorter, easier, and quicker than the wearisome 'trek' from the Cape. But what were the experiences that confirmed and extended those ideas? Why did he come to think that the 'opening-up' of Central Africa was not merely an aid to missionary enterprise but its necessary prelude? Why did he feel that missionaries could do little in the dark interior by themselves, that Commerce must play its part besides Christianity in the task of civilization?

The answer to those questions first appears in a letter written from the River Zonga in 1851 (No. 37). He had discovered that the Slave-Trade, the old-established curse of West Africa, had recently penetrated to the neighbourhood of the Upper Zambesi. Not only a marauding native tribe but some Portuguese (or half-Portuguese, one suspects) had been bartering guns and cloth for young slaves. If Portuguese came so far inland in pursuit of this nefarious traffic, why, Livingstone asked, should not British traders take the same road and do more lawful business? He was convinced that it would pay. There was a great demand everywhere for cloth and other European goods and a great supply of ivory. 'I feel assured if our merchants could establish a legitimate commerce on the Zambesi, they would soon drive the slave dealer from the market.' (No. 38.) On his next journey northwards he saw and heard more of the Trade. It 'seems pushed into the very centre of the continent from both sides', he noted in his diary in 1853 (Blaikie, 122); and on his way to the Atlantic and back he sometimes passed those gangs of chained slaves on the march which were to become so terribly familiar to him later on.

It is not too much to say that Livingstone's first encounter

Introduction

with the Slave-Trade was a landmark in African history. For centuries past Europe and Asia had been committing this monstrous crime against their neighbour-continent. Europeans, mainly in the West, had been raping Africans away from their homes into slavery oversea at the rate of many thousands a year. Arabs in the East had been doing the same thing on a smaller scale for a much longer time. When Livingstone pushed his way into the centre of Southern Africa he found, as he said, the two currents of depredation meeting. Despite the legal abolition of the European Slave-Trade and the ceaseless efforts of the British Navy to enforce the law, the business of smuggling slaves across the Atlantic was still at its height, though soon to decline and in fifteen years or so to peter out. But, just at this time, as it happened, the Arab Slave-Trade from the East, based on Zanzibar, had begun to expand. Within a few years it had not only reached the Great Lakes, but swept beyond them into what are now Northern Rhodesia and the Belgian Congo. It seemed, indeed, that if nothing were done to stop it, the Arab Trade would follow up the ebbing European Trade almost to the Atlantic coast. As it was, great areas of Mid-East Africa were fast being devastated and to some extent depopulated.

The suppression of the Slave-Trade, in East Africa as in West, was the almost single-handed achievement of the British people. Thereby they made what amends they could for having previously taken the lion's share in the European part of the Trade. For just as the Slave-Trade was the greatest injury, its destruction was the greatest service ever done to the African peoples. And it was the British people, not a party or a group, that did it. The anti-Slavery movement was in the full sense of the words a national crusade. But crusades must have their leaders; and if Wilberforce did more than anyone else to awaken the conscience of his countrymen and spur it on to the abolition of the Slave-Trade in the West, it was Livingstone who did most to revive, with regard to the Trade in the East, the humanitarian ardour which Wilberforce and his fellow

Introduction

'Saints' had inspired half a century before. On each of his subsequent journeys the conviction that had come upon him in those earlier days on the Zambesi was strengthened by what he saw; and the vast and varied picture he painted in his letters and journals of the new world he had discovered was steadily overspread and darkened by the shadow of the Slave-Trade, till at last all his desires, all his appeals for helpless Africa were concentrated in a single prayer. 'All I can say in my solitude is, may Heaven's rich blessing come down on any one—American, English, Turk—who will help to heal this open sore of the world.'

That far-away call from the wilderness of Central Africa was heard. In those last years of Livingstone's life the descriptions he gave of the horrors of the Slave-Trade 'really took hold', as Sir Bartle Frere put it, 'upon the mind of the people of this country'. The result was a new spur to the efforts which British Governments had been making for a generation past to persuade the Arab Sultan of Zanzibar, the commercial centre on which the whole of the eastern Slave-Trade converged, to prohibit his subjects from engaging in the Trade and to close the great slave-market at his capital. Successive Sultans had agreed under diplomatic pressure to restrict the scope of the Trade; but since it was so profitable to their subjects and to their own revenues, they had persistently refused to contemplate its complete suppression. Now, however, something more than diplomatic pressure was employed. In 1873 Sir John Kirk, Livingstone's old companion on the Zambesi and now British consul and political agent at Zanzibar, whose practical work on the spot was the essential complement of Livingstone's propaganda, was instructed to inform Sultan Barghash that if the sea-borne Slave-Trade were not prohibited and all the slave-markets closed, Zanzibar would be subjected to a naval blockade. The threat of force sufficed. On June 8, about a month after Livingstone's lonely death in the interior, a proclamation was posted declaring the transport of slaves by sea illegal and the markets closed. That was much, but not quite enough. Desperate

Introduction

slave-hunters drove their gangs overland along the coast to the Somali ports in the north whence they could be smuggled over to Arabia. In 1878, therefore, at Kirk's suggestion, Barghash signed another proclamation forbidding the passage of slave-caravans by land. Then at last the monster that for so many centuries had been feeding on the vitals of East Africa could be destroyed. Spasmodic smuggling continued for some years, but at the close of the century the Trade was dead.

Several influences and personalities combined to bring about that great achievement of British humanitarianism; but the dominant factor was the impression made on British public opinion by Livingstone's character and the long, exciting, tragic adventure of his African life—the adventure which began when he wrote so eagerly from Bechuanaland that he was going North.

R. COUPLAND

LIST OF LETTERS

1.	*To the* REV. HENRY DICKSON	*8 May 1840*	5
2.	*To the* REV. GEORGE DRUMMOND	*25 July 1840*	7
3.	*To* T. L. PRENTICE	*27 Jan. 1841*	10
4.	*To* MISS CATHRINE RIDLEY	*24 Feb. 1841*	12
5.	*To* T. L. PRENTICE	*5 Mar. 1841*	16
6.	*To the* REV. GEORGE DRUMMOND	*10 Mar. 1841*	19
7.	*To* THOMAS PRENTICE	*3 Aug. 1841*	22
8.	*To* HENRY DRUMMOND	*4 Aug. 1841*	24
9.	*To* MRS. JOHN PHILIP	*5 Aug. 1841*	27
10.	*To* DR. J. RISDON BENNETT	*22 Dec. 1841*	28
11.	*To the* REV. J. J. FREEMAN	*3 July 1842*	32
12.	*To the* REV. J. J. FREEMAN	*18 July 1842*	37
13.	*To the* REV. GEORGE DRUMMOND	*20 June 1843*	40
14.	*To the* REV. DR. TIDMAN	*24 June 1843*	42
15.	*To* DR. J. RISDON BENNETT	*30 June 1843*	49
16.	*To* HENRY DRUMMOND	*29 July 1843*	59
17.	*To* THOMAS L. PRENTICE	*9 Oct. 1843*	62
18.	*To the* REV. DR. TIDMAN	*30 Oct. 1843*	64
19.	*To the* REV. DR. TIDMAN	*9 June 1844*	68
20.	*To the* REV. GEORGE DRUMMOND	*21 Nov. 1844*	74
21.	*To the* REV. DR. TIDMAN	*2 Dec. 1844*	76
22.	*To the* REV. DR. TIDMAN	*23 Mar. 1845*	78
23.	*To* DR. J. RISDON BENNETT	*26 Dec. 1845*	83
24.	*To the* REV. DR. TIDMAN	*10 Apr. 1846*	87
25.	*To* CHARLES WHISH	*9 Oct. 1846*	90
26.	*To* CHARLES LIVINGSTON	*16 Mar. 1847*	94
27.	*To the* REV. DR. TIDMAN	*17 Mar. 1847*	96
28.	*To* ROBERT MOFFAT JNR.	*13 Aug. 1847*	110
29.	*To the* REV. D. G. WATT	*13 Feb. 1848*	115
30.	*To* HENRY DRUMMOND	*19 June 1848*	118
31.	*To the* REV. DR. TIDMAN	*1 Nov. 1848*	123
32.	*To* CHARLES LIVINGSTON	*16 May 1849*	129
33.	*To the* REV. J. J. FREEMAN	*24 Aug. 1850*	133
34.	*To the* REV. WILLIAM THOMPSON	*27 Aug. 1850*	139
35.	*To* BENJAMIN PYNE	*4 Dec. 1850*	141
36.	*To the* REV. DR. TIDMAN	*30 Apr. 1851*	144

List of Letters

37.	*To the* REV. DR. TIDMAN	*1 Oct. 1851*	148
38.	*To the* REV. DR. TIDMAN	*17 Oct. 1851*	153
39.	*To the* REV. DR. TIDMAN	*17 Mar. 1852*	164
40.	*To the* REV. DR. TIDMAN	*26 Apr. 1852*	168
41.	*To the* REV. WILLIAM THOMPSON	*9 June 1852*	170
42.	*To the* REV. WILLIAM THOMPSON	*Probably June–July 1852*	171
43.	*To the* REV. WILLIAM THOMPSON	*6 Sept. 1852*	174
44.	*To the* REV. WILLIAM THOMPSON	*30 Sept. 1852*	178
45.	*To the* REV. WILLIAM THOMPSON	*12 Oct. 1852*	181
46.	*To the* REV. DR. TIDMAN	*2 Nov. 1852*	184
47.	*To the* REV. WILLIAM THOMPSON	*24 Nov. 1852*	189
48.	*To the* REV. CHARLES LIVINGSTON	*6 Feb. 1853*	192
49.	*To the* REV. WILLIAM THOMPSON	*17 Sept. 1853*	198
50.	*To the* REV. DR. TIDMAN	*24 Sept. 1853*	202
51.	*To the* REV. J. FREDOUX	*28 Sept. 1853*	210
52.	*To the* REV. WILLIAM THOMPSON	*11 Oct. 1853*	212
53.	*To the* REV. DR. TIDMAN	*8 Nov. 1853*	215
54.	*To the* REV. WILLIAM THOMPSON	*14 May 1854*	217
55.	*To the* REV. CHARLES LIVINGSTON	*8 Nov. 1854*	223
56.	*To the* REV. DR. TIDMAN	*14 Jan. 1855*	227
57.	*To the* REV. WILLIAM THOMPSON	*13 Sept. 1855*	233
58.	*To the* REV. WILLIAM THOMPSON	*27 Sept. 1855*	236
59.	*To the* REV. DR. TIDMAN	*12 Oct. 1855*	240
60.	*To the* REV. WILLIAM THOMPSON	*2 Mar. 1856*	255
61.	*To the* REV. DR. TIDMAN	*2 Mar. 1856*	257
62.	*To the* REV. WILLIAM THOMPSON	*8 Aug. 1856*	258
63.	*To the* REV. WILLIAM THOMPSON	*17 Sept. 1856*	262
64.	*To the* REV. WILLIAM THOMPSON	*31 Oct. 1856*	264
65.	*To the* REV. WILLIAM THOMPSON	*4 Oct. 1858*	266
66.	*To* JOSEPH W. STURGE	*11 Dec. 1858*	268
67.	*To the* REV. DR. TIDMAN	*10 Nov. 1860*	270
68.	*To the* REV. WILLIAM THOMPSON	*Nov. 1872*	272

LIST OF ILLUSTRATIONS

David Livingstone, from the portrait by T. and R. Annan and Sons, Glasgow . . . . . . *Frontispiece*

Map of Livingstone's journeys xxviii

Part of Livingstone's letter from Mabotsa dated Dec. 2nd, 1844, announcing his engagement to Mary Moffat (see letter No. 21) facing p. 76

Part of a letter from Boatlanama, to Dr. Tidman, dated April 30th, 1851 (see letter No. 36) . . . facing p. 146

Part of a letter to Dr. Tidman, dated March 2nd, 1856 (see letter No. 61) . . . . . facing p. 258

A BIOGRAPHY IN DATES

1813 David Livingstone born at Blantyre, March 19.
1823 Began work in a cotton mill.
1836 Entered Glasgow. Classes in Medicine and Greek.
1837 Studied Theology under Dr. Ralph Wardlaw—Glasgow.
1838 Offered his services to the London Missionary Society.
1839 Further tuition under Rev. Richard Cecil at Ongar.
1840 Attended medical lectures at Charing Cross Hospital. Took degree. L.F.P. & S. (Glasgow) (Nov.). Ordained, Nov. 20. Sailed, Dec. 8.
1841 Arrived Cape Town, March 15. Arrived Kuruman, July 31.
1843 Settled at Mabotsa.
1844 Encounter with lion, April.
1845 Married to Mary Moffat, Jan. 2.
1846 Removed to Chonuane.
1847 Settled at Kolobeng.
1849 Crossed Kalahari desert. Reached Lake Ngami, Aug. 1.
1851 Discovered Upper Zambesi River, Aug. 3.
1852 Mrs. Livingstone and children returned to England; left April 23. Kolobeng raided by Boers, Aug.
1853 Journey to west coast began, Nov. 11.
1854 St. Paul de Loanda reached, May 31. Left again, Sept. 20.
1855 Discovered the Victoria Falls.
1856 Crossed Africa from west to east, reaching Quilimane, May 20. First return to England, Dec. 9. Reception at Freemasons Tavern, Dec. 16.
1857 Wrote *Missionary Travels and Researches in South Africa*—published Nov. Received Freedom of the City of London. Made D.C.L. (Oxford) and LL.D. (Glasgow). Resigned official connexion with the London Missionary Society. Addressed British Association in Dublin, Aug.
1858 Audience with Queen Victoria, Feb. 13. Made Fellow of Royal Society. Appointed Consul. Sailed March 10.
1859 Discovered Lake Nyassa. Explored Shiré Valley.
1860 Explored Zambesi River. *Ma-Robert* foundered, Nov. 21.
1861 Explored Lake Nyassa.
1862 Mrs. Livingstone died, April 27.
1863 Recalled to England, July 2.
1864 Crossed Indian Ocean in *Lady Nyassa*, April 30–June 13. Reached England, July 23.
1864–5 Wrote *The Zambesi and its Tributaries*.
1865 Death of his mother, June 18. Lost his son Robert, aged 19, in

A Biography in Dates

American Civil War. Commissioned by Government and R.G.S. to open up Central Africa. Sailed for last time to Africa, Aug. 13.

1866 Arrived Zanzibar, Jan. 28.
1867 Reached Lake Tanganyika, April 1. Discovered Lake Moero, Nov. 8.
1868 Discovered Lake Bangweolo, July 18.
1869 Arrived at Ujiji, March 14. Explored the Manguema country.
1871 Reached Lualaba River, March 29. Witnessed slave-raiding massacre, July 15. Returned to Ujiji, Oct. 23. Found there by Stanley, Oct. 28.
1872 Stanley departed, Oct. 28.
1873 Last day of travel, April 29. Died in Chitambo's village, May 1.
1873-4 Carried by faithful hands to Zanzibar.
1874 Remains arrived at Southampton. Buried in Westminster Abbey, April 18.

ABBREVIATIONS IN FOOTNOTES

Blaikie: *The Life of David Livingstone*. By W. G. BLAIKIE. (John Murray, 2s. 6d.)

Travels: *Missionary Travels and Researches in South Africa*. By DAVID LIVINGSTONE. (John Murray.)

Campbell: *Livingstone*. By R. J. CAMPBELL, D.D. Abridged edition, 1939. (Livingstone Press, 2s. 6d.)

BOOKS ON LIVINGSTONE AND THE ARAB SLAVE-TRADE

D. LIVINGSTONE, *Missionary Travels and Researches in South Africa* (Popular edition, London, 1912).

— *Narrative of an Expedition to the Zambesi* (London, 1865).

— *Last Journals* (ed. H. Waller, 2 vols., London, 1874).

W. G. BLAIKIE, *Personal Life of David Livingstone* (6th ed., London, 1910).

R. J. CAMPBELL, *Livingstone* (London, 1929).

R. COUPLAND, *The British Anti-Slavery Movement* (Home University Library, 1933).

— *Kirk on the Zambesi* (Oxford, 1928).

— *The Exploitation of East Africa* (Oxford, 1939).

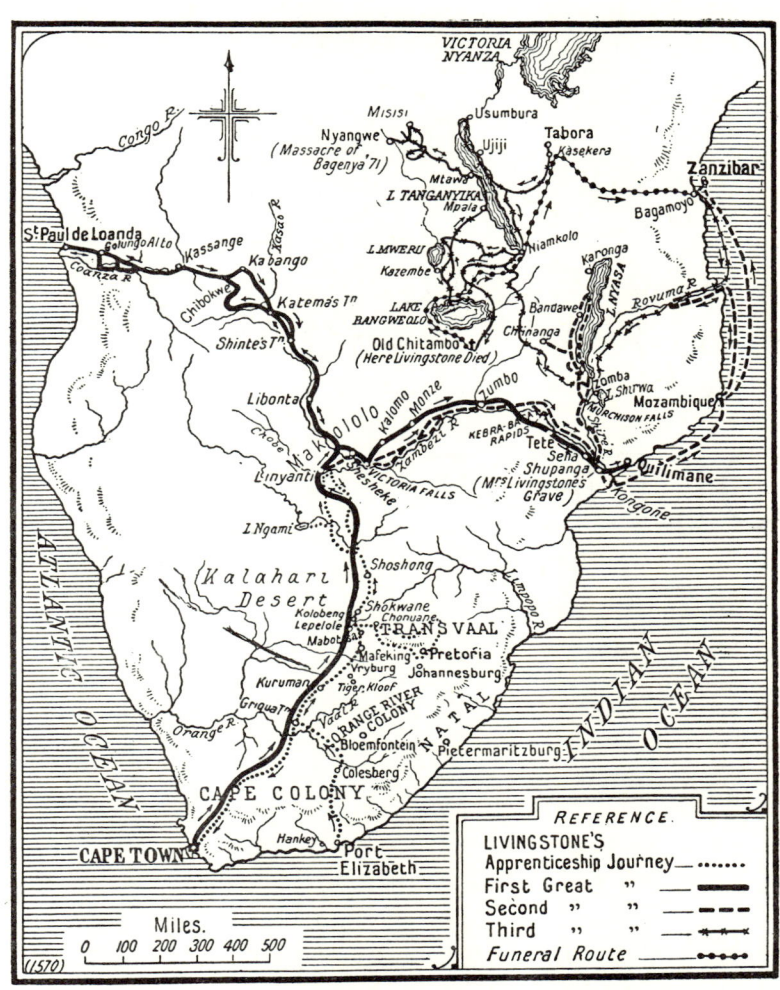

MAP OF LIVINGSTONE'S JOURNEYS

LETTERS FROM LIVINGSTONE

THE first document in Livingstone's handwriting in the collection of letters now available is dated 'Blantyre Works, Sept. 5th 1837' and consists entirely of his views on Christian doctrine, his motives in offering to become a missionary, and his religious experiences. The statement is written with scrupulous care: no other letter from the writer is as neat and legible as this. Livingstone's doctrines were orthodox of the period and he adhered to the Congregational, or Independent, form of Church government, while in the bringing of full conviction regarding the inner life and future destiny he avows his particular indebtedness to Dr. Thomas Dick's *Philosophy of a Future State*. This letter was addressed to the secretary of the London Missionary Society.

In the January following, a Form containing seventeen questions was furnished by the Society to which the candidate appended answers. Among these, two are of special interest. One question asked, 'What do you apprehend are the proper duties of a Christian missionary?' to which the following answer was given:

'His duties chiefly are, I apprehend, to endeavour by every means in his power to make known the Gospel by preaching, exhortation, conversation, instruction of the young; improving so far as in his power, the temporal condition of those among whom he labours, by introducing the arts and sciences of civilization, and doing everything in his power to commend Christianity to their hearts and consciences.'

Here, in words written before he began his life's work, Livingstone reveals the roots of that widely diffused philanthropy—the expression of his faith—which in later years distinguished him above all men of his time.

The other question related to marriage: its shape may be guessed by the sweeping reply—

'Unmarried; under no engagement relating to marriage,

Tutor's Report

never made proposals of marriage, nor conducted myself so to any woman as to cause her to suspect that I intended anything relating to marriage; and, so far as my present wishes are concerned, I should prefer going out unmarried, that I might be without that care which the concerns of a family necessarily induce, and give myself wholly to the work.'

The answers to the seventeen questions were read to a small Committee of Directors of the Missionary Society on July 23, 1838, and the candidate travelled from Blantyre to London to meet the Committee. Twice he was interviewed (August 13 and 20), and as a result he was accepted on probation and assigned to the tutelage of the Rev. Richard Cecil of Ongar, for three months. At Ongar he lodged in a room over the entrance arch to the Chapel yard, and boarded at the tutor's residence, Roden Lodge, with other students.

On January 26, 1839, Mr. Cecil, the tutor, reported thus:

'Mr. Livingstone gives me pleasure in some important respects. The objection I mentioned, his heaviness of manner, united as it is with a rusticity, not likely to be removed, still strikes me as having importance, but he has sense and quiet vigour; his temper is good and his character substantial, so that I do not like the thought of his being rejected.

'Add to his stock of knowledge and then I trust he will prove after all an instrument worth having—a diligent, staunch, single-hearted labourer.

'If the decision were now coming on I should say accept him.'

On January 28 the Committee did as they were advised; their Minute reads that Livingstone was then 'fully admitted under the patronage of the Society'. He remained at Ongar, and on July 2 wrote as follows to the Society:

'Having been informed a few days ago by Mr. Cecil that there had been some intimation of a wish on the part of the Directors that I should be employed in the West Indies in preference to South Africa, and being desirous to enter upon

Proposed appointment to West Indies

that sphere of labour and, I trust, that only, in which I may be able most efficiently to advance the great cause of our Blessed Redeemer, permit me to state the following particulars for their consideration, previous to coming to a final decision on my case—

'... It appeared to be in accordance with the will of Providence that I should attempt to obtain a medical education in order to render service to the cause of Missions by that means; after much exertion and overcoming considerable difficulties, in which I was sensibly assisted by the good hand of providence, I spent two years in that study, all which time, in the event of my being sent to the West Indies, might be considered as lost, for I could not use the knowledge which I have obtained, without in all probability incurring the displeasure of medical men who have gone thither for the sake of gain, and it is well known how easily medical men can destroy each others' influence and usefulness, when an unsuccessful case occurs, as many hundreds of young men have experienced in this and other countries. In this manner might not only that means which I had hoped to have exerted to subserve the cause of religion, be rendered inoperative, but likewise my moral and religious influence be weakened.

'... Settling in the West Indies has always appeared to me so much like the ministry at home that my thoughts have not at all been attracted in that direction, but always to other parts of the world.

'I beg leave to state likewise in reference to a proposal to send me out in the present year, my earnest desire for more education. This has always been my wish and the more I contemplate the magnitude of the work the greater does the necessity of good preparation for it appear to be ....'

This letter had its effect. On July 8 the Committee decided that Livingstone should remain at Ongar till next year 'at his request'. On the 22nd of the same month it was resolved that after Christmas he should 'attend the B. & F. School of Medicine,

Life in London

to fit himself for some station in South Africa or the South Seas'.

The year 1840 was an eventful one for Livingstone. He removed from Ongar to London on January 2, and took lodging with Mrs. Sewell, 57 Aldersgate Street, where he had put up for a time when he first came from Blantyre in 1838.

Dr. Risdon Bennett[1] was Physician to the Aldersgate Street Dispensary and Lecturer at Charing Cross Hospital. Livingstone attended the Dispensary practice and the Medical School, then held in Charing Cross Hospital, taking Medical Practice, Midwifery, and Botany. His letters show that the pressure endangered his health. Bennett's father was minister of Silver Street Chapel, Falcon Square, close to the Aldersgate Street address, and there Livingstone attended, being recorded as an 'occasional communicant'. This was the church referred to in Livingstone's letter to his parents (quoted in Blaikie, p. 89), in which he said: 'I was a member of the very church in which John Howe the Chaplain of Oliver Cromwell preached and exercised the pastorate.'

[1] Afterwards Sir John Risdon Bennett, President of the Royal College of Physicians, London.

LETTER I

(Original at Scottish National Memorial, Blantyre)

To REV. HENRY DICKSON, *Navigator's Islands*[1]

London 8 May 1840

MY DEAR FRIEND

After having neglected writing so long I scarcely know how to begin my letter   I know I ought to have written ere this time even though I had received no word from you for I feel persuaded that your ship has neither touched at the Cape nor fallen in with anyone coming home, so that you could not transmit any communication to me. I had many opportunities of sending letters & have not embraced any of them save one but though I have had opportunities of sending I have been so situated during most of the period which has intervened since we parted that I could not do as I wished in relation to writing— I wrote you a long letter from Ongar which I hope has reached its destination. Will you please to mention whether you have received it or not? I ask this because I could not come to London to look after it myself. . . .

Since parting from you I have been to Ongar for more than 4 months—came up to London on the 2d January /40 have lived in Mrs Sewell's & persued my medical studies untill the present time   I have enjoyed excellent health during the whole of that time wh. is a great blessing, . . . I have had & still have excellent opportunities to acquire medical knowledge, by the end of summer I shall have completed the curriculum of medical studies, I daresay however they wont grant me the wherewithall to pass my examinations for a diploma but it's no great matter I shall be able to practise medicine amongst the Bechuanas as well without as with the Licence of the Royal College of Surgeons—usefulness is the grand matter to be attended to—. . .

This is the period when the annual meetings are held. The

---

[1] H. Dickson (a fellow student at Ongar) did not live to reach the Islands. He died at Sydney on the way out, Feb. 4, 1840.

Penny Postage

Bible Society was held yesterday & the Tract Society tonight—ours will be held on Thursday next when great lamentation over the fate of poor Williams[1] will be made, of course you know all about his lamented end—it has created great sensation in this country—a beautiful edition of his work at 2/6 sells amazingly quick, it was well that he was kept faithful to death, for really the praises heaped upon him were sufficient to turn any man's head

Mr Thos Prentice[2] . . . has now succeeded in his addresses to Miss Ridley[2]—has been received graciously, I believe she has a true missionary spirit but she will require it all I should think as the difference between the elegant little carriage which they used to drive & the Bullock waggon of S. Africa is very great. . . .

Be sure & write as often as you have an opportunity   I shall not fail I hope to do the same when I get to Africa. I have been very much pressed by the studies in which I have engaged since I came to London & when in Ongar I had to preach every Sunday besides my usual studies in Greek & Hebrew.

You cant imagine what a convenience we have now conferred upon us in the new post office regulations—only a penny to convey a letter from Ongar to the Orkneys—We can write to friends as often as we please   I wonder when we shall have a penny post in Africa & South Seas?

Mrs Sewell desires to be kindly remembered to you & Mrs Dickson & hopes you are as happy as she wishes you to be

Now dear friends I bid you farewell wishing you every needful blessing especially that yours may be the portion of those who turn many to righteousness—May we meet in joy at last—believe me your very affectionate brother in Christ

D. LIVINGSTON

[1] John Williams, the martyr of Erromanga; died Nov. 20, 1839.
[2] Friends of the Ongar days: see the next following letters.

LETTER 2

(Original at Scottish National Memorial, Blantyre)

To REV. GEO. DRUMMOND, *Papaoa, Tahiti*

London. 25th July 1840

MY DEAR BROTHER,

... I leave London in two days in order to pay my farewell visit to my parents etc. in Scotland. I have resided in Mrs Sewell's[1] since the 2nd of January 1840 & have during that period been almost entirely occupied with the study of medicine —it is now settled that I shall sail for my destination in the Bechuana country South Africa in the month of November next this it seems is the best time for travelling inland. The importance of fixing it so is evident when we take into consideration the fact that I must travel about 600 miles inland immediately after I have quitted the ship at Algoa Bay—I must remain at Kuruman till I have acquired the language & then I may be located about 500 miles beyond that amongst the Wanketzes— But though I may be placed so far up the country you must not forget to write me & you may depend on me I won't neglect to do the same to you in return. I am quite delighted with your proposition to do so for I assure you my affection is not the least diminished by the distance which now separates us, it is rather greatly increased & I never cease to pray for you as one whose welfare & usefulness I am greatly interested in—I hope our affection shall never abate, no it cannot for we are joined together in bonds which death cannot sever ...

I would have written a letter specifically to Mrs D but it is with some difficulty that I write this as I have been poorly during the last fortnight in consequence of having, I suppose, inhaled too much of the effluvia of sick chambers, dissecting rooms etc during my stay in London. I now hasten away that I may breathe once more the caller air of my native land....

About Mr Ths Prentice. He came off surprisingly well in the examinations at University College carried off three prizes in

---

[1] See page 4. The site is now occupied by the makers of Stephen's Inks.

Teetotalism in Ongar

three different classes namely Latin, Greek & German. Both he & Cathrine seem possessed of the true missionary spirit for when I told him I thought she was too much of the lady for a missionary's wife he said that ever since she thought of becoming a missionary she wrought just like a servant & did a great part of the household work baking the bread etc & expected when she went out to have to do a great deal more. This I think shows that she has not got the romantic ideas of mission work wh. some have had. She sent me the other day a watch guard made by herself & an elegantly bound copy of Bridges[1] on the 119th Psalm as a sort of keepsake from T & herself till we shd meet in Africa.

I dare say you wonder if I am going to be married myself... I really don't know. If people would just let me alone I am quite easy but there are so many giving me advice, & all gratis, that I don't know what to think I think if I know my own heart that I want to do what will render me most useful but whether my usefulness will be augmented by getting a wife I really dont know. So here I am in a pretty mess you will allow as deep in the mud as any man was; can't see three inches before me. and am free as to any engagements. What may turn up you shall hereafter hear.

I look forward with greater interest than ever to my mission. I can't say I have the least regret in leaving my native shores for ever. I rejoice that so great honour is to be bestowed upon me. how much reason have we to say 'I thank Jesus Christ our Lord who hath enabled me for that he counted me faithful, putting me into the ministry, ...

Mr Cecil has been poorly but is now recovered & a most interesting thing in connection with his character is his recent conversion to Teetotalism. He has become not only an advocate but a most strenuous one. They have got a Teetotal Society in Ongar wh numbers about 16 members. Mr Fison

---

[1] *An Exposition of Psalm CXIX.* By the Rev. Charles Bridges, M.A., Vicar of Old Newton, Suffolk. Of many editions and issues there was one in duodecimo at 7s. See also letter to Miss Ridley (No. 4).

News for fellow student

T Prentice & Mr Cecil each gave addresses on the subject at Stowmarket last week. Mr P tells me he never heard Mr Cecil speak so earnestly on any subject as on this. Nay more, Mrs C has been experimenting in order to do without yeast in making bread. . . .

Before I left I preached every sunday either at Tylor's Green[1] or Blackmore—Sometimes at both places on same Sabbath but this was too much as I could not get on with my other studies as I wished. Since I have been here I have not done much in theology. I have bent all my powers to medicine as I am to be the only medical man in the Bechuana Mission—The Pynes[2] are just as they used to be, as kind as ever. Miss Marshall is still with them & all moves on as before only they have fewer scholars I have not had it in my power to visit them since I came to London but have written frequently I sent them your letter to peruse it—they were highly gratified with it. I mean to visit them before I leave & will write you again if I can before I sail from England—address me in the Bechuana country—of course sending it first to the Mission House . . .

I wish I could tell you something about the old Cumnoch[3] but I know just as much about it as about the affairs of the antipodes —some of your other friends must supply that deficiency— Mr & Mrs Wright now living in London desire their very kind regards also Mrs Sewell, her son Charles has passed the College of Surgeons & his first examination for the degree of Bachelor of medicine & will come up for examination at Apothecaries Hall next week to what purpose these honours will be put, is a question to which there are no evidences that a satisfactory answer will soon be given—He gained last year also a gold medal— . . .

Now I must bid you adieu May the Lord bless you both & make you blessings to thousands who are now perishing— My very affectionate Christian regards to yourself & Mrs

---

[1] Blackmore is 4 miles east of Ongar, and Tylor's (or Tyler's) Green about the same distance westward of the town.

[2] The Pynes. See Letter 35.

[3] Cumnoch was Drummond's birthplace. He met Livingstone at Ongar.

Catherine Ridley

Drummond . . . Now don't forget to write as often as convenient although you don't hear from me for some time after my next letter—I am yours Dear Brother & Sister in the best bonds

DAVID LIVINGSTON

You must excuse this unconnected scrawl for I am not well

LETTER 3

(Original at Rhodes Livingstone Institute)[1]

Barque George at Sea, off Rio Janeiro
27th. January 1841

To MR. T. L. PRENTICE,[2] *Stowmarket*
MY DEAR FRIEND

You have returned from the celebration of Christmas and settled down quietly to your studies for some time now. But have you remembered your promise to write your humble servant when you had done so? If you have not you must understand that I fully expect a letter from you when I reach Algoa Bay advising me of the state of our dear friend C's[3] health (I make known my expectation in order that when you receive this some remorse may seize you as a punishment for your negligence) I shall be sorry if I dont. I wish I could hear now for I have often thought of you both and wished you were here I should have been delighted to have assisted you when passing through that grievous ordeal sea sickness. . . . I promised to tell you all the disagreables. This is No. 1 and a regular bad one it is. . . . Perhaps you may not be in such a pitiable state from

---

[1] The letters here reproduced by courtesy of the Trustees of the Rhodes Livingstone Institute at Livingstone, Rhodesia, should not be reprinted without the permission of the Trustees.

[2] Mr. T. Lomas Prentice (an Ongar student) afterwards married Miss C. Ridley to whom Letter 4 was addressed.

[3] 'Our dear friend C.' was Catherine Ridley (Livingstone spelt her name 'Cathrine'). She was descended from a brother of the Martyr, Bishop Nicholas Ridley. In the company of students at Ongar there were two other friends of Livingstone—Joseph Fison and Manning Prentice (younger brother of Thomas)—who married sisters of Catherine Ridley.

Hints for travellers

seasickness as my poor friends Mr. and Mrs. —— were for our little vessel went reeling and staggering over the waves as if she had been drunk, our trunks perpetually breaking from their lashings, were tossed from one side of the cabin to the other, everything both pleasant and unpleasant huddled together in glorious confusion. You have been on board a steamer; that is nothing to a little sailing vessel in a stormy sea such as we had when about the Bay of Biscay, she writhed and twisted about terribly. Imagine if you can a ship in a fit of epilepsy. My nervous system not being over sensitive enabled me calmly to contemplate the whole scene and certainly I never beheld such a mess before, it might be called 'the world upside down'. The storm I wont attempt to describe. It is beyond description and I hope you will see one yourself. . . . What delightful weather we have had since reaching the latitude of Madeira—10 days after leaving Gravesend we bade farewell to the cold and now while you cant keep your fingers straight and Mr. Fison has to rub his chilblains I enjoy a climate more genial by far than even summer in England. It will however be hotter on land. The atmosphere has been really delightful. If I were writing to C. I should tell her of the beautiful appearance of the sea and sky in the evenings, etc. but you I am afraid wont thank me for such observations, therefore I shall proceed to mention some things which I think worthy of your attention in prospect of undertaking a voyage—Get a swinging cot to sleep in instead of a mattress—a swinging tray—Take no edibles except perhaps a very few oranges or apples, some seidleitz Powders and a few lemonade and soda Do. Not more than 2 trunks for the Cabin. Let these contain all you require for the voyage, part of them of easy access. Have all your other goods in air tight boxes and dont open them while at sea. Some Wesleyans last voyage of this ship examined their dresses after being 3 weeks at sea, found them all right, but the act of opening them admitted the sea air and when they looked about 3 weeks after that found all of them completely spoiled. Expect to be sick and take nothing from your trunks untill that is over except your Bibles, if you

Visit to Rio

escape sickness it will be an agreeable disappointment. You will require a lantern for your birth   A folio is perhaps better than a writing desk. Get your bedding and every thing else arranged previous to sailing and you need not be downcast although I have told you of the disagreable ordeal through which you have to pass. Take every thing as easily as you can is the best advice I can give you in prospect of changing land for sea life—

I wrote you from the Downs. Did you get that? We had our foremast split by the wind a few days ago and in consequence have been obliged to put into Rio de Janeiro for a new one and a supply of water. We are, while I am writing, in sight of land and expect to get on shore tomorrow. We had only 30 days water on board when the accident happened and we were in Lat. 23 S. Long 28 W. Had we pursued our course to the Cape the probability is that the first gale having taken the mast right away, should have so disabled the vessel as prevent her gaining land for perhaps double that period. As a prudential measure the Captain puts in here for a new mast and a supply of water...

(Signature missing)

LETTER 4

(Original at Rhodes Livingstone Institute)

To MISS CATHRINE RIDLEY[1]

On board the barque *George* Lat. 33 S. Long 12 W.
24th. Feby. 1841

My Dear Friend,

You must not be surprised at the liberty I take in addressing you so for I can claim relationship to you through a third party whom we both consider a dear friend. I hope you are now completely recovered from the indisposition you laboured under when I left England and I confidently expect the first letter I receive will apprise me that such is the case. But should it be otherwise we know that the hand which afflicts is guided by a heart of infinite love and that this is one of the all things

---

[1] See notes 2, 3 to letter No. 3, page 10.

Verdure of Brazil

which are to work together for our good. We have only to throw our whole being into His hands and all will be well.

I know you regard with feelings of interest the course which I am now pursuing as, if in accordance with Our Father's will, you hope to follow in a similar track. I shall therefore tell you a little about Rio de Janeiro, to which harbour we paid a most delightful visit. Had you been there I am sure you would have enjoyed it as much as I did, even although you are more attached to home than I am. I don't think that the recollection of what you had left behind would have had even so much effect on you as it had on me for you know Scotchmen have a very great love to their cold barren mountains and warm hearted relatives. I was so delighted with the beautiful scenery, the lofty green hills covered with wood to their summits and everything else so new and strange and interesting that my thoughts never soared beyond Rio, except perhaps when I betook myself to my couch at night—The country is delightful but perhaps it appeared more so to me on account of having been for 7 or 8 weeks cooped up on shipboard. I could not cease gazing at and admiring the beautiful mountains which meet the eye in every direction and then there was so much in the people wh. called for observation. They are said to be revengeful and have little regard for human life. I believe it is true but I know they are capable of shining hospitality, at least some of them are as I myself experienced. As I wished to see a little of the interior of the country and nobody else was inclined to endure the heat and fatigue of a walk beneath an almost vertical sun I set off alone and having walked about 6 or 7 miles got into a Brazilian Forest. Really it is a fine sight. I have read good descriptions of them but the sight is much better. Orange and cocoa nut trees were the only trees I could claim acquaintance with. Butterflies and grasshoppers of gigantic size in great abundance. Lizards and scorpions with vegetation on a most luxuriant scale. Parasitical plants in immense variety. After spending some time admiring the strange productions of nature I travelled on and saw many vallies lovely beyond description. Their sides covered

Hospitality at Rio

with plantations of coffee, sugar cane, Indian corn, etc. and the little shed-like cottages of the natives scatterd here and there and peeping out from beneath orange trees or the spreading leaves of the banana—Being desirous to obtain some fruit I descended one of these vallies intending to seek a supply at the first cottage I came to, but no sooner had I emerged from the wood to an open space in front of one, than I was surrounded by three half starved looking dogs who seemed inclined to make an end of me but having a good stick in my hand I soon convinced them that I was not a member of the Peace Society. The row brought out the inmates and the dogs were called off. By means of a few words of Latin for I had no Portuguese I made them understand I wished to purchase some fruit, but they had none ripe. They however beckoned me to come into the cottage and partake of their dinner. The good lady pressed me to every dish they had. Beef, fish, rice, bananas, bread and cheese and tapioca, and as an inducement to eat well her husband brought out a stone bottle and filled up a glass of some sort of liquor. On my declining this he produced another and presented a glass of that. I could not tell him I was a teetotaller but kept asking 'aqua'. I never had such a strong temptation to break my resolution to abstain from these drugs as at this exhibition of disinterested kindness. Notwithstanding my partaking freely with them they would take nothing by way of remuneration although I offered to pay them in their own coin. I got the children to take a few coppers and the parents an English halfpenny as a memorial of my visit. The good lady asked whether I were 'Englees' or 'Americana'. On my answering I was the former she gave her children a long account of the English occasionally turning round to me for confirmation to what she was saying but presently recollecting herself she explained to me that she had forgot and then again remembering that not even that was understood smiled and shook her head and when I was coming away she folded two bananas in a piece of paper and put them in my pocket. Perhaps she herself had a son in a distant land and I wished I had

Riotous sailors

had some Portuguese tracts with me. May Heaven direct the steps of some missionary with the bread of life to your pretty cottage, Ye kind hearted Brazilians. The husband seemed surprised that an Englishman should refuse ardent spirits for Eng. and Am. seamen continually disgrace themselves in the streets of Rio by getting into a state of intoxication. The sailors of all other countries behave themselves like men, except ours and the Americans. They get into scuffles with the inhabitants and they soon use their knives, rob and stab them. I saw a case of this kind in the Misericordia Hospital. He was lying in a fit of raging delirium, secured by a strait jacket and the blood still flowing from his wound. The Portuguese menials understood not his language and only laughed at his vain attempts to get up. My heart warmed to my countryman. I sat on the edge of his bed and vainly endeavoured to lead his mind into a train of thought, if I got 2 collected sentences the 3d was sure to be about blue devils or gin, etc. He was a young man of about 22 and had got this from what he calld skylarking the day before. I turned away with a heavy heart for I knew from the nature and position of his wound that he could not with his system impregnated with alcohol survive another night. O How much need have the Christians of Britain to exert themselves in behalf of seamen—

On the bed from which he expected never to arise lay another who could speak English. He was an old Frenchman and had acquired the English language during the time he was a prisoner in England. He thought if he were sorry for his past sins and did well as he could God would forgive him. I explained his mistake and gave him some tracts and left him never to see him more untill we appear before that Bar where it shall be made apparent whether we have cast all our dependance on Christ or have trusted to a refuge of lies.

That you and all whom you love may meet there with joy is my sincere wish and for this end I pray that Christ may be made of God unto us wisdom and righteousness, sanctification and redemption.

A shower-bath needed

Please write to me and ask any questions you choose. I dont know very well what kind of information you would like. Name the different subjects you should like to know and I will give you all the information in my power. Is it the difference in the mode of life? or clothing or work you feel most interested in? You know I am not very well acquainted with the feelings of those who have been ladies all their lives. A hard bed might be a greater sacrifice to one than sleeping on the ground to another. If you ask me freely I shall tell you as plainly as I can the real state of affairs on missionary stations and what you have to expect and do. I cant of course tell you the feelings with which you will meet them. All I can do is to tell you how I like them. I gave Mr. Prentice some hints about the voyage. Now I beg leave to cancel these in case you find it quite different and think I was mistaken—the only advice I shall give about it is in Scotch 'Aye put a stout heart to a steye brae'. Always put a stout heart to a steep declivity and dont be put out by trifles. I have your 'Bridges'[1] always by me in my birth and often get my heart warmed by his heavenly minded reflections. Many thanks for it. May every blessing attend you is the prayer of Yours affectionately   DAVID LIVINGSTON

LETTER 5

(*Original at Rhodes Livingstone Institute*)

To MR. T. L. PRENTICE, 22 *Gower Place, London.*

Barque *George* Lat. 35 S. Long 3 E
MY DEAR FRIEND   5th. March 1841

One thing you must not leave England without or you will be sorry for it. I mean a shower bath; you can't do without something of the sort in a warm climate. The aparatus for forming the shower will do, the rest you can construct for yourself. That with flesh brush and perhaps a pair of horsehair gloves will do more towards the preservation of your health

---

[1] See note to Letter 2, p. 8. Livingstone had given Miss Ridley a little book of verse, *Lays from the West*, by Miss Sigourney, inscribed: 'with the best wishes and Christian regards of DL London 28 June 1840'.

Adventures at Rio

than all the drugs in my medicine chest. I was fully convinced of this before we put into Rio for we have not convenience for sponging, etc. on board. Many times I longed to have a dash into the sea but the occasional appearance of enormous sharks prevented any of us from enjoying that luxury. When I got out into the country and into the woods I found a fine mountain stream came dashing down the side of one of the lofty hills with which Rio is surrounded. I went up the bed of it untill I got to a little waterfall. You can form no idea of the pleasures connected w. a thorough ablution under a natural shower bath after 7 weeks almost total abstinence from anything of the kind and many of these weeks in a warm atmosphere—I told the Captain and Dr. Grant of my good fortune on the day we sailed. So much did they envy me that I daresay the Captain could easily have been persuaded to remain another day in order to get one. But I unconsciously ran the risk of getting all my clothes stolen while in the state in which Adam was when he pruned the trees which no doubt would have caused me to look unutterably foolish. In these forests live great number of runaway slaves, who frequently commit depredations. I did not know this and when I did not return till late to Mr. Spaulding's all were in great consternation lest I had been robbed. A man and his wife having gone to the same place a few days before; he was stript of every thing he had not even excepting his wife. . . . You see I have written Cathrine and sent it unsealed not because I thought you would be offended with the liberty I take, but I dont wish to increase the weight of this packet. I could not send it to her address, for that I dont know. Please forward it. . . . It would be well for her if she has recovered to look a little into the Sitchuana Testament. I think it would be of great advantage to her afterwards for there are many gutterals and aspirates in the language which though no difficulty to a scotchman are a plague to those who have not been accustomed to them. G. is always gutteral, h is pronounced as the spiritus asper of the Greeks, and n as the ringing ing a nasal sound—'nonarega' (to murmer) is one of the most difficult

American Hospitality

words and is pronounced as if it spelt ngongarexa the x pronounced scotch fashion. g is always pronounced so or like the Hebrew ח Heth. The other letters are sounded as in Dutch, a as in father, e as in clemency, ē as ai in Mail, i as ee in seek, c as ch in church as caka is sounded chaka, o as in pot or pole, u as oo in cool. Every letter is sounded and she might very soon read the testament by comparing it with the English   I mention this because I should like her to get the language well and not merely be able to say such sentences in it as a cockney in our language 'Bring me the Hegg of the 'en' or 'You 'eet me 'ard' for you hit me hard. I should like her to practise the gutterals and aspirates although she learnt none of the language. You can get Testaments at the Bible Society House. Please pay Mr. Moffat a visit. He will give you better instructions than the above if you should consider it desirable to act on my hint. The gospel acc/ John is very easy. I have begun to make a Dictionary for my own use and have got nearly all the words in John and Acts and part of Luke. . . .

We were most hospitably received by the Revd. Justin Spaulding an American Miss. at Rio. He sent an invitation as soon as he knew that there were Missionaries on board requesting us to make his house our home during the period of our visit. He can distribute as many tracts and bibles in Portuguese as he chooses without molestation from the priests but what can he do single handed among a population of from 150 to 200,000 which the Town contains, and he has to devote a great portion of his time to Eng. and Am. seamen. He received us with great affection although of course we were entire strangers and during the whole week of our stay did every thing in his power to render our sojourn agreable. It was truly refreshing to meet a brother disciple of the Lord Jesus in a place when we expected to find nothing but the heathenism of Popery. He introduced us to some other christian friends who treated us kindly and for the purpose of gratifying us they planned an excursion round a part of the Bay to the Emperor's gardens. The gardens are very fine.   All sorts of fruits were in great abundance, mangoes, bananas, caju apples, custard apples, oranges, etc. The best of it however was that every one is allowed to eat as much of the fruit as he chooses. Did I neglect the opportunity? . . .

We expect to land at the Cape in a few days. I write this before coming to land lest new scenes should for a little drive old friends out of my head. You cant imagine with what a light heart I visit these foreign shores. Everything is so different from the idea I formed of them while reading. The actual sight and the imagination are two very different things. This is really a fine world we live in after all. Were it not that hateful rebellion against God, it would be quite a Paradise. I see more clearly now than ever the necessity of casting our whole being into the hand of Jesus. Our interests cares and sorrows upon Him who careth for us. Why should we burden our hearts with these and go moping and melancholy beneath a cloud of our own vapours when he offers to look out for us. . . .

If possible I shall write you from Algoa Bay. I hope you have written me, advising me how you both are. I dont know why I feel so much interest in your good lady, perhaps selfishness, the prospect of having both as fellow labourers.

Affectionately Yours D. LIVINGSTON.

March 17th. Cape Town—We have been 14 weeks on our passage. Fine Town this—warm but not roasting: am in Dr. Philip's[1] house. D.L.

LETTER 6

(*Original at Scottish National Memorial, Blantyre*)

To REV. GEO DRUMMOND, *Tahiti*

On board the Barque *George*, Lat. 35. 40 S. Long. 17. E.
10th March 1841

MY DEAR BROTHER,

We are within 50 miles of land & hope to anchor tomorrow morning in Simon's Bay where our vessel discharges part of her

[1] The Rev. John Philip, D.D., Superintendent of the London Missionary Society's African Missions.

Dr. John Philip

cargo. My colleague & I go by land to Cape Town & remain there until she comes round to Table Bay for us. We then proceed in her to Algoa Bay where we expect Waggons are now being built to carry us overland to our destination. This is all I can say about myself & voyage except perhaps that it has been on the whole a fair passage, & I have enjoyed it all very much having had no sea-sickness nor anything else worth mentioning.

Your humble servant is very much the same as when you saw him. Here he sits in the after cabin striving to keep himself from reeling to leeward while the poor Barque *George* is staggering over the waves before a furious North Wester as if she were tipsy. He does feel a little thankful that he is permitted the precious privelege of carrying the message of mercy to his perishing fellowmen.

Have you seen Finney's work on Revivals of Religion? If you have it please to read it. You will see in it our responsibility & the necessity for ministers being well acquainted with the laws & operations of mind in order efficiently to discharge their duty. They must be able to adapt the means so as in every peculiarity of individual cases, produce the end proposed, even the salvation of souls—He wants the wisdom & if sinners are not saved the blame is his, their blood will be required at his hand. I was so well pleased with Finney, that when in Rio, I purchased another of his works & gave 12/- for what I should have got in London for 4/-.

18th March. Cape Town. We arrived here on the 15th currt & are now living in Dr Philip's house. I find the Dr a very amiable man although I came out prejudiced against him for many complaints are made against him by some missionaries. He does not however appear so bad to us as he is represented at home I hope we shall go on comfortably together. He claims no superiority over us, I was always determined not to submit to any bishop & am therefore happy to know he does not wish to dominer—My colleague[1] is a secession man & has a good

[1] William Ross appointed to Kuruman.

Emancipation at Work

deal of the 'Act & Testimony' in his composition but I am determined to live in peace & goodwill. I won't quarrel on any account & May God give me wisdom to conduct myself aright. I see it is of great importance that missionaries should be united & not spend time grinning at each other while the Devil is leading sinners around down the sides of the bottomless pit. . . . You find a good deal of Scrofula in Tahiti. Try if you can get Iodine & its preparations, the iodide of Iron Hydriodate of potass & ascertain the doses. You I have no doubt might do a good deal of good to many by means of this excellent medicine—It is an excellent remedy in that disease I saw that Scrofula abounded in Tahiti in Bennet & Tyreman's travels & immediately thought of you & Morrison's Pills. . . .

We hope to leave this place in the course of a fortnight & then proceed inland on bullock waggons. It will be at least 3 months before we can reach Lattakoo—In the meantime we intend learning a little Dutch as we proceed & when we have arrived we intend devoting all our energies to the acquistion of the Setchuana. . . . The Boors are again shooting the Caffirs—levying their cattle & making their prisoners slaves but our Govt. has just sent up a detachment of soldiers with 4 pieces of cannon to protect the natives—This may be considered a sort of preliminary step to taking Port Natal altogether—That colony or independent state as they call it has been supplied by the dissatisfied Boors of this colony leaving & establishing themselves where they think they may treat the natives as they please Most of the Boors are exceedingly vexed with the British Govt. for emancipating the slaves here O when shall the time come in which every man that feels the heat of this sun shall be freed from all other fetters but bonds of love to our Saviour. . . .

D. LIVINGSTON.

Arrival at Kuruman

LETTER 7

(*Original at Rhodes Livingstone Institute*)
To MR. THOS PRENTICE, 22 *Gower Place, London*

Kuruman, 3rd. August. 1841.

MY DEAR PRENTICE,

I have at last reached this which is to be my resting or rather halting place for a little. We left Algoa Bay on the 20th. of May and reached this on the 31st. July, a pretty long period you think but through the whole, it has been so pleasant I never got tired of it. My waggons are very comfortable affairs indeed, little houses in fact so you may expect to set up housekeeping long before you are surrounded by mud walls. I could tell you a great deal about the country but any book of travels will supply a better acct. of it than I can. I go on to the operations carried on in it and first of all I want to set you right with respect to Dr. Philip concerning whom I was entirely wrong when in England. I came to the Cape full of prejudice against him but after living a month in his house and carefully scrutinizing his character that prejudice was entirely dissolved and affection and the greatest respect took its place. I have heard a great deal said against him but now I am fully satisfied it is all, or at least the greatest portion of it, sheer downright calumny. He may have done some things which appeared tyrannical but it must have been from a conviction that the part he took was the path of duty and the only way whereby he could advance the interests of the Saviour's cause. Do keep your judgement suspended untill you see him and if you ever have that pleasure you will agree with me that both he and Mrs. P. are eminently devoted and humble christians. Their worth will be known better when they have gone to reap the reward of their labours and when the name and memory of their calumniators shall be sunk in the shade of cold oblivion. He stated to me that he is only the money agent of the Society and does not wish to interfere with the modes of operation or plans of any man, but the Society had compelled him frequently to act a part he had

Capetown church

no inclination to, by referring disputes to his decision. Whichever way he decided generally one party has become his enemy —he appears most desirous to get the cause forward and if men will only work they may be sure of the co-operation and friendly regard of the Dr. He has been the means of saving from the most abject and cruel slavery all the Hottentots and not only them but all the Aborigines beyond the Colony. The Boers hate him cordially. Many of them would think it doing God service to shoot him. They have an inveterate hatred to the coloured population and to him as their friend & advocate, you can't understand it, it is like caste in India. Can you belive it? Some of the missionaries have imbibed a portion of it. I name none but you find none of that feeling amongst the friends of Dr. Philip. . . . I am now heartily sorry I ever retailed anything said to me by missionaries whilst I was in England. I am no partizan but I am and always have been on the side of civil and religious liberty.[1]

I find this a pretty spot but as it is winter it wants most of its charms. The church is the largest place I have seen on any Mission Station. The walls are built of stone and so strong they resemble those of a battery. The gardens are excellent but the number of the people is much smaller than I expected to find. This being the hunting time most of them are out pursuing their occupation. This is a point between light and darkness. About two months hence I am going into the regions beyond in company with Mr. Edwards of the station. The Church Miss. Soc. have abandoned their mission to the North of us and recalled Mr. Owen one of the best of men, whose praises we heard sounded through all the colony. From all accounts he is an admirable man, every one regrets his departure. I shall see the state of the country and learn its

---

[1] Livingstone preached to Philip's Congregation. In a letter to Richard Cecil of Ongar dated May 13 1841 he wrote: 'I was *honoured* by them with the character of being heterodox. They asked my companion Mr. Ross, to remain as candidate.' This seems evidence against the statement (Blaikie, p. 31) that Livingstone was invited to the pastorate of the Capetown Church.

language at the same time. It is an easy language, the only difficulty is I have to make my own vocabulary. Dont forget a good gun and learn to shoot it. Also some carpentery with tools. How is Cathrine? You did not write me at Christmas. How can I write you long letters when you serve me so? I shall be away perhaps half a year. I write this in great haste for the only opportunity of sending for a long time now presents itself. . . . We visited Griqua Town and were much gratified by a little intercourse with the brethern there. They are excellent men and have been very successful in their labours. Waterboer is a remarkable character and if you come through Graaf Reinet you will see the prettiest town in all Africa and two christians worth going a hundred miles to make the acquaintance of. I mean Mr. and Mrs. Murray.[1] He is a Scotchman and is the Dutch minister of the town. . . . This climate is most salubrious. Through the whole colony this is famed as a remedy for consumption. Several cases even of that desperate malady are said to have been cured by a residence here. . . This climate is certainly much more agreable to the feelings than the English one. Remember me to your Father, Cathrine, etc. etc. Remember me at the throne of Grace that I may be kept faithful unto death.

Yours affectionately,
D. LIVINGSTON

LETTER 8

To HENRY DRUMMOND, ESQ,[2] *Hamilton, Lanarkshire.*

Kuruman,
4th August 1841.

MY DEAR BROTHER,

I have been ten weeks on the journey, but having visited the various missionary institutions lying near our route, I have not

---

[1] Rev. Andrew Murray, Senior, an Aberdonian.

[2] Henry Drummond, described as a lace manufacturer, was at different times addressed at four places—i.e. Hamilton, 62 Queen St., Glasgow, St. Enochs Square, Glasgow, and as H. & W. Drummond, 153 Argyle St., Glasgow. As will be seen in later letters, he sent out supplies of clothing and drapery to Livingstone.

Livingstone's programme

been more than two months in continuous journeying. Oxen are slow paced, resembling much in this respect the common cart horses at home, and then we have such terrible roads it is frequently difficult to get along at all—I intend (D.V.) to remain here about two months for the purpose of acquiring a little of the colloquial language, and then with the hope of fully mastering the whole, I shall proceed to the Northward and live excluded from all European society. Mr. Edwards, of this station, intends to accompany me to an extensive population at the distance of about a fortnight or three weeks from this. We shall collect information respecting their state and the state of the surrounding country, and if circumstances are favourable for the formation of a new Mission. After two months more, leaving me, he will revisit his family, and afterwards return, and we shall proceed to the erection of houses, etc. This course of exclusion from European society is almost absolutely necessary for one beginning the language. I must form my own vocabulary, and nearly construct my own Grammar, and I must so mingle with the natives as to learn accurately their mode of thinking, or I shall never be of much use as a preacher. I hear Mr. Moffat intends publishing a Grammar and dictionary. These will be truly invaluable to all future missionaries. In the meantime I must take the only course left for me, I go forward to mingle in a state of society of which you in Scotland can form but a very faint idea. In the Colony, and even far beyond it, civilization has exerted a powerful influence, men and women are ashamed to be seen in a state bordering upon entire nudity, but immediately beyond the range of the itineracies of this station you have all living in a state of complete savageism. I have seen several specimens pass through this, and really they give me a much better idea of what pure heathenism is than ever I possessed before. Bows, arrows and assagais, which in the hands of those under missionary influence seemed puny instruments, now look terrible weapons when bristling around the wild, restless, sparkling eye of the real savage, smeared all over with red paint. . . . The Churches at

Bechuanas against Sunday travelling

home know comparatively little of the success which has attended the labours of missionaries in this country. . . . In many places it is truly delightful to behold the Christian deportment of the natives—their sense of Christian propriety is really astonishing. On one occasion we had to travel a long way without water, and as it was Saturday we hurried on till late, but failed to reach water that night. Both on our own account and for the sake of the oxen we were obliged to travel next morning. Before we had arrived at the water however, we were reproved by a Bushman for travelling on the Sabbath. He said it was very wrong to travel on Sunday. We explained, but it did not seem to satisfy him. Near the spot where we came to the water stood a Bechuana village, consisting of about 100 houses. It had a native teacher connected with the Griqua Town Mission, had seldom even been visited by a missionary, but they hold service regularly in a house appropriated for that purpose, and for holding school. After morning service the Chief, with the native teacher and principal people of the village, came and requested an explanation of our conduct. That being given it was next demanded why we had not come to Church since we had come early enough for that. We knew not that they had a Church but were glad to meet with them in the afternoon. Next morning they purchased many Sitchuana Testaments from us. I never saw such thirst for the Word of God before, all seemed eager to possess a copy. A mighty work is going forward here, and much more might be done were there means for the employment of native agency. Believers everywhere among these people preach as soon as they feel the value of the Gospel, although they have much opposition to contend against, and no worldly support save what results from their own industry, they persevere amazingly. The Bechuanas are great retailers of news, every circumstance that occurs is handed from one to another. They are, too, perpetually on the move from one spot to another. We have people here who have come several hundreds of miles from the interior. This nomadic life is very favourable to the spread of the Gospel, although it is opposed

Journey to Kuruman

to the spread of civilization. Ought the Churches at home not take advantage of their news-telling propensities? I think they ought, for I am told it is no uncommon thing for a Bechuana, after he has heard a sermon, to sit down among his friends at a distance, and relate the whole of it word for word. Native agency (I am fully convinced) although it has many evils connected with it, is the only thing that can evangelize the world. . . .

D. LIVINGSTON.

LETTER 9

To MRS. JOHN PHILIP, *Cape Town*

Kuruman 5th August 1841

MY DEAR MRS PHILIP

Through gracious care of our Heavenly Father we have at length reached this distant station in safety. The way has appeared long, very long indeed But having frequently been cheered by the fellowship of our bretheren at the different stations we called at, We have managed to get along comfortably. We visited Untenhage, Graaf Reinet, Colesberg, Phillippolis, Campbell & Griqua Town and remained with the bretheren in the latter place 9 or 10 days. Mr Hughs[1] had just got over a severe attack of fever & His youngest child was very ill of an inflammatory affection of the chest. Both now I am happy to inform you are in a decidedly convalescent state. We have been kindly treated by all but more particularly by Mr Murray & our bretheren whom we have just left. Mr Hughs having lent me his oxen hither & I having given mine a little rest by hiring a span from Colesberg to Phillippolis (*Here follows a list of the expenses incurred in the waggon journey from Algoa Bay to Kuruman.*) . . .

I find the bretheren are opposed to everything having the least relation to trading. I shall follow their example although I was made to believe by the good folks at the Bay that goods

---
[1] Isaac Hughes of Griqua Town.

Bechuana life

were absolutely necessary for getting along I wont even give goods instead of money which is all I ever intended if the cause is to be in any way injured by it. I am at present living in a room in Mr Moffats house & board with Mr Edwards. A new house is not at present needed & should there be hereafter there is a prospect of the traders house being for sale. He talks of going to live at Griqua Town. Please present my kind regards to the Dr. & Mr & Mrs Williams if present with you. I shall have an opportunity of writing the Dr about a month hence at present I am obliged to content myself with a mere note to you on money affairs as our men are very impatient to get off to the wives & families in Bethelsdorp. I advised you formerly of £30 which I drew to acct of salary at Algoa Bay.

I beg leave to subscribe myself
Yours truly
D. LIVINGSTON

LETTER 10

(Original at Scottish National Memorial, Blantyre)

To DR. J. RISDON BENNETT, *London*

Kuruman,
22nd Decr. 1841.

MY DEAR SIR,

I wrote you last Octr. but having had no opportunity of transmitting it for a long time afterwards the letter became so old I was ashamed to send it. I have now been longer in the country & having lately returned from a long journey in the Interior perhaps the information I can now give will be more acceptable than that I should have given by sending the other. . . .

Towards the North by West the country is a dreary desert with scarcely a drop of water to be found, but even here there exists a tribe of Bechuanas. They have no cattle, cultivate no ground & have no fountains yet they love their liberty & very generally they fled from us lest we should seize them & take them away. Providence seems to supply this destitution of

Plants in the desert

water in a wonderful manner. Even in these most desert places on the burning sand a species of bitter water-melon grows in great abundance, these they collect, making incisions into them, the juice flows out into their vessels and with this bitter stuff they quench their thirst. Probably like the Laplanders with their sowthistle & some folks with medicine, it now tastes sweetly to them. The seeds of this plant roasted and many other edible roots which they dig up, serve as food while a few skins of animals they happen to snare serve as clothing to these hardy sons of the desert. They have a great number of esculent roots & some of them very good. The manner of growth of one of them struck my mind very forcibly. Above ground you see nothing but a single tendril or two of a slender creeping plant: dig down for perhaps two feet and you have still a slender thing of a root but beyond that perhaps three feet from the surface and quite away from the immediate effect of the burning sun on the sand, it suddenly swells out in many instances thicker than one's thigh, and quite succulent and perhaps a foot and a half long. Young ones about two inches in diameter & 3 in length very much resemble a young turnip but the old ones have an astringent taste. I have got another root very much resembling these in size. It ·is saturated with gallic acid & something else. The natives tan their skins with it. It is powerfully astringent & when tasted immediately constringes the mouth & decomposes the mucous of the tongue. I have tried it in some cases where an astringent seemed to be indicated, with success. It will prove I hope a means of saving my English medicines of that class. As I am talking of plants, I may mention a plant which grows in abundance in this quarter & when in flower, scents the whole atmosphere with its delightful odours. One of the French bretheren being delighted with its fragrance thought it might be a good substitute for tea, and made an infusion of it. Of this both he and another partook a little and presently their whole nervous systems were strangely affected. I cannot give you an accurate account of the symptoms for they are not able to give them in English. But the effect of

Patients come 130 miles

the remedy was curious. A large dose of vinegar seemed as soon as it entered the stomach to run along the nerves to the extremities of the limbs as if cold water had been gradually poured over them beginning at the centre, and pouring gradually out to the tips of the fingers & toes. After this they very soon became well. I should not have mentioned this, but this is one of the plants the Bushmen make use of in poisoning their arrows, and when I made a decoction & tasted it, it caused a burning sensation on the tongue and roof of the mouth with a sense of stoppage in the nostrils. When however I added a little acetic acid to the decoction it made it quite bland. Would I be justified in trying this in a case of Rheumatism? I cant get dogs on which to try its physiological effects. I have thought the compound which seems to be formed by the acetic acid might be useful in the same manner some of the preparations of other virulent poisons are, but I am scrupulous about trying. I have felt no effects from it myself, even when taken in drachm doses. I shall feel obliged by your spending an hour on me at your leisure. I feel the benefit often of your instructions. . . . I have patients now under treatment who have walked on foot 130 miles for my advice; and when these go home others will come for the same purpose. This is the country for a medical man if he wants a large practice, but he must leave fees out of the question. The Bechuanas have a great deal more disease than I expected to find amongst a savage nation. But little else can be expected for they are nearly naked and endure the scorching heat of the day and the chills of the night in that state, add to this they are absolutely omnivorous. Indigestion, Rheumatism & Ophthalmia are the prevailing diseases, the latter is caused by the hot winds which coming over the extensive sandy plains to the North West load themselves with myriads of fine particles and produce a disease which for its virulence deserves to be called the Bechuana purulent opthalmia. When in the interior, many bad cases were brought to me at every village & sometimes my waggon was quite besieged by these blind & halt & lame. What a mighty

Africans: good patients

effect would be produced if one of the seventy disciples were amongst them to heal them all by a word. The Bechuanas resort to the Bushmen and these poor people that are in the desert for Doctors. The fact of my dealing in that line a little is so strange and new, my fame has spread far and wide. But if one of Christ's apostles were here I should think he would very soon be known all over to Abyssinia. The great deal of work I have had to do in attending to the sick has proved beneficial to me, for they make me speak the language perpetually, & if I were inclined to be lazy in learning it they would prevent me indulging the propensity. And they are excellent patients too besides, there is no wincing, everything prescribed is done instanter, their only failing is they become tired of a long course. But in any operation even the women sit unmoved. I have been quite astonished again and again at their calmness. In cutting out a tumour an inch in diameter they sit & talk as if they felt nothing. 'A man like me never cries' they say 'they are children who cry' & it is a fact the men never cry. But when the Spirit of God works on their minds they cry most piteously. Sometimes in Church they endeavour to hide themselves from the eye of the preacher by creeping under the forms or hiding their heads with their Karosses as a remedy against their convictions. And when they find that wont do they rush out of the church & run with all their might crying as if the hand of death were behind them. One would think when they had got away there they would remain but no there they are in their places at the very next meeting. It is not to be wondered at that they should exhibit agitations of body when the mind is affected as they are quite unaccustomed to restrain their feelings. But that these hardened beings should be moved mentally at all is wonderful indeed. If you saw them in their savage state you would feel the force of this more. . . .

Yours affectionately,
D. LIVINGSTON.

Journey to the interior

LETTER II

To the REV. J. J. FREEMAN[1]

Kuruman 3rd July 1842.

DEAR SIR

On the 10th of February last I left this Station and having proceeded into the interior of the Bechuana Country remained there during the Months, March April, May, and part of June. . . . The objects I had in view were the following:—That I might by exclusive intercourse with the Natives facilitate my labours in the acquisition of the language,—that I might for a season be freed from all attention to Medicine—and that, though still but imperfectly acquainted with their tongue, I might make an effort for the eternal welfare of the tribe or tribes, with whom I should sojourn, by means of Native Agents. In order the more effectually to carry into operation the last and principal object I had in contemplation I took with me two natives, members of the Church in this place, and with two others, connected with the management of the waggon, we proceeded in a direction nearly North East of Moteeto. This route brought us near to none of the tribes which lie East and West of it, and consequently we saw no people, save a few of the Bakalihari and Bushmen, until after twelve days travelling we arrived in the valley of the Bakhatla—there we saw three villages, each of which may be said to contain a population of 400 souls. The situations of these are very inviting for the valley is both beautiful and large, not less I think than forty miles in length, and from two to four in breadth; and, besides abundance of iron-stone, it contains no fewer than seven fountains, each of which pours out a copious supply of excellent water. . . .

Nearly directly north of the Bakhatla and a little more than one hundred miles distant, lives Bubi, one of the Chiefs of the Bakwain (Baquane) and one of the most sensible of his class I have yet seen. To him we next proceeded, and the very

---

[1] Joint Foreign Secretary of the London Missionary Society 1841 to 1846.

Digging a Canal

friendly reception Mr Edwards and I met with both from him and his people last year, the very favourable character he bears among all the tribes, and the fact that Mr E. found them entirely ignorant of the Gospel, induced me to prefer making a commencement for a native teacher with them. The beginning of the School for the Children was as favourable as we could desire. The Chief expressed much joy at the thought of having the foreigners as his friends and went himself and collected the children. He supplied me with Milk regularly and when payment was offered he promptly declined. His under chiefs continued to supply my people with food during most of our stay and although the waggon attracted crowds of visitors daily, on no occasion did we miss a single article. Not long after our arrival it occurred to me that it would be advantageous if we could lead out for irrigation the fine stream which winds round the foot of the hill on which their town is built. And this because it would both furnish the teachers with an available garden and also help to convince the people that they might by a little industry render themselves independant of those impostors called 'Rain Makers'. I accordingly explained to the Chief and his principal men our mode of irrigation and was glad to find that they were quite delighted with the idea. The Chief said he would send as many men as it needed, if I would only shew them how to do the work (two of those he sent are his principal underchiefs and another is his own favourite doctor or rain maker) I had not thought of engaging in a work of this nature when I left Kuruman and had none of the necessary implements with me, but seeing it would not do to lose the favourable season when all were eager to work, I commenced with such as I could invent. Sticks sharpened to a point served for digging a canal between four and five hundred feet in length, three in width and in some places more than four in depth; the earth was lifted out in handfuls and carried to the dam in Karosses, wooden bowls, and tortoise shells. . . . The Bakwains shewed surprising industry and perseverance in this work, and . . . although the dam was twice

Visit to Bamangwato

swept away by floods and I was unable, in consequence of getting both legs and arms severely sunburned, to stimulate them by my example, they did not seem in any way discouraged but laboured on to the end. . . .

Having remained with the people of Bubi for nearly a Month I proceeded northward in order to visit the Bamangwato, Bakaa and Makalaka, three tribes having their countries in Lat. 22° S and stretching from 28° to 30° E. Long. The last named is the smallest of the three, but it is a section of a people of very considerable numbers who speak a language differing very decidedly from the Sitchuana . . . their manners too are somewhat different from the Southern tribes, inasmuch as they are not entirely dependant on the rude Kaross for covering, but manufacture cotton cloth for shawls &c. And, besides the knowledge how to manufacture iron and copper, one of the five tribes into which the Makalaka are divided, called the Mashona, fight with guns instead of the Assagai. These they obtain from the Portuguese on the eastern coast, and from some circumstances which have come to my knowledge; I am inclined to believe they procure them in exchange for slaves. . . .

Our route to the Bamangwato skirted the sandy desert which flanks the Bechuana country to the westward and as the sand proved very fatiguing for the oxen, when within 40 or 50 miles from that people they were unable to proceed farther and I had to leave both oxen and waggon and perform my visit on foot. But I had not the least reason to regret having done so, for the Chief (Sekomi)[1] was evidently pleased that I had thrown myself on his bounty without the least appearance of distrust; indeed before I had been 10 minutes in his company and while sitting surrounded by hundreds of his people he began to shew his satisfaction by feeding me with the flesh of the Rhinoceros and some other things which they consider dainties. He then took me to the house of his Mother presented me with a large Elephant's tusk, more food, and as we became better acquainted

[1] Sekomi was the father of the famous chief Khama. The latter was a youth at this time.

Lions abound

he frequently and emphatically exclaimed 'you have come to us just like rain', and 'if you had brought your waggon I should have detained you at least a Month looking at you'—Sekomi has a large number of people under him—In the town alone I numbered 600 houses which is a number considerably larger than I have been able to count in any other Bechuana town in the Country. But they are all very small and cannot contain many individuals each. The one in which I lived was quite as large as any in the town and three of us could not sleep in it without touching each other, unless we put out our fire. The population is sunk into the very lowest state of both mental and moral degradation, so much so indeed it must be difficult or rather impossible for Christians at home to realize anything like an acurate notion of the grossness of that darkness which shrouds their minds. . . . The Country abounds with Lions and so much are they dreaded by the Natives, one man never goes out alone. The women have always some one to guard them when they go to their gardens and they always go in companies to draw water for the sake of the protection which numbers give—nor are these precautions unnecessary—for a time I would not believe but that they were. But the earnestness with which the Chief remonstrated with me for going a few hundred yards from the town unattended, and the circumstance that he always sent an attendant if at any time he saw me going out afterwards, together with the fact that a woman was actually devoured in her garden during my visit and that so near the Town, (I had frequently walked far past it) fully convinced me that there are good grounds for their fears and precautions. . . .

I was much gratified by the hospitality shewn by the Bamangwato to myself and the two natives who accompanied me. We came among them without anything to insure us a good reception, and after living for a fortnight entirely upon the bounty of the Chief when we left he sent 30 of his people to guard us and carry the presents he had given to both myself and people safely to the waggon. Four of these he instructed to proceed with me to Kuruman, and bring him back a faithful

Treachery of the Bakaa

report of all the wonderful things I had told him—they are an underchief of his and three servants—I wish and pray that I may be useful to them so that when they return they may not only tell the strange customs of the 'Makuas' but also the 'wonderful works of God'.

I have finished what I had to say about the Bamangwato, but my visit to them was not accomplished in one space of time. I walked to the Bakaa who live about 24 miles East by South of Sekomi—remained there a few days—proceeded to the Makalaka who lie about 15 miles north by west of the Bakaa and then returned to the Bamangwato, thence after two days across the Sands I reached the waggon in safety.

The Bakaa have a bad name among all the other tribes and I believe they fully deserve it, for a few years ago they destroyed by poisoning both water and food the second white man that ever visited them—he was a trader and when he with two of his people fell victims to the treachery of the Bakaa, a fourth still lingered under the effects of the poison but they put a leathern thong round his neck and finished him. They burned the waggons in order to get the iron work of them, and devoured the oxen. As I happened to be the first European who has visited them since this deed of darkness, their conscience loudly accused them, and when I came into their town, except the Chief and two attendants, the whole had fled my presence. These were in the usual place of meeting and in their faces they had evidence of perturbation such as I never saw in black countenances before. Nothing I could do in the way of appearing perfectly at ease, and squatting down beside them, could remove the almost ludicrous expression of fear until they had got a dish of porridge cooked; and when they saw me partake of it without distrust, the act seemed to excite their confidence but lying down to sleep in consequence of the fatigue of the long walk seemed to have the full effect I desired and they soon came round me in considerable numbers. There seemed to be something horrid in the appearance of these people but perhaps the impression on my mind may be accounted for by the fact

First speech in vernacular

that I saw as ornaments round their necks pieces of gun-locks &c, and one had a piece of sail cloth round his head which I felt sure must have been taken from the waggon of the unfortunate Gibson. They however during the few days of my stay with them treated me with kindness and I had more than ordinary pleasure in telling these murderers of the precious 'blood which cleanseth from all sin' and I blessed God that he has conferred on one so worthless the distinguished privilege and honour of being the first messenger of mercy that ever trod these regions. It being also the first occasion in which I had ventured to address a number of Bechuanas in their own tongue without reading it renders it to myself one of peculiar interest. I felt more freedom than I had anticipated but I have an immense amount of labour still before me ere I can call myself a master of Sicuana. . . . When I left the Bakaa the Chief sent his son with a number of his people to see me safe part of the way to the Makalaka. I shall not however say anything more respecting them untill I get better acquainted with their actual condition. . . .

7th July. I beg leave thankfully to acknowledge the receipt of your kind favour of the 18th February last, which has just come to hand. I look anxiously for your next as I hope it will contain something definite respecting the interior.

I beg leave to remain
Affectionately Yours
DAVID LIVINGSTON

LETTER 12

To REV^d J. J. FREEMAN

Kuruman 18th July 1842

DEAR SIR

A period of twelve months has now nearly elapsed since my arrival in the country of the Bechuanas. And though during that time ample opportunities have been afforded me for ascertaining the real state of this mission, I have not untill now felt it to be my duty to make any definite statement to the Directors

Testimony to Colleagues

respecting the amount of amelioration of which, by the devoted labours of the missionaries and Divine favour, the Bechuanas here have been the subjects. And I am not at all sorry that I have refrained so long, for, in gradually becoming conversant with their condition, some things exceeding and others falling within my expectations would probably have swayed my judgement & prevented me coming to a calm conclusion, had I written sooner on this point. Untill lately too, I was not fully aware of the proper point from which to view the improvement which has been effected. We must not only be conversant with the present condition of the Bechuana converts. We must be intimately acquainted with others sunk low in the same depths of degradation, from which these have been raised, before we can appreciate the magnitude of the change. To me lately arrived from England the condition of the converts presented many features of pleasing interest. But not untill after I had visited the tribes in the Interior which may be called the facsimiles of what the converts were, was I able to see in all their greatness the wonderful works of the Lord. The contrast between what they were, and have now become is most striking, and it forces on my mind with greater power than ever the conviction, that the gospel has lost none of its pristine efficacy. . . . I can the more freely bear testimony to the mighty effects which have and do still follow the faithful and devoted labours of my elder bretheren in this place, as my instrumentality has in no way contributed to the result. And from my knowledge of the character of M$^{rss.}$ Hamilton and Edwards I believe in their communications to the Directors they must have always kept considerably within what they might have told of the progress of the cause of Christ through their instrumentality. . . .

It is with much pleasure I can thus bear my humble testimony to the efficiency of the bretheren who have preceded me in this part of the missionary field, and while I magnify the grace manifested both in and by them, I pray to be enabled to walk with humility and zeal in their footsteps. May the same power which supported them ever uphold and cause me to be faithful.

Extension approved

The church is in a most flourishing condition, and though there are still some points in the character of the converts which require the exercise of charity and forbearance in us, a visible improvement is going on. It is not a stand-still church. It is making headway against the world, and in several instances the truth is beginning to prevail over their selfish national character, the person who conducted my waggon into the Interior on one of my journies is an instance, for when I paid him eighteen dollars as wages, he immediately laid down twelve as his subscription to the Auxiliary Missionary society. May the Holy Spirit be poured out on us more abundantly, so that the spirit of benevolence may be increased, and all the dark places of the Interior soon feel its blessed effects.

I am Dear Sir
Affectionately yours
DAVID LIVINGSTON

¶ The Foreign Secretaries of the Society wrote to Livingstone from London, on January 29, 1843: 'It affords us unfeigned pleasure to express our entire approval of the measures you have pursued, and our grateful satisfaction at the vigor, perseverance and fidelity with which they were prosecuted. Nor do we hesitate to state our cordial concurrence in your sentiments as to the desirableness of extending the permanent operations of the Society among the tribes to whom your attention has been directed. It is on this principle we have appointed the Brethren by whom Mr. Moffat is accompanied on his return to Africa, and we trust arrangements will be made at an early period towards carrying these views into effect.

'We refrain from entering, on the present occasion, into any enlarged detail on the important subject of native agency in reply to your communications, as you will have ample opportunity, in your official capacity as a member of the District Committee, of explaining and advocating your views or proposing any specific measures which you may deem desirable, and you may rest satisfied that the recommendations of the

Committee, in support of such views and proposition will always meet our ready and cordial consideration, inasmuch as we highly appreciate your exertions and cherish an earnest desire to respond to your solicitudes and encourage your efforts on behalf of the native tribes.'

LETTER 13

(Original at Scottish National Memorial, Blantyre)

To REV. GEO. DRUMMOND, *Island of Savaii, South Seas*

Kuruman. 20th June 1843.

MY DEAR FRIEND,

I recieved your most welcome & long expected letter a few days ago, & I assure you my heart was made white by its perusal. . . . Inglis is married & now on his way up here, so is Moore & now on his way to your quarter. Prentice is married to Cathrine & has a child I believe he got her because he intended to be a missionary. Now he is stuck up in his fathers country house at Stowmarket & John Hay is expected home to be noosed to Lucy. Thus you see the world goes on & all my good example is lost upon it. O tempores & mores! You thought I should turn foolish at the Cape. What nonsense man Do you think I would take a thing in hand & not carry it through. . . .

I have not been allowed to attempt anything of a permanent nature in consequence of an interdict of the Directors. They forbade the formation of any new station untill the whole mission should be organized, this organisation was to take place after the arrival of Mr Moffat & the other bretheren. . . . A committee it is to be alias a presbitery, this is as much against the grain with me as a bishopric is. But if it will advance the cause I wont spend time quarrelling. They've not the least confidence in the wisdom either collective or individual of our S. African bretheren. There has been too much jarring & now a committee the result of a jar It does not bode well. I shall

Expected departure North

give it the go by if I see nonsense springing up. O that none of my life may be spent in vain jangling after I have had such an opportunity of devoting it to Him who died to save me.

This mission has been pretty successful among the Bechuanas. But a stranger coming here would not know it, indeed he would feel disappointed if he read the accounts respecting it. They are far below the Hottentots in point of civilisation & general information as well as morality. Of a church composed of more than 300 I dont know half a dozen of whom I could say with confidence the man appears to have consecrated himself to the Redeemer. But notwithstanding this the change among them upon the whole has been wonderful, the difference which exists between professed believers & the professed heathen is such as to make one feel there must be something more than outward conformity notwithstanding all the darkness & perversity with which it is associated. The pure heathen are as degraded in soul body & spirit as it is possible to concieve humanity to be. . . . Very soon I expect to depart for the interior & assist in the formation of a station at the Bakhatla tribe. They are the iron smelters of whom Mr Campbell[1] heard but was not permitted to see & they are situated very near the spot where he faced round to go away home. It is also very near the spot where Mosilikatse was seen by Mr Moffat. You will read an account of him in Mr M.'s book. You will see numerals in that book, for instance the immense armies of Mosilikatse, cut off a few cyphers always & then you will have the truth. . . .

Salome Cecil is very ill of some complaint of the liver. You have probably heard of Mr Wright's death. I mean Mr Wright of Ongar. Mr Wright of Griqua Town is also dead. He was an able & efficient missionary & his place will not soon be filled up. May we who are spared be enabled to work while we are alive & glorify the Father in Heaven. My very kind regards to Mrs D. & believe me yours most affectionately.

D. LIVINGSTON.

[1] Rev. John Campbell of Kingsland, London, who made two important tours in South Africa for the Society.

Native agents

LETTER 14

To REV. A. TIDMAN[1]

DEAR SIR   Kuruman 24th June 1843

    Your kind and encouraging letter I found a few days ago on returning from another tour in the Interior, and I now beg leave gratefully to acknowledge the encouragement it imparted to my mind. It afforded me unfeigned pleasure to be informed that the measures I felt it my duty to adopt had met the approbation of the Directors. Their satisfaction in my labours I hope at all times to feel anxious to secure. And I earnestly pray the Great Head of the Church may condescend so to guide my operations, as that all may be for His glory. If that prayer is answered I have no doubt but that I shall obtain not only the testimony of my own conscience but also the approbation of all His eminent servants.

    In reference to two topics adverted to in yours viz. Native agency and the appointment of a District Committee It will be gratifying for you to be informed that having written some of my Christian friends in Scotland on behalf of the former I have recieved some very encouraging promises of support. One has already remitted the sum of £12 to the Society, and others promise to make an effort to raise other two such sums as soon as the then depressed state of the country had been got over. But with respect to the latter measure I confess I entertain no very sanguine hopes of its being successful. I only know of two of the bretheren viz. M^{rss} Moffat & Ross at all desirous of its establishment. This and the fact that the others will join simply because such is the expressed rule of the Directors, seem to augur ill for its prosperity. For my own part although a warm admirer of the principles on which the Congregational Unions of England and Scotland are formed my short experience among missionaries makes me not quite so sure of the propriety

[1] Rev. Arthur Tidman, D.D., was principal Secretary to the London Missionary Society during the years of Livingstone's missionary career. From the Society's head-quarters at 14 Blomfield St., London Wall, E.C., he conducted with much authority an extensive foreign correspondence.

Doubtful value of Committee

of missionary unions. The salutary influence of enlightened public opinion which these possess is here entirely awanting and without it I believe we may in our corporate capacity do what as individuals no one of us should ever dare. I however endeavour to repress my private feelings on the subject and I do so with the hope that the measure may be productive of all the advantage to the cause which a well conducted combination is calculated to effect. But the Directors will not I trust consider me guilty of any impropriety if when yielding a prompt compliance with their wish I feel constrained to add I must reserve to myself the power of withdrawing from that committee if at any future time I feel that to be my duty. If compelled to dissolve my connection with it I earnestly hope it may not be in consequence of having indulged a spirit inimical to brotherly union, but that it may be the result of a humble prayerful deliberation and with grief that the measure has failed to answer my expectations.

I shall now endeavour to give you some account of the manner in which I have been employed since the date of my last viz. 18 July /42. . . . The population here is very small indeed, the majority are professors of religion and the remainder being very few there is no scope for more than two missionaries at most. The greater portion of my time I employed in itineracy to the agacent tribes But when here I took part in the routine business of the station, preaching, working occasionally at the printing press, assisting at the erection of a small chapel got up by Mr Edwards and myself at one of the substations, administering to the wants of the sick many of whom come great distances for aid, and other duties which though differing entirely from those of the minister at home all require to be cheerfully performed. To think of standing upon what some people at home call 'clerical dignity' in the sense they have of it, would be as much out of place in a missionary in Africa as his becoming entomologist would be. The work of God has been going on steadily here ever since we arrived, but I am not aware of its having received any visible impulse through our instrumentality. It must therefore be attributed under God entirely to the machinery previously set in motion by our honoured predecessors. If you could realize this fact as fully as those on the spot can, you would be able to enter into the feelings of inexpressible delight with which I hail the decision of the Directors that we go forward to the dark Interior. May the Lord enable me to consecrate my whole being to the glorious work.

Most of my period of suspense here was one of great commotion in the interior. One tribe after another was attacked either by the Southern tribes or by the more to be dreaded Matibele. These wars & rumours of wars seemed to occupy the minds of those under the preaching of the gospel to the exclusion of everything else, this proved a great hindrance to the work of conversion. But by the month of February last the ferment had so far subsided I was at length able to find people to conduct the waggon.

I left this on 21st of February and after 12 days travelling arrived at the village where Sebeqwe[1] with the remains of his tribe had taken up his residence.

. . . . . .

After remaining a few days with Sebeqwe and partaking of such hospitality as his reduced circumstances now enable him to bestow I passed on to the Bakhatla who live a few hours to the North-West. Their situation is peculiarly well adapted for missionary operations, more so indeed than any I have seen in the country, there is as great a population collected in one spot as in any other point in the Interior and their population seems attached to the soil—there are abundant facilities for a more improved mode of agriculture even should that be adopted by a much more numerous population than at present exists. The manufactory of iron seems to have been carried on here uninterruptedly from a very remote period. The ore is found in the immediate vicinity of the villages, and is scarcely anywhere covered by any depth of soil. It was very near to this spot where Mr Campbell faced about to go home and very probably the

[1] Sebeqwe = Sebehwe, cf. Blaikie, p. 42.

Sechele's child cured

iron founderies which he heard of but was not permitted to see are the very same as belong to them. They always refuse admittance to those who have had intercourse with the other sex since the period of the year when they annually commence smelting, lest they should bewitch the iron. . . . Iron bewitched is when it is burned to a cinder from a too brisk use of the bellows. When the chief & principal families of this tribe fled along with Sebeqwe on account of the inroads of the Matibele the majority of the tribe remained and carried on their works in iron as usual. . . . I lately asked the chief of that tribe if he should like me to come and be his missionary. He held up his hands & said 'O I shall dance for joy if you do. I shall collect all my people to hoe for you a garden and you will get more sweet reed & corn than myself'. No instructions on the subject of an Interior Mission having then come to hand I could only say in answer to his enquiries, that I should inform my Christian friends in England of his desires for a missionary. I need scarcely add that his wish although sincere does not indicate any love to the doctrines we teach. It is merely a desire for the protection & temporal benefit which missionaries are everywhere supposed to bring. It is however as much as we can expect from the Heathen. If we have security for life & property we trust the Lord will give us, in His own time all the rest our hearts long for.

The village of Sechele chief of the Bakwain is five days beyond the Bakhatla. Last year he was exasperated with me for remaining a month with Bube another Bakwain chief whom Sechele considers as in rebellion against him. He made known to some of the believers of this station his determination to do me mischief should I ever attempt to pass his country again. But the Lord was my shield and Sechele was kinder than I ever saw him before. His only child was sick when I arrived and the child of one of his principal men was reduced to a skeleton by dysentery, the means I employed were with the Divine blessing useful to both and Sechele did not seem able to speak a single angry word. . . .

Drivers refuse to go forward

The Matibele of Masilikatze during their last inroad upon the tribes in the Interior took many of the women prisoners, these are constantly making their escape & returning to their respective tribes. When still at the town of Sechele I saw a party of these fugitives which had just arrived. They had travelled nearly two months from the period of making their escape, collecting the roots of the desert for subsistence by day and climbing any high rock they saw in their way for protection by night. The hardships they had undergone had reduced them almost to skeletons and it was most affecting to listen to their tale of woe. But on the part of their fellow countrymen the recital of their sufferings seemed to excite not the smallest sympathy. They were 'women only' and the men sat & listened with the greatest indifference Truly Heathenism has no bowels of compassion. The tale of these females although it had no effect on the Bakwains, had a powerful effect upon the people of my waggon. I could not prevail upon them to go an inch farther for to go any nearer the Matibele than they were seemed like rushing into the jaws of death. Their very hearts seemed ready to die within them. I was thus reduced to the necessity of either giving up my tour & returning, or going forward on oxback. I chose the latter and although it has some inconveniences, it possesses some advantages over the waggon. I visited no fewer than four villages of the Bakalihari to which with the waggon I could not have come. And as they are much more attentive to our instructions than any other Bechuana tribe the pleasure of proclaiming the message of mercy to those who had never before seen a white face, far outweighed any fatigue incurred in reaching them. By far the happiest portion of my late journey was when sitting by their fires & listening to their traditionary tales I could intermingle the story of the cross with their conversation. They are a poor degraded enslaved people. The other tribes consider them as their inferiors—keep them constantly hunting for them and although they procure all the skins which the other tribes sew into Karosses they can scarcely keep as many as

Locusts and wild honey

cover their own nakedness—their gardens are always situated far from their villages in order to secure the produce from the exactions of their masters. And they are always found far from water in order to get as few visits from the servants of the chiefs as possible. To us Europeans it is wonderful how they live. But though they are in want of much that we consider almost necessary to existence a kind Providence has supplied them with many substitutes. They have shewn me more than 40 different kinds of roots and above 30 kinds of fruits which the desert spontaneously yields them. And many of these are by no means unsavoury esculents. 'Locusts and wild honey' abound to them. Perhaps I may be excused if I mention the Physiological effects of the Baptist's food, the former is excessively constipating and the latter has quite the opposite tendency. The locusts pounded & mixed with honey are as good if not better than shrimps at home. It is not probable that he confined himself to that diet. If however 'locusts and wild honey' were as plentiful in the wilderness of Judea as they are now in the desert of the Bakalihari he would have had very little difficulty in finding a constant supply. During a period of twelve months I saw no fewer than nineteen swarms of locusts and yet no particular damage was done to the crops of the natives in consequence; and had I myself attended all the calls of the 'honey bird' I should never have been without a sufficiency of honey.

When at the Bamangwato I saw a son of Conrad Buys, a name both known and dreaded by the early missionaries. He is apparently about 30 years of age,—is dressed & speaks the language exactly as a native. He is one of their lowest menials & is kept to tend a garden in a sort of slavery. His father, Buys, after committing many acts of injustice & murder among the more southern tribes proceeded to the North East of the Bamangwato and there fell a victim to fever. The natives took possession of everything belonging to him even his children of whom by different native wives he had seven, the different chiefs took and distributed among their servants. This man

Ruins of Mosilikatze's town

had been given by a former chief of the Bamangwato to his present master, two brothers he informed me are still alive but in servitude to another tribe. He has forgot all about God & Jesus & only remembers that his father sometimes collected his children—and a book, and then knelt down to pray. He does not remember a single word of Dutch although I tried to recall it to his memory by frequently addressing him in that language. His owner would not consent to part with him so I was obliged to leave him in his sad position. And I could not help thinking that the passage 'the seed of evil doers shall never be renowned' has found in him something like a fulfillment.

Both Bamangwato, Bakaa & Makalaka have been visited during the last year by the commandoes of Mosilikatze and they are all in a much more impoverished condition than when I saw them last. The caverns of the Bakaa & Makalaka saved their lives; their property has all been carried off. The Bamangwato in addition to the loss of property have been considerably reduced in numbers in consequence of having been without retreats in which to hide themselves. Internal dissension too, during which the chief killed his own brother have tended to the same result.

.   .   .   .   .   .

I might have proceeded farther into the Interior but as I was more than 200 miles North from the waggon and the people of it not very trustworthy, I deemed it more prudent to return. The only new people I saw besides the Bakalihari were a portion of the race of Makalaka. They live much farther North than the other tribe mentioned above and are within 2 days of Mosilikatze. They assured me that that Tyrant was still alive and still pursues his career of blood. In returning I walked over what was once the site of his Town near Mosiga and where he suffered his last dreadful defeat by a handful of Boors. The grass had recently been burned off the country so I got a good view of the whole and a few human bones were all that remained of what once belonged to the marauder. And these

Prospects in China

will soon be removed for the hyaenas are so plentiful in a few years they remove everything by which one could discover a recent field of slaughter. Mosilikatze is living at the distance of 12 days or about 200 miles north east of the Bamangwato....

I must also state that I have since hearing of the delightful prospects opened in China felt again the glowings of heart towards that country which were familiar to my mind when I dedicated myself to the mission work there. I feel it is wrong to think more of another field than that to which in the Providence of God I have been called & endeavour to suppress my feelings But I tell you them that you may judge how much ought to be deducted from the force of these statements by taking the existence of these feelings into consideration

I am Dear Sir
Affectionately yours
DAVID LIVINGSTON

LETTER 15

(Original at Scottish National Memorial, Blantyre)

To DR. J. RISDON BENNETT, *London*

Kuruman, 30th June, 1843.

MY DEAR SIR,

Your most welcome letter I found a few days ago on returning from a tour in the Interior, and I assure you the perusal of it afforded me a great amount of enjoyment. Every topic to which you advert is interesting, indeed everything from home is peculiarly so, just like cold water to a thirsty soul, so you must not imagine it was unworthy 'a passage accross the Atlantic'. I thank you heartily for it and earnestly hope you may find it convenient soon to give me just such another.

I am not surprised you have not seen any account of my labours in the magazine, the reasons are, I am not yet settled, the Directors expecting their Mr. Moffat would soon follow, instructed me to remain at Kuruman till his arrival, and this in order to obtain the benefit of his local knowledge of the

Sebehwe's people attacked

country in the choice of a suitable location for a new mission. Mr. M's departure having been delayed, my labours have been mixed with those of the elder missionaries. Good has been done but I believe it has been effected chiefly through the instrumentality of my predecessors I have not felt at liberty to advert to it in my letters to the Directors except in a vague and general manner. . . . Makabba, who was the terror of the Interior in Mr. Campbell's time, has been succeeded by a son called Sebehwe, who is the bravest of all the Bechuanas; Mosilikatse could never overcome him, for he retired into the great Bakalihari desert, and there, by his tactics, cut off detachment after detachment of Mosilikatse's people, sometimes he finished them so completely not one returned to tell the tale. Last year when I was in the Bakwain country, Sebehwe sent messengers to me to say that he was now anxious to leave the desert and return to his own country, and requested me to tell him if it might be a safe movement. I told him although the people of Mosilikatse had been driven away, many of the Batlapi (people of Kuruman) refused the gospel, and having now got guns would certainly attack him for the sake of his cattle. Several of the believers of Kuruman happened to be in that country at the time when S. contrary to my advice, did leave the desert. They visited him and were most kindly received, but, unfortunately, during the very time of their visit, Mahura with his Batlapi pounced upon them. The people of Sebehwe, being quite unused to guns, fled in dismay, and the Batlapi murdered as they chose. The believers, although commanded by Mahura to fire, refused obedience to their chief, on the ground that they served a higher Master than he. But, as they are Batlapi, a most injurious prejudice was excited in the minds of all the natives in the Interior against the gospel by the circumstances in which they were placed at the time. A gun had been fired the night previous to the attack. This Sebehwe thought must have been the signal by which these believers apprised Mahura of his situation, the singing at family worship their incantations for success, and the fact that one of the party, a deacon in the

Lake Mokhoro

church here, was in the act of collecting the people for worship (it being Sabbath morning when the attack was made) when the shout of war was heard was considered by all the heathen as only a pretext by which to aid the work of slaughter. The believers, it was universally believed, had been the betrayers of the brave Sebehwe. The object of my last tour, which commenced on the 21st Feby. last, was by my presence and explanations to disabuse the minds of the heathen, particularly that of Sebehwe, of the unfavourable impression received. He, with the remains of his tribe, lives at a village 10 days N.E. of this, and near to the town of the Bakhatla. The driver of my waggon was one of the party of believers above referred to. When I entered the village, Sebehwe, with his remaining warriors, was seated on the ground; I squatted down beside him. But neither looks nor words betokened complacency to my driver who, during a most uproarious recognition, looked anything but comfortable. Sebehwe demanded of me why I had destroyed all his people and stolen all his cattle. I, being a Scotchman, returned for answer, 'Why did you refuse to listen to my advice, and then destroy yourself?' His messengers of last year then recognised me, and we were soon good friends. . . . Having arrived on a Saturday, I explained the nature of the following day, and desired to have an opportunity to address his people. Next morning, before daybreak, I heard his herald proclaiming the chief's orders that no one should do anything that day but 'pray to God and listen to the words of the foreigner'. At the different services he seemed much interested and frequently asked sensible questions concerning the strange things I had brought to his ears. By the way, I may mention here that fevers seem the greatest barrier to the evangelisation of Africa we have. A short distance beyond my farthest point North there is a fresh water lake called Mokhoro, or the lake of the boat, on account of the canoes which are found upon it. The banks are level with the water, and the surrounding country flat. Hippopotami, alligators, fishes, etc. abound in it. Bamboo and other reeds grow in its banks. There fevers abound, and

Travel on ox-back

this lake stretches away an immense distance to the North East and South West. A small boat carried to it would be an excellent mode of exploring a large portion of the interior. Many nations live upon its banks and trade upon its waters. They are armed with guns, which they procure from Portuguese on the East coast. I hear Mr. Moffat intends revisiting this lake. I hope he won't fall a victim to its fever. Last year, a strong native who accompanied me was seized with it, and I had great difficulty in getting him through it. The effects, however, are still apparent upon him. Then to the North and N.W. and then to the North East we have a fly which bites the oxen, and the very first rain that falls afterwards seems to excite its poison to activity, for they all die. Several traders have lost every one of their oxen by them. And then towards the coast at Delagoa Bay fevers are exceedingly fatal. Several parties of boors have been cut off by them. I have anxiously looked for an account of that which cut off so many of the Niger expedition in order to compare it with this case of it which I saw. But it has not appeared in any periodical that has come my way yet.

After parting with Sebehwe, I went Northwards to the Bakwain country, which is situated on the tropic, and meeting some of the escaped captives there, my people would go no farther. The idea of going near Mosilikatse was too much for them. Their hearts were ready to die within them, so I left them in charge of the waggon and proceeded on oxback. I think I see you smile at the idea of such a conveyance. It is rough travelling, as you can conceive. The skin is so loose there is no getting one's great coat, which has to serve for both saddle and blanket, to stick on. And then the long horns in front with which he can give one a punch in the abdomen if he likes, make us sit as 'bolt upright' as dragoons. In this manner I travelled more than 400 miles. I visited the Bamangwato, Bakaa, and Makalaka, and many villages of the poor enslaved Bakalahari, which, but for this mode of travelling, I should never have seen. Their villages are usually so far in the desert no waggon can approach them. They are much oppressed by the other

Desert Life

Bechuana tribes. All the skins which the other tribes sew into karosses are procured by them, and yet they can scarcely keep as much of what they kill as to cover their own bodies. They always live far from water in order to avoid coming in contact with their masters (the other tribes consider them inferior) yet their wants are wonderfully supplied by Providence. They have shewn me between 40 and 50 different kinds of roots, and more than 30 different kinds of fruits, which they use as food, and some of them are by no means unsavoury. They were more attentive to my instructions than any other, which made me feel much interested in them. The other tribes mentioned above live on the summits of a range of lofty black bassaltic rocks once the scene of active volcanic operations. When standing on their tops, we see in every direction immense cup-shaped cavities, some of them as large as Finsbury Square,[1] and at least 300 feet deep, their flat bottoms are covered with vegetation, but their almost perpendicular sides have not yet formed a vegetable mantle, while on the outside patches of the same colour, and destitute of vegetation take the form of streams running down to the plains below. Some end in a point half way down the hill, others gain the bottom and then spread out, just as we suppose streams of lava would do. These rocks are rent and riven in every direction. The huge angular fragments which have slipped down have, by impinging on each other and the rocks below, formed innumerable cavities and into these the Bamangwato, Bakaa, and Makalaka fly for shelter from their fierce enemies the Matabele; One which I entered could hold a hundred individuals. The entrance was so small and crooked, a dozen men could stand and defend it against the ingress of a single individual, crouching on all fours. Into another a whole village entered, and when the Matebele besieged one entrance, the people had another by which at night they went to draw water and bring wood for cooking. The Bakaa have a bad

---

[1] Finsbury Square is an oblong 161 yards by 136. It was at that time well known as a residential square. Secretary Tidman lived at No. 27, within a short walk of his office at 14 Blomfield St.

Broken finger-bone

name among all the other tribes because a few years ago they killed a trader and all his people by poison. When I visited them last year I saw pieces of his gun locks, tin jugs, and sail-cloth of his waggon worn as ornaments by them. Last year a native who was with me became ill during our visit to the man himself and all the other tribes believe he was poisoned. I however, do not believe it, for I saw symptoms of indisposition before we arrived there. The Bakaa determined this year to give us nothing at all, and thus avoid a similar imputation. There was no game near, so we had to feast for two days on the delectable things we saw in our dreams. This low diet had a good effect on me, for when descending their lofty rocks, after having addressed them, I felt so much interested in the questions they were putting concerning what they had heard, I forgot for a moment where I was going, and then feeling as if about to fall, made a violent effort to save myself. But, though I succeeded, I struck my hand with so much violence on a sharp angle as produced a compound fracture of the finger bone. The Testament served as a rest between which and the rock my finger was injured, and a very good splint was made of a piece of reed. The fasting, I suppose, prevented irritative fever, and although I did not rest a day on account of it, it was about to heal kindly. But one night a lion began to roar tremendously and very near to the bush at which we were all fast asleep. It was nearer than from your room in the dispensary to the open street. My ox leapt in among us. My poor Bakwains shrieked for fear, and I, half awake and stupid seized a pistol with the disabled hand fired at the monster, but the rebound rebroke my finger. When we got him driven away the poor Bakwains (three of that tribe went with me as guides, my own people being all with the waggon) seeing the blood running, said, 'You have hurt yourself, but you have redeemed us. Hence forth we shall swear by you'. . . . The second fracture was worse than the first, but as I can bear a little pain pretty well, it did not hinder me as much as I expected it should. It prevented my obtaining provisions by my gun, and the whole party being entirely

Locusts and wild honey

dependant on it, we should have been put to shift had it not been for the kindness of the Bakalahari. They generously gave what food they had, and although some of it is absolutely indigestible, and undergoes no alteration by being subjected to the action of the stomach, I never enjoyed better health. I don't remember ever to have seen the physiological effects of the food of John the Baptist (I don't suppose the Baptist lived constantly on locusts, etc., but suppose he had, if the locusts were as plentiful as here, he would find no difficulty in obtaining a constant supply. In less than a year I have seen 18 swarms besides others not yet furnished with wings, and no damage was done to the crop worth speaking of) noticed by commentators. The locusts are the most constipating food I ever ate; they taste just like the vegetables on which they subsist, generally like the soft juicy parts of a stalk of wheat, which perhaps you may have tasted, and far better than shrimps at home. The wild honey has the very opposite tendency, the two combined form one of the best kinds of food the Bakalihari have. We find the honey by means of a bird, the skin of which I shall send you. They call us by a peculiar kind of chirping, and following it we very seldom are disappointed. I have followed them four or five miles, and when hungry was sure of finding a meal at the spot she pointed out. I have resolved to deviate from your instructions respecting sending anything large. I intend sending with the other things a skin of a spring buck. It is the most beautiful of all the antelope tribe and will make an elegant ornament to your receiving room. It is as large as a greyhound, but I am sure when you see it you will not grudge it a corner. To the other things I shall make additions, and as soon as a conveyance can be got down to the Bay (Algoa), I shall dispatch them for you. I send, in the course of a few months, a box to Revd. E. Williams of Hankey, who has been obliged to go home on account of Tracheitis or something of that nature. I shall desire him to hand you a Kaross, which I shall be obliged to you to accept as a token of my remembrance until I can send you something more substantial. It will make a comfortable covering

Rarity of Hydrocephalus

for your study chair in winter, or a lining for the cloak of your little boy. Your very kind offer as to the medicines, instruments etc., I shall gladly avail myself of, as I purchase them at a great disadvantage at the Cape. But, as I have lately obtained a supply, it will be next year before I take the liberty of writing you on that subject.

I must now advert to the other topic in your letter but I am ashamed to send so much egotism as is contained in the above but perhaps you will be able to glean something of the state of the country from what I have said. We are not gentlemen missionaries, but rough it wherever we go. And we do not grudge our efforts if they only conduce to the advancement of our Redeemer's glory. When I first saw the manner in which the native women carry their children viz. slung on the back with the head exposed (to) the piercing rays of the sun, I felt certain that affection of the head should be of frequent occurrence. I have, however, never met with a single case of either congestive or inflammatory affection of the brain; the above custom put me on the 'look out' for Hydrocephalus, but have not as yet observed one case in the least degree resembling that disease. On enquiry amongst the missionaries who have paid most attention to disease, I find it is exceedingly rare among the native children, while among the children of Europeans it is as common as meningitis. During a period of twelve years, Mr. Edwards, a very accurate observer of these matters, has only seen one case of it. Having seen the disease in European children, and being well acquainted with its symptoms, I think his testimony can be relied on. Whilst during a shorter period of observation, and among the Mission families (French and English) not amounting to 40 individuals in all, I am informed no fewer than 4 infants have fallen victims to that disease. You remark 'that it is probable Hydrocephalus does not often appear among the natives', from this, and the corroboration of your view which my enquiries seem to elicit, I infer, whatever your views of the cause of that disease may be, they seem to be correct. . . .

Cure of Consumption

With respect to consumption, I saw it prevailing very extensively among the Hottentots, especially those near the sea coast. This district is reputed in the Colony as peculiarly favourable for the cure of that disease. I have made many enquiries on the subject, and the only reasons for the idea are the following. Two individuals are reported to have been nearly in the last stage, but, having removed to this part of the country, soon lost every symptom of Phthisis, and are now living in perfect health. One is a Hottentot and the other a Motchuana. The former I have not seen, but the latter I had under my care for enlargement of the right ovary, with shooting pains and tenderness in the situation of the other. She told me (she) got married soon after her arrival here from the Colony, became pregnant and was delivered of a still born child before the usual period. Soon after that event pains commenced in the right ovary, and not long after that she felt the tumour (which was, at commencement of my treatment last year about the size of a large fist, and visible to the eye on looking at the abdomen) and it continued to increase for several years. About twelve months before I saw her the pains shifted from the right to the left, but no swelling took place. I gave her solution of iodine internally in large doses, with occasionally a Plummer's pill, and applied a large mercurial plaster over the situation of the tumour, and in the space of three months the pains in the left and swelling in the right had entirely disappeared. I examined the lungs frequently with the stethoscope, but could discover nothing to indicate they had ever been the seat of tubercle. I was at first disposed to think that possibly her former medical attendant had been deceived in his diagnosis, and that the case might have been one of Bronchitis rather than of Phthisis. But I find she was under the care of Dr. Chalmers of Algoa Bay, who seems well acquainted with the use of the stethoscope, one of his own lungs being completely condensed—the effect of pleuritis—and the other frequently attacked with bronchitis, have led him to a careful investigation of lung diseases. So there is the less probability of a mistake having been made. I ought

Climate of Bechuanaland

to have mentioned that it is now 9 or 10 years since she left the Colony on account of bad health. She is now strong, and if I could, in answer to her importunate begging, give her medicine to enable her to get a child, she would be one of the happiest of women. Perhaps this case may be accounted for by the same mode of reasoning as the arrest of the progress of consumption for a time by pregnancy, the salubrity of the climate helping to complete the cure. Among Bechuanas I have only seen one case of consumption. She lives about 50 miles from this, has been about two years ill, and is now much spent. I regret I have not had an opportunity of treating her, for if any climate would assist the curative effects of medicine I believe this would. It is dry, not excessively hot during summer, and the winters are bracing. It differs much from that of the Interior, and a journey is almost always beneficial to invalids. The Indian officers who come here are usually quite fat before they come this length. The chief excellence of this climate I conceive is its dryness, and almost entire absence of sudden changes of temperature. The cold weather comes on very gradually, and when it is warm during summer the nights are also warm, and except immediately after rain, which, however, seldom falls, we never see dew. I slept during my oxback journey for three weeks and four days on the sand with only my great coat over me and a little grass under, and yet I never once caught a cold. . . .

This is a *parvum in multo* letter, but you must (pardon) its many blunders. My sentences sometimes come tailforwards, as in Bechuana, and require many corrections. Will you be so kind as to present my Christian regards to your much respected father and mother and your partner, with whom I hope you will long live in much domestic happiness.

Believe me,
Yours affectionately,
D. Livingston.

LETTER 16

To MR. HENRY DRUMMOND, *Glasgow*

Kuruman,
29th July 1843.

MY DEAR FRIEND,

I believe it is usual when one receives a letter from a far country to expect to find something in it, and I shall be sorry if your expectations are raised by the sight of this, for it will contain nothing at all but a request for your assistance to refit, or rather replenish, my wardrobe. I have transmitted, through a dear friend of mine, who has been compelled to leave for England, on account of an affection of the throat, the sum of ten Pounds to be sent to you for the above purpose. I don't know exactly what I need, but I shall give you an account of what the country needs, and then I leave you to supply me to the best of your judgment. The country then being one of the most thorny in the world, needs some sort of thing which will prevent it reducing us to the necessity of going with our bare legs, like old Dr. Vanderkemp. We don't need waterproofs, we require thorn-proofs only. If you have any of the latter in your shop—please let my trousers be of this. I wear common cloth trousers but they are not at all strong enough. On my last journey I wore out two pàirs of them in less than three months. I have thought strong moleskin would be better, and should like to try. It does not matter what colour, it might be scarlet, for colour is nothing—strength everything to one in this region. Please let them be made without pockets and open in front.

I should like a jacket or two of the same material, made with a single row of buttons, a plain collar shaped like those of soldiers, but made to lie flat on the shoulders, and inside pockets. Also some sort of duffel jacket and trousers for the winter. If it would not much increase the expense I should prefer the jacket to be something of the surtout shape, or rather common hunting jacket. The winters here are not cold to one

Order for clothing

from Europe, but to one from the interior they are piercing. When last in the interior I slept for three weeks, and four nights on the ground with only a little grass between me and it. My greatcoat and one skin blanket were my only coverings, and yet I was all the time quite comfortable. No sooner, however, did I pass to this side of the Bakhatla than I was more miserable with cold than ever I was in Europe. It seems here to go through to the very marrow of the bones, and yet the thermometer does not indicate cold current. The winter dress might be of tartan,[1] lined with green baize. I wear one of that sort now and it is very good. It has one fault, but it is a peculiarity of all the goods brought from Europe by traders to this country—the stuff is so useless it is done for directly. But I am going to the country where it will not be needed, and when I return it will be summer with us.

Half-a-dozen strong cotton shirts, striped blue, and a pair of boots, if the money will go so far. You must be good enough to give the value of the chief part of the money in strong trousers, the others on the list you must leave as soon as the tail of the money leaves you. A plain overcoat, or two, if you please.

With respect to the measure, I give you a measurement made by a London tailor, but as it is in his own hieroglyphics it may be of no use to you, the length of leg from the fork to the foot, is 2 ft. 8 inch, to the knee 1 ft 3 in. Girth of thigh, 1. 11, of seat 3 ft. 1 in, of waist 2 ft. 8 in, whole length of trousers measure on the outside 3 ft 7.

With respect to the jackets, as you and I seem very much of the same dimensions your measurement will answer me very well. Mr. Nasmith has my measure for boots, if you get him to make them for me—tell him he cannot make them too strong, the thorns are really dreadful in this country, there are some the very oxen won't go near. The Dutch call them 'Wait a

---

[1] See *Travels*, ch. 1. A tartan jacket worn by Livingstone in his encounter with a lion was thought to have removed the virus from the animal's teeth. The tartan which the Highland Livingstones are entitled to wear is the hunting tartan of the Clan Stewart of Appin.

The land drying up

little' for if you happen to come in contact with them they will compel you to wait and unloose, or else leave your garments in their power. Africa seems to have got a larger share of the curse of thorns than any other country, yet this sort of vegetation is entirely confined to the plains, on the hills we have no thorns, but a totally different race of plants and trees, which seem to have been formerly the inhabitants of the plains. They have been expelled from their former habitat by the increasing heat of the climate. Perhaps you are not aware this country is becoming warmer, the fountains are drying up, and there is the strongest evidence that at one period this, instead of being as it now is, chiefly a sterile waste, was one of the finest watered countries in the world. The channels of these are still visible, and being covered with a different kind of vegetation from the surrounding country, their forms are easily detected. The natives always call them rivers, although now not a drop of water ever flows in them. One I travelled in must have been as broad as the Thames at Westminster, and when I came to the point of junction with what must have been a large Lake, there in a mound formed at the former confluence of the water, were beautiful collections of fossil bones—the bones were harder than the rocks, and as the latter had been washed away by the rains the former stood out on the surface in bold relief. The teeth, although of stone, were in such a perfect state of preservation, the radiated structure of the channel, the black tartar; the little hole for the transmission of nerve and blood vessels, were exactly as in recent specimens. But I am away from my purpose in writing this letter. . . .

I am just on the point of starting for the country of the Bakhatla, a people with whom I expect before long to be located. It is the Sheffield of the interior, and seems a fine part of the country. We have good prospects of effective permanent settlement there. But we don't know the future, the cause is, however, that of the Lord, and greater is He who is for us than all that can be against us. We shall have the Boors of Port Natal, etc, about three days to the East of us, a most ignorant, half-civilised, but generally hospitable race. They are as formal in religious observances as any of our worthy Church-going Scotch folk in country parishes, much disaffected towards the Colonial Government, and indeed in open rebellion against the measures of the Home Government, for the abolition of slavery is the great root of bitterness among them. They had the finest farms in the Colony, unprincipled Englishmen, seeing that these could be turned to their own benefit as sheep farms, took advantage of their discontent and ignorance, fanned the flame until they got them to sell their lands for almost nothing. The Boors believed everything they saw in print must be true, left the Colony in thousands, determined no longer to submit to British rule. A worthless Tory journal, edited by a Wesleyan, has been the main instrument in this disaffection. Boors are again stealing the children of the natives in order to make them slaves. The Government will not allow this, but there will be bloodshed before it is put down. . . .

I am Dear Friend,
Yours affectionately,
D. LIVINGSTON.

LETTER 17

(Original at the Rhodes-Livingstone Institute)

To MR. THOMAS L. PRENTICE, *Violet Hill, Stowmarket, Suffolk*

MY DEAR FRIEND PRENTICE,   Lattakoo.[1] 9th. Octr. 1843.

'Hope deferred maketh the heart sick, but when the desire cometh it is a tree of life', is the passage which sprung into my mind when I saw your letter. I cannot tell you how much I longed for it nor how often I have thought of you and C. . . . I got it on returning a few days ago from the erection of a hut at the Bakhatla a tribe situated a little more than 200 miles north of this. It is the nearest point in the Interior where an eligible spot can be found, and we have by this step taken possession of it for a station. A lovelier spot you never saw, a hill in the rear is called Mabotsa (a marriage feast). . . .

[1] Lattakoo, an earlier name for Kuruman.

Waggon upset

I have been in journeyings oft since I last wrote you. These were necessary because the Directors imagining that we[1] should be fully employed in acquiring the language untill the arrival of Mr. Moffat directed us to remain at Kuruman for that purpose. I did not however find it so difficult as was expected and very soon set off to gain local knowledge for myself, that being the sort Mr. M. was expected to assist us by in selecting a proper site for a station, I have been further in the Interior than any other European and have repeatedly had the privilege of preaching beyond every other man's line of things. Many merciful escapes I have met with. Poor Birt[2] I hear lost his wife by the overturning of his waggon. That accident happened to me twice during one journey and not a hair of my head harmed in consequence. On one occasion I was sitting reading with my legs across the waggon and all I felt was an instantaneous transference from the sitting to the standing posture. I only looked back to see books, bed, bags, boxes and guns making all haste to the leeward in glorious confusion. Had my head been where my feet were a box might have finished my chapter.... We have not so many people as in some countries but this I am inclined now to look upon as an advantage, for we can bring the truth to bear on one individual again and again while in India for instance they seldom see the same person twice at services—This climate is delightful, indeed I cannot speak too highly of it. I really pity you in your cold damp one, only think I slept three weeks and 4 days at one season on the ground and although riding all that time on a pack ox I never had a cough.... How is old Mr. Ridley? and Susan and all. I like much just to hear how it is with everyone I ever knew.... May His presence be with your dear Cathrine and comfort her as He only can. I hope your little boy will be a missionary. Please give him a press to your heart for me. Please present my affectionate salutations to Cathrine. I cant think of her as Mrs. P. and will always name her as she was

[1] 'We', W. Ross and himself.
[2] Rev. Richard Birt of Kafirland.

Everything slow except time.

when I first saw her. To your Father Mother and Brothers. Surely Fison might as easily give me a note as write some nonsense from Greek plays.

Ever affectionately yours
DAVID LIVINGSTON.

I shall answer every letter of yours that reaches me.

LETTER 18

To REV. ARTHUR TIDMAN

Lattakoo 30th Octr 1843

DEAR SIR

In my last dated 24th June, I informed you that there were again by the establishment of peace, favourable prospects for the Missionary cause in the Interior. And I likewise gave you some particulars respecting a tribe called the Bakhatla which is situated at the nearest inhabited & at present most eligible spot northwards. At that time I had no other intention than that of remaining here untill by the arrival of the bretheren the committee of which you advised me should be constituted and final arrangements made for our future operations. But after waiting more than a month in suspense & daily expectation of witnessing their arrival a letter arrived from Mr Moffat stating that both he and his companions were detained near the coast and that probably two or three months more might elapse ere they could reach Kuruman. No one out of this country can imagine how grievously slow everything in it moves except time But it cannot be otherwise so long as the heavy Dutch waggon and tedious pack ox are the only permanent conveyances This disadvantage has a great effect on most missionary movements and not unfrequently presses heavily on our spirits. For with scenes such as those of Exeter Hall living and burning on our recollections, and the remembrance of the shortness of our lives, together with the sad prospects of the Heathen immortals before us, it is felt hard to be called on to wait or indeed do anything unconnected with the movement onward—

Help of Edwards

While here I could generally find a sufficiency of work by attending to the wants of the sick who come in crowds from great distances as soon as they hear of my arrival But as I believe the expenditure of much time and medicine is not the way in which in this country I can do most for the Redeemer's glory, I usually decline treating any except the more urgent cases, These with a share of the duties of the station might have filled up my time untill the formation of the committee But having always felt an intense desire to carry the gospel to the regions beyond, And Mr Moffat having intimated that 'The Directors would have no objection to Mr Edwards removing to the Interior'; and it being a fact too that a little delay would throw the commencement of the new mission by whomsoever formed into the most unfavourable season for health, or else produce a much longer delay viz. untill the hot season had passed. I concluded that it would be proper to proceed immediately and erect a hut on the spot selected near the Bakhatla. And in this decision I was cordially joined by the bretheren Hamilton & Edwards. The latter indeed resolved to accompany me and I feel happy in being able to state that on account of his superior knowledge of the use of tools He was a much more efficient agent in the labour that ensued than I was. He also afforded me much assistance by allowing me the use of a waggon, my own having previously been sent off to the Colony with Mr Ross in order to assist in bringing the luggage of the bretheren who are coming to join us. This proceeding in as far as I am concerned does not preclude my being subject to the arrangements of the committee either with respect to my location or associate in labour. For though I believe the spot selected is the very best at present inhabited in the Interior. This too being the opinion of three Indian[1] gentlemen. One an Aide Camp to the Governor of Madras who visited it with us. And though I should be delighted to

---

[1] 'Indian gentlemen.' The term is used elsewhere also, they were not Indians but men from India of whom Captain Steele of the Coldstream Guards, the aide-de-camp here referred to, was an example.

Invited to dwell with the Bakhatla

call it the centre of the sphere of my labour I shall try to hold myself in readiness to go anywhere provided it be forward. And with respect to my future companion, as Mr Ross feels it to be his duty to remain near Kuruman, I should prefer from a variety of considerations one of the younger, especially Inglis, to any of the older brethern. But these with all my cares I desire to cast on the Lord. And I earnestly desire He may lead me in that path which shall be most for His glory. My short experience of missionary life fully convinces me of the excellences of the hints contained in pages 18 & 19 of the Printed letter of Instructions. Indeed close attention to them will enable one to get on pretty comfortably with even the strangest tempers. And it might have prevented much unpleasantness in Africa. May the Lord clothe me with humility and make me more like Himself.

We left this in the beginning of August, and after a fortnight spent in the journey we arrived in safety among the Bakhatla. The chief eagerly enquired whether I had as promised told my friends of his desire that I should live with him. And on my replying on the affirmative, and that the object Mr Edwards and I had in this visit was to talk on that subject, he expressed himself much satisfied. We afterwards in a grand 'Peecho' or assembly of his people stated fully our objects in proposing a residence with them, and desired his counsellors to mention their objections if they had any, to our coming to teach them. One man said he had heard, if any one 'put himself under the word of God he should be obliged to put away his superfluous wives'. To this the only objection offered, another of themselves replied before we could, 'That he had been to Moteeto and saw that the missionaries there acted entirely on the voluntary principle, and neither claimed nor exercised authority over any one.' We then explained that our province was not to compell, but to teach the commands of God, to entreat and warn. But should men refuse to obey God, Guilt would be incurred before Him, and He will require it. The rest were unanimous in expressing their wish that we should come &

Settlement of Mission Station

live with them. But alas their motives in giving us a cordial welcome are very different from ours in desiring to accept of it. They wish the residence of white men, not from any desire to know the gospel, But merely as some of them in conversation afterwards expressed it 'that by our presence and prayers they may get plenty of rain, beads, guns &c &c. And be secure from death by the warriors of Mosilikatse. May the Lord enlighten their benighted minds.

On enquiring whether they intended to remain on the spot they then occupied, We were delighted to find that they had had in contemplation for some time previously to remove to the very locality selected. They however put it in our option whether they should remove or remain where they were. We preferred the former as the removal was to an adjoining valley much better adapted for agricultural purposes than that they then occupied. A portion of land might have been appropriated to our use but we preferred purchasing with the use of the streams on each side of it. I drew up a short statement of the transaction, read it over in Sitchuana the chief repeating it word by word after me and when both chief & counsellors perfectly understood its nature, they expressed entire satisfaction by affixing their marks.

We then proceeded to the erection of a substantial hut 50 ft. by 18. But in this work we got scarcely any assistance from the Bakhatla. Hard work in many of the Bechuana tribes devolves entirely on females so the males become as unfit as they are unwilling to bear it. One of the four men we took with us feigned sickness during most of the time. But Mabalwe a deacon of the church here rendered us invaluable aid He is willing and anxious to go with us as native teacher and the bretheren here think him well qualified for that purpose So I have concluded he is a proper person to recieve the assistance tendered by a friend of mine in scotland. I have not however made any definite arrangement with him as I feel anxious to hear the plans of the Directors in the committee before doing so. I have given him a portion of the sum I have drawn in his name

Mebalwe instructed

viz. £12. not as remuneration for his services as I think it undesirable to convey even in a remote way the idea of wages in the Lord's service, But as part of the assistance a believer in another country is desirous of rendering to one who spends most of his time in endeavouring to do good. The remainder will remain in my hands till definite plans are promulgated by the committee; in the mean time I am endeavouring to give instruction in order to qualify him for greater usefulness.

The Indian gentlemen above mentioned came to this country in order to have their health restored by the exercises of hunting and travelling, they were totally unlike some others of the same class who have visited this country, for they behaved with great propriety before the natives, and towards us with the greatest kindness, on various occasions supplying us liberally with game and skins to assist in building, which with the economy we endeavoured to maintain will render the whole expense of journey & building a very small item only in the expenses of the Interior mission.

We have been here nearly a month again and the bretheren do not yet appear. But we recieved information yesterday which leads us to conclude that they must now have reached Colesberg. Patience has her perfect work here if anywhere

Believe me Dear Sir
Yours Affectionately
DAVID LIVINGSTON

LETTER 19

To REVD. DR. TIDMAN

Mabotsa,
9 June 1844.

DEAR SIR,

The Lord having in tender mercy restored me to my wonted health I have much cause for gratitude in being able again to communicate with you. The affliction[1] from which I have been

[1] The lion incident is fully described in *Travels*, ch. 1. The news of the affair was sent to Tidman by Robert Moffat. See below.

The broken arm

raised was both painful and protracted, as the wounds discharging profusely prevented the union of the fragments into which the bone was broken, and these having been seldom properly secured, every motion of the body produced a grating irritation which reacted on the wounds. But through the mercy of our Heavenly Father the whole has healed well beyond my most sanguine expectation, and the bone is perfectly straight and firm. It was a severe trial of patience to be laid aside so long and at a period, too, when every assistance that can be rendered is required. But though I fear I have not learned all that was intended by the chastisement, I trust I have realized much, which though I knew, I did not fully feel before. And I hope I am now more anxious than ever that my spared life may be entirely consecrated to the glory of my great Deliverer.

The Bakhatla are at present busily engaged in removing from their former location to the spot in which we reside, and it is cheering to observe the subordinate chiefs have, with one exception, chosen sites for their villages conveniently near to that on which we purpose to erect the permanent premises. We purpose to build a house to serve as school and meeting-house, as soon as possible, and then we hope our efforts to impart a knowledge of saving truth will assume a more regular form than at present. Among a people so degraded as Bechuanas, no very decided result can be expected unless there is a continuous application of the truth to their minds, and for this missionaries in Africa have superior advantages to those in countries more densely populated. There the mass of the population cannot be addressed very frequently, or the address followed by continued and pointed appeals to the same individuals. While here we generally have opportunities of directing the light on to the same minds continuously, and it appears by the Divine blessing to ensure greater results than desultory efforts between which considerable periods intervene. Conversion among Bechuanas is in general by no means a quick process, their depravity being *sub-natural*, some time elapses ere they are raised to the level of sinners in other countries, and

Animal tribal names

then they seem to require time again before they can accommodate their minds to the change of thought and motive. There may be a leaning to the side of holiness for a long period, but generally a thorough revolution is wrought out before their convictions become embodied in action. I visited the Bakhatla frequently before the establishment of the Mission. But it was not until my fifth visit that sufficient confidence was inspired to draw forth a cordial invitation for me to settle among them. And this is the only good I can ascertain effected by my itineracies to them. The reason seems to have been too long periods intervened between each journey to produce any lasting impressions. And this is not to be wondered at, for nothing can exceed the grovelling earthliness of their minds, they seem to have fallen as low in the scale of humanity as human nature can. At some remote period their ancestors appear to have been addicted to animal worship, for each tribe is called by some animal, by it they swear, and in general neither eat nor kill it, alledging as a cause that these animals are the friends of their tribe. Thus the word Batlapi, literally translated is '*Men* (of the) *Fish*', Bakwain '*Men* (of the) *Crocodile*', Bakhatla '*Men* (of the) *Monkey*', etc. But if the conjecture is not wrong, they have degenerated from even that impure form of worship, and the wisest among them have now no knowledge of it but suppose some of their ancestors must have been called by these names. They have reached the extreme of degradation. When we compare the Bakhatla with the inhabitants around Lattakoo, the latter appear quite civilized. And their present state of partial enlightenment shews that the introduction of the Gospel into a country has a mighty influence even over those by whom it is either not known or rejected. I am not now to be misunderstood as speaking of the converts nor of the new phases of character the transforming power of the Gospel has developed among them. But I allude to the unconnected, and to those other than saving influences of Christianity which so materially modify the social system at home. On many these influences have operated for years and they have not operated in vain.

Mebaloe risked his life

Hence the mass of the population in the Kuruman district are not now in that state the Gospel found them, and in which the poor Bakhatla now are. There the existence of Deity is tacitly admitted by nearly all, the exceptions denying it rather on account of attachment to their lusts than in sober seriousness. And I believe the number is but small, who have not the idea floating on their minds that this life is but the beginning of our existence, and death but one event in a life which is everlasting. But the Bakhatla have had no thoughts on the subject, their mind is darkness itself, and no influences have ever operated on it but those which have left it supremely selfish. It is only now that Christians have begun to stop the stream which has swept generation after generation of them into darkness. And O may the Holy Spirit aid our efforts, for without His mighty power all human efforts will be but labour in vain. That power exerted over Bechuanas—raising them from the extreme of degradation—and transforming them into worshippers of the Living God, constitutes the wonder and the cause for gratitude in the Bechuana Mission.

Our native assistant Mebaloe has been of considerable value to the Mission. In endeavouring to save my life he nearly lost his own, for he was caught and wounded severely. But both before our being laid aside and since recovery he has shewn great willingness to be useful. The cheerful manner in which he engages with us in manual labour on the station, and his affectionate addresses to his countrymen, are truly gratifying. Mr. Edwards took him to several villages near the Kurrechane lately in order to introduce him to his work, and I intend to depart tomorrow for the same purpose in several villages of the Makone, situated at convenient distances around us, and we each purpose to visit them steadily. It would be of immense advantage to the cause had we many such agents. But after being assured by bretheren on the spot, whom I presumed to be intimately acquainted with the state of the Mission, that many such could be got; and after most earnest pleading for, and receiving assurances of support from my friends at home,

Secretaries and lion incident

I am sorry to say I cannot succeed according to my desire. Suitable individuals are generally so wedged and dovetailed among their relatives, I fear some time must yet elapse ere that means of spreading the Gospel can be extensively brought into operation. Still, believing that it is extremely well adapted to the state of this country, and having seen that it has been extensively blessed for the conversion of souls, I shall never lose sight of it. And constantly pray that God may incline the hearts of his converts to feel more compassion for their countrymen.

Believe me,
Dear Sir,
Yours affectionately,
DAVID LIVINGSTON.

¶ Having heard of the attack made upon Livingstone by a lion while at Mabotsa the Foreign Secretaries wrote on September 11th, 1844: 'You will be assured it was with strong and affectionate solicitude we received the intelligence of the alarming disaster which occurred to you at Mabotsa, in the month of February last. The information reached us in a letter from Mr. Moffat, which was dated on the 24th of that month, and since it arrived we have received no further communication on the subject. You will therefore judge of the anxiety we have felt, and continue to feel, as to the results of the serious injury inflicted on your person, under circumstances and in a situation which would render it all but impossible to obtain proper surgical treatment. . . . We hope that an event which so nearly proved fatal will impress you with the necessity for being very careful for the future how you expose yourself to similar risks. . . .

'Your letters of October 21 and January 24th, have reached us in due course, and to the former of these we have already, in preceding parts of this communication, substantially replied. Your letter of January explains two or three points to which we would now briefly advert. With reference to the District Committee we are gratified that you so readily accepted your appointment from the Directors to act as a Member of that body, and we trust experience will have removed any appre-

Theory of Committees

hensions you might have felt in the first instance as to the satisfactory working of a plan which has been long tried and found highly beneficial in other parts of the world. The affairs of our Missions in India, the South Seas, and the West Indies, are all conducted by Missionary Committees similarly constituted, and no objection has hitherto been raised against such a mode of operation by those who have to carry it into effect. The power of a Committee is precisely of the same nature as the power of the Board of Directors—in both cases, it is a delegated power and no more, and the objections which would be fatal to a Committee would also be fatal to a Board, as they are both based simply on the principle of representation and possess no absolute or final authority. The Committee is accountable to the Board, and the Board is accountable to the Members of the Society, to whom, in every case, there is an appeal from the decisions of the former two bodies. In such cases no individual Missionary can suffer wrong from a Committee—If wrong be attempted he has the remedy in his own hands, by referring the case to the Board, or, (if he fails to receive redress there) to its constituents to whose decision he must clearly either submit, or retire from the service of the Society. We have thus endeavoured to give a correct idea of the nature of a District Committee because we feel persuaded that when viewed in its true light, no reasonable objection can be urged against the appointment and agency of such a body for conducting the local affairs of an extensive Mission.

'Your statistical notices of the population of the Bechuana Country will be useful for our future guidance, in the adoption of measures for extending the Gospel in that part of Africa. On a comparison of its population with that of India or China, we fully agree with you as to the superior claims of either of the latter Countries on the resources of the Christian Church, and we shall certainly feel it our duty to act upon the principles which you have so properly and earnestly urged upon our attention. At the same time, there will be no diminution of our interest on behalf of the Bechuana Mission, nor shall we ever

'In Love'

feel that your own energies could be better employed than in labouring to widen its boundaries and multiply its triumphs.'

LETTER 20

(Original at Scottish National Memorial to Livingstone, Blantyre)
To REV. GEORGE DRUMMOND, *Navigators' Islands*

Mabotsa. 21st Nov. 1844.

MY DEAR BROTHER DRUMMOND,

Your welcome & excellent letter written at some queer outlandish place[1] ... found me in my monkish cell a few days ago as happy as any of you domesticated animals and (*mirabile dictu* just on the eve of becoming one myself. But I cannot leave the bachelor life myself without a sigh. What infatuation you labour under to rejoice after having had your nose held to the 'grun-stone' for such a length of time and what infatuation I am under myself. In love!! words yea thoughts fail so I leave it to your imagination & recollection—I am it seems after all to be hooked to Miss Moffat (Mr Moffat's eldest daughter) in about three weeks hence. I am just finishing my house. It is something like your own I suppose only rather more primitive. 52 feet in length & 20 broad, walls 18″ thick & 11 feet high. Veranda 6 feet broad, containing a study, bedroom & parlour—& pantry, kitchen apart from the house. Is it stone do you think? Nay but a much easier material to mould, very plastic mud. We dash it on about a foot thick & then cut it straight with a spade & such is the heat of the luminary as Fairbrother[2] would call the sun over our heads before two hours you would wonder where the water has gone. Indeed one hour's exposure makes it difficult to cut. We run up walls in no time after the foundation is laid & they are as hard as brick almost....

Our chiefs are generally an imbecile race. 'Gowks' & 'Sandy Macfarlanes' their power is of the feudal sort & they are exceedingly jealous of our approaches. Everything we do is thought

[1] Savaii, Samoa.
[2] William Fairbrother, of Tutbury. He had sailed for China in October after training at Ongar.

African nakedness

to be an attempt to draw people to our party & power The 'Boguera' or circumcision is more (or rather entirely) a national civil rite than religious observance. It takes place every four or five years & all of nearly the same puberty age are subjected to it, thòse who have gone to the circumcision together are bound into a cohort under one of the chiefs sons or brothers for ever afterwards & have to render service go whereever he is sent, do whatever he likes under pain of death untill that event takes place,This ceremony was looked upon by the early missionaries as sinful, They keep it secret in a measure & perhaps this was one portion of the reason why the missionaries came to the conclusion. You will percieve that war proclaimed against this might easily be interpreted as war against the feudal system which exists & it was so, & thus jealousy for the existing form of government was very extensively engendered. This has been a great hindrance to the spread of christianity. Each chief is absolute lord of his people. He knows all their affairs & they can't transact any business without his consent, this was the state of matters out at Kuruman & vicinity when the mission began. It is not so now, but it is so here. Mahura the chief of the Batlapi was very much opposed to the gospel untill lately, & so long as he continued so no one living near him embraced the gospel. He has lately become more favourable & Mr Ross has gone to live with him & we have hopes of good being the result. . . . You seem to have been shocked with the indecency of the dress of the males. A short apron reaching half-way down the thigh is the Bechuana female dress when working, the men have a nondescription always & the Caffers go stark naked. I have seen the men stand in the presence of European females with as little consciousness of impropriety as G. D. does with his trousers on. The Matebele too go *in puris naturalibus* & one & all of them wonder what makes us thrust our pins 'into bags which can only hinder us from running fast'. . . . Peace & mercy be with you & Mrs D. & children.

Give her my most affectionate salutations.

D. L.

Livingstone's Marriage

LETTER 21

To REV. ARTHUR TIDMAN, D.D.

Mabotsa 2^d December 1844

DEAR SIR

Having in my communication of June last, adverted to the causes which prevent native agency being called more extensively into operation, you will readily percieve the reason why in the enclosed I have recommended that £15. of which Mrs Philip recently advised me as 'collected by a Sunday school in Southampton for the support of a native teacher' should for the present year be appropriated to the general objects of the society. And the reason why I venture to address the contributors is, if the plan of correspondence with this school is calculated to increase or keep alive the interest they already feel in the cause of Christ, I may be honoured to do in one school what you at home now so successfully attempt in all. For though situated as Roman soldiers once said of Britain, 'out of the world' we look with intense interest on the grand efforts made for enlisting the rising generation, and we have no doubt but by the Divine blessing a phalanx will be raised destined to effect more noble achievements than those of Caesar's soldiers. If you think my letter calculated to draw on the contributors in the path of liberality untill I find a laborer whom I can conscientiously recommend be so kind as address it to the proper quarter. Various considerations connected with this new sphere of labour and which to you need not be specified in detail having led me to the conclusion that it was my duty to enter into the marriage relation, I have made the necessary arrangements for union with Mary, the eldest daughter of Mr Moffat in the beginning of January 1845.[1] It was not without much serious consideration & earnest prayer I came to the above decision and if I have not decieved myself I was in some measure guided by a desire that the Divine glory might be

---

[1] The marriage took place at Kuruman on Jan. 2, 1845, according to an entry made by Robert Moffat in the Church book there.

Various considerations connected with this new sphere of labour and return to you need not be specified in detail having led me to the conclusion that it was my duty to enter into the marriage relation, I have made the necessary arrangements for union with Mary, the eldest daughter of Mr. Moffat, in the beginning of January 1845. It was not without much serious consideration & earnest prayer: I came to the above decision and if I have not deceived myself I was in some measure guided by a desire that the Divine glory might be promoted in my increased usefulness. I hope this rule be considered the

Part of Livingstone's letter from Mabotsa, dated December 2nd, 1844, announcing his engagement to Mary Moffat

(see letter No. 21)

School teaching

promoted in my increased usefulness. I hope this will be considered a sufficient notification of the change contemplated and that it will meet with the approbation of the Directors. I may mention that I do not regret having come out single. I rather think it would be advantageous if many of our young missionaries would spend at least as much time previous to marriage as would enable them to acquire the language and become acclimatized. In cases where young men would be kindly cared for by older bretheren a much longer delay would be advantageous for the mission. But when there is an almost total deprivation of European society & civilization long delay would be improper.

The arrangements connected with the above caused an absence from this station of nearly two months lately, and probably an equal period will be lost by my next visit to Kuruman But the necessary supplies being obtained at the same time will enable me to devote myself unremittingly to the great work for the future. On my return lately I found that Mr Edwards had nearly finished the walls of a small but substantial school. On its completion the native assistant Mebaloe and I commenced the instruction of the children and though we found them exceedingly shy at first we by degrees overcame their fears. The attendance however is extremely irregular Sometimes we have fifty at other times not five But we hope to overcome all difficulties connected with it by perseverance. The attendance on our other services is also very fluctuating & when we have a good meeting it is entirely by the influence of the chief. All are at present much deluded by a rain maker concerning whom I shall furnish some information which may be appropriate for the Juvenile magazine. May we be enabled to be faithful to their souls for if we are there is no doubt but that the Divine blessing will attend God's own word

After the school was finished I commenced the erection of a dwelling house and it is now nearly finished, the dimensions are 52 feet by 20 ft. and it is built of the same material as the school. Mud is heaped on about a foot in thickness at a time,

Building with mud

then cut straight and the heat of the sun is so great in a day or two it becomes both hard & strong. It is therefore both a cheap & easy mode of building. This you will understand when I mention that though my house is large enough to be a church for the station, the whole expense is about £25. the greater heat of the climate required greater dimensions than at stations farther south.

Having engaged to furnish information to a Welsh missionary Magazine through the late Red^d E. Williams I am unable to furnish it directly to the Editor Mr Roberts of Llanbrynmair in consequence of being ignorant of his address

If you kindly forward a letter which I send by this post to your care you will very much oblige

Yours Affectionately
DAVID LIVINGSTON

LETTER 22

To REV. ARTHUR TIDMAN

Banks of the Molopo 23^d March 1845

DEAR SIR

As an attempt at response to your circular respecting the Juvenile Magazine I beg leave to enclose a sketch of the station Mabotsa kindly furnished by A. H. Bain, Esqre a gentleman who recently visited that quarter. . . . the spot from which the sketch was taken does not afford the most picturesque view of the station, But it takes in the range of Kurrechane in the extreme distance & I preferred it on that account to any other. We can look to Mr Campbell[1] as a missionary pioneer with something more than satisfaction for though there is now comparatively no danger in traversing these regions, scientific expeditions have as yet penetrated but a very small way beyond him.

[1] Rev. John Campbell of Kingsland, London, was the first visiting inspector or Deputation sent out by the London Missionary Society. He went twice to South Africa, in 1812–14 and in 1818–21. See his *Travels in South Africa*, 1 vol., 1815; 2 vols., 1822. His last visit to the Kurrechane district was in 1820.

Bakhatla ideas

The following information concerning a 'rain maker' is presented with the same object. And it may be well to remember that the Bakhatla among whom we dwell, in some respects resemble the Batlapi of old. All the maxims of their conduct are based on the absolute importance of the present life, the body, with its appetites and desires, is regarded as the whole of man. Unlike the Batlapi of old, however, they treat missionaries with respect. Yet notwithstanding the deference paid us, they cling with astonishing pertinacity to their antient superstitions; unlike what young people might suppose, they have no curiosity about God and eternity, and this although all that can be said of their own vaguely floating ideas on these subjects is, those who are better informed think they can distinguish in them something like broken planks floated down on the stream of ages from a primitive faith. I have sometimes asked them why since we had come so far to tell them of these things, they never question me about them. They reply by another question, Do we know to ask? the subject too has to be pressed upon them, and they appear as persons dosing towards one who would wake them up, they prefer to get rid of the disturbance that they may again quietly compose themselves to sleep. Alas they know not that the sleep of sin is the sleep of death.

A belief in witchcraft is characteristic of all the tribes, many if not all have a fear lest by means of the mysterious powers of plants & roots some of their neighbours may influence the prosperous or adverse events of their lives. And like those in our own country who are subject to superstitious fear they never investigate the cause of it. It is exceedingly difficult to induce them to examine for themselves. In the case of the Rain maker who came to Mabotsa I found it impossible. He came with large pretentions—was called 'Morimo' or God and asserted that he had power to cure diseases make rain, and charm game for the hunters. He is most insignificant in appearance. Of low stature,—his hair twisted or plaited like that of a female, the numerous wrinkles around his eyelids nearly obscure the white of his small cunning eyes—wide nostrils—and irregular teeth.

Powers of rain maker

His body was without ornament and his 'Karros' filthy, yet some of the most intelligent among the Bakhatla were literally afraid of him. One man who has scars on his body shewing that twenty three have fallen by his hand in battle, confessed that he was afraid of him, and took off some of his ornaments as an offering to the Rain Maker. On the day of his arrival the clouds seemed propitious. But though on that and several other occasions he experienced pointed disappointment, the people could not, or would not percieve that the excuses he advanced were mere pretences. Having spoken to him in private on the folly and wickedness of his course, I was very soon afterwards blamed as the cause of the departure of the clouds. The chief sent for me and enquired in the presence of a number of his counsellors, why I had driven away their rain. I repeated all I had said to the Rain Maker and added, I was sorry to see my friends decieved by an impostor. One asked if I did not know that he could not only give rain, but kill people by lightning: Having besought them to put his powers to the test by experiment. An old man gravely remarked, that God had made white men wise in many respects But those who had come forth of Loey (a cavern in the Bakwain country with marks in the rocks around somewhat like foot prints from which Bechuanas imagine they were produced in the beginning) these were skilled in other things of which white men were ignorant White men know how to make guns and black men know how to make rain, and the latter ought not to be interfered with: Having admitted our ignorance of rain making, and induced them to confess our mutual obligations to instruct each other, I offered myself as pupil to the Rain maker. Nothing daunted he made allusion to the fee of an ox I offered three if he would only exhibit his power by collecting the clouds during the time we were sitting. He excused himself by saying that he must first go and dig medicines, but promised to bring the clouds in our presence in a few days. But though I placed the whole of my waggon oxen at his disposal he declined to have me for a pupil when I stipulated that he should make some little difference

Workers in iron

between his rain, and the 'rain from Heaven' such as causing it to rain on my garden one day and on none of the others; or on all the other gardens, & not on mine. I wished to test his godship before them by killing a kid by prussic acid and then offer a little of it to him. But the people were afraid of exasperating him, for several called out 'We have done with him' evidently anxious that I should not proceed to provoke him. By inducing him subsequently to name the periods in which he would give rain his failures were pointed out again and again. And on one occasion when making a great smoke by burning old bones, bulbs, roots &c. for the purpose, of as, he said, healing the clouds, when it was pointed out to them that his smoke was all going to the leeward while the clouds were all situated in the opposite direction, many laughed outright. But though they did so, they still continued to fear, honour, and sing his praises, and instead of believing that we wished to undecieve them, the endeavours seemed to produce the impression that the missionaries did not wish them to obtain rain. They think it is enough to be as their fathers were—content in the power of superstition and the very indefiniteness of their superstition seems to hold together the system. Power Divine and that alone can burst the chain which holds them in bondage.

It may not be known to the Directors that though the Bakhatla have the reputation of being workers in iron only a very few families in the tribe possess the knowledge of the art, the rest believe that it can be smelted only by means of certain medicines, and that though others who have not the knowledge of these medicines should attempt to smelt the ore, their attempts would prove quite abortive; there are not half a dozen families in the tribe who work in iron. Being now with my partner in life on our way to resume our labours in connection with that mission, I purpose on our arrival to commence in addition to our other services an evening lecture on the works of God on creation & Providence. And endeavour so far as in my power to illustrate the subject on the following day I intend to commence with the goodness of God in giving iron ore by

Difference with Edwards

giving, if I can, a general knowledge of the simplicity of the substance &c endeavour to disabuse their minds of the idea which prevents them in general from reaping the benefit of that which abounds in their country. If this fails I shall try other means to break the power of this superstition; I intend also to pay more particular attention to the children of the few believers we have with us as a class for whom as baptized ones we are bound especially to care. May the Lord enable me to fulfill my resolutions. I have now the happy prospect before me of real missionary work All that has preceded has been preparatory

       Believe me
       Dear Sir
        Yours Affectionately
         DAVID LIVINGSTON

¶ Livingstone wrote a long letter (7,000 words) from Mabotsa on October 17th, 1845, explaining with great candour and good feeling the difficulties which had arisen in his relations with R. Edwards, his senior colleague at the station. They were differences such as might easily arise when an energetic young man with ideas, becomes harnessed to an older man disinclined to allow him any initiative.

The points of disagreement seem trivial at a distance. Livingstone did his best to put matters right, but felt he had to take some action when Edwards displayed a letter he proposed to send home to the Directors.

The younger man felt compelled to appeal to them also and he did it promptly—The letter from Edwards was never sent; Livingstone announced his intention to remove to another place. The root of the trouble may be guessed from a phrase used by Edwards when he declared that he would not be 'a mere appendix' to the young man.

No doubt the feeling was mutual, but Livingstone was grievously ashamed of the business. He wrote: 'the degradation involved in answering these childish charges is more harmful than any sacrifice I have yet been called to.'

Treatment of arm

When his letter of October 17th was penned Livingstone had already made a start at Chonuane, the new station among Sechele's people, the Bakwains.

LETTER 23
(Original at Scottish National Memorial, Blantyre)

To DR. J. RISDON BENNETT, *London*

Chonuane. 26th December, 1845.

MY DEAR FRIEND,

As I have not yet received any answer to my last I presume it may not have reached its destination. And as I cannot without an effort afford to lose your correspondence, I take this gigantic sheet in order to stir you up to think on a poor 'dweller in the wilderness'. The longer I am absent from home the fewer my correspondents are likely to become, and as you are in heart engaged in the same cause, you must not leave me entirely to the wearisome round of news furnished in this benighted region. We have wars and rumours of wars untill the heart is sick of them. Right pleasant indeed then comes the stimulus of a letter from home. I have seen and was glad in reading a notice of your promotion to St. Thomas's and wish you every degree of success which will be for your good. . . .We commenced a new station[1] about 200 miles north of the Kuruman, or Lattakoo, and shortly afterwards I was much injured by a lion. The failure of strength in consequence of a profuse discharge from eleven gashes was so great I could not move my limbs. And while lying in my little native hut I often saw you in my dreams. And I shall not soon forget the lively disappointment I as often experienced on finding that all surgical aid was still on the other side of the Atlantic. When only partially recovered I had to begin the erection of my house and a jerk received in lifting a stone has led to a false joint in my left humerus. I often think of putting a seton through it but never have been able to plan a six weeks leisure. It is not however

[1] Mabotsa.

African diseases

a great hindrance even in heavy work—the chief inconvenience is the want of power to steady the arm when extended —the fissure is oblique and being situated in the upper third of the bone seems to run into the socket.[1] The point of bone ... starts out when my arm is extended and the hand in the supine position and appears as if it would burst through the skin. But the biceps being situated internally to it I could easily put the needle through. I can use the adze & hammer and lift heavy weights notwithstanding, and if I try the seton I shall let you know how it succeeds. But I must not speak so much about ego. I shall give you a little information concerning the diseases of this country and then proceed to missionary intelligence.

Compared with other countries this has very few maladies indeed. I have only seen one case of consumption and only two of scrofula in a period of four years. Amongst the Hottentots in the Cape Colony the former disease is by no means rare but let them come up to the dry and healthy climate of Lattakoo and they invariably recover. I am no believer in the curability of Phthisis in general. But some cases which have occurred have quite astonished me. One young woman I carefully examined and found no evidence of her former disease although that had been pronounced by a medical man well acquainted with the stethoscope as a real case of consumption. She became the subject of tumour in the ovarium, and this having been dispersed by Iodine she is now quite well. Poor Mr. Williams of Hankey was dissuaded from coming up here, the medical men in the Colony having about as much knowledge of this climate as of the planet Mars. I felt extremely sorry that he followed their advice, and went home to your cold wet cloudy climate. I conceive there is not a better than this for patients with pulmonary complaints in the world. I have not seen one patient from either India or England return unbenefited by their sojourn. It is now in consequence of the abundance of game of all sorts become very common for Indian invalids who

---

[1] A plaster cast of the fractured humerus is in the Museum of the Royal College of Surgeons, London.

can afford it to take a trip up here and from their enthusiastic statements it is probable it will become much more so. I wonder why the medical men connected with our Society do not recommend our Indian missionaries to come here instead of going home. The East India Company find the plan of sending to the Cape good. The same plan adopted by our society might save a great deal of the funds. As I remember Mr. Arundel[1] once mentioning that they considered you as one of their staff I take the liberty of speaking to you on this subject. And as I intend to make a series of observations in reference to this subject I shall be glad of any hints you may feel inclined to give. We are, if my thermometer can be depended on, nearly three thousand feet above the level of the sea. The climate is dry and clear, and the nights are never so warm as to prevent sleep. The winters are always bracing, and disease is decidedly rare. I have been through the whole country and though well acquainted with the inhabitants I cannot say they have more than three diseases at all common among them. Neither natives nor Europeans are subject to any other maladies but Ophthalmia, indigestion and occasionally a kind of bilious fever. I have not yet been able to ascertain in any part a mortality equal to ten per thousand. Have seen only six cases of Pneumonia and all these were infants except one. Only two cases of Hydrocephalus in native children and two in European infants have come to my knowledge, one only of these came under my own observation. The venereal disease has often been communicated to Bechuanas but invariably dies out. Rheumatism and disease of the heart occur occasionally, but surprisingly seldom when we think on the habits of the natives. In travelling they sleep on the ground and have but few precautions against damp. I have heard it remarked that in certain climates injurious effects are produced by exposure to the influence of the moon in sleep. Nothing of the sort is ever known here. I have myself slept for weeks on the bare ground

[1] Rev. John Arundel, Home Secretary of the London Missionary Society, 1819–46.

Place for a misanthrope

and often looked up to the beautifully clear orb untill I have fallen asleep. Yet I have felt nothing in consequence nor have I heard the natives ascribe anything baneful to her rays. If it is true that in other countries malaria acts with increased virulence at certain lunar periods, the entire absence of effects at these periods in relation to the production of disease would seem to show that malaria is not abundant here, and that where it is in existence it is at least ponderable and acted upon in somewhat the same way as the tides. There have been no epidemics except influenza and whooping cough since I came into the country. A kind of madness previously unknown to the natives appeared last year among the dogs, but it differs essentially from Hydrophobia. As a precautionary measure I have excised the bitten parts of all those who applied for assistance. The disease appeared to be communicated to a child and a calf. Both died. The long illness I was subjected to by the lion and my subsequent building operations have produced a great hiatus in my examinations, etc. in the materia medica of the country. Many roots etc. have been spoiled by long keeping so I must commence all over again. . . .

Towards the South the progress of evangelization is steadily advancing. The fruits of the long continued labours of our predecessors are now apparent everywhere. I cannot give any details as we have not heard from Lattakoo for many months. Indeed in reference to conveyance you are about as near New York as we are to Kuruman. A misanthrope who did not wish to hear any more about the civilized world would find this almost as good for his purpose as one of the silent system establishments in America. But all will come right at last.

Will you kindly remember me to your honoured father,[1] and believe me

Yours ever affectionately,
DAVID LIVINGSTON.

[1] Rev. Jas. Bennett, D.D., Minister of the Church in Falcon Square, London.

Lifting Cattle

LETTER 24

To THE REVD. ARTHUR TIDMAN.

Mabotsa,
10th April 1846

DEAR SIR,

As the commotions which occur among the tribes in this region usually possess features of interest in relation to our Mission, I shall relate a few particulars concerning the more recent changes which have occurred; and though these are calculated to awaken emotions more of pain than pleasure, the information may tend to excite prayer, that He who is head over all things to His Church may overrule the course of events for the establishment of His glorious kingdom.

Wars, or rather expeditions for plunder, seem to have been of frequent occurrence in this country from time immemorial, and the narration of the deeds performed in their forays forms a prominent feature in native conversation. But though generally the occasions of the most wanton cruelty they are regarded in much the same light as our own wars were thirty years ago. As with the antient Highlanders 'Lifting cattle' is not considered by the Bechuanas synonymous with stealing. Some do not like the term robbery to be applied to these deeds of plunder, while they could talk with composure when the term 'Lifting' is applied. In former years more severe scourges swept over the tribes by the irruptions of Mantatees and Matabele—compared to these, Bechuana marauding inflicted but little lasting injury. All the tribes in the interior were dreadfully thinned by these sweeping scourges, so there are but few old men now alive to tell the history of bygone years. Old Makabba, mentioned by Mr. Campbell. fell by the hands of the Mantatees, and his son, Sebeqwe[1] was driven away into the desert. More recently Sebeqwe was driven by fever from the banks of the Lake Mampoore back to the country of his father, and there his power was

---

[1] Sebeqwe. See also Letter 14 and Blaikie, pp. 39–42, where the chief's name is spelt Sebehwe.

Chief Bubi killed by explosion

completely broken by an attack of Mahura, Chief of the Batlapi. This latter event seemed very unfavourable at the time, as the natives here could not be expected to understand that though Mahura had for many years heard the Gospel he had no connection with believers. But the ruin of Sebeqwe's influence allowed the Chief of the Bakhatla to escape from a state of vassalage to him and collect the scattered remnants of his tribe into one body at Mabotsa. They now enjoy privileges they might not have had under Sebeqwe. The severe trials through which all have passed were probably designed to produce humility and make the native mind more susceptible to the influence of the Gospel.

The Bakwains, were formerly divided into two portions under Bubi and Sechele, the division having been effected by the murder of Sechele's father—the two parties were always at variance. In August last, Bubi, having received some gunpowder in a present from Sechele, and conceiving that coming from such a quarter it must be bewitched, he endeavoured to dissolve the charm by holding some medicines, in a state of combustion, over it. But his incantations were interrupted by an explosion which inflicted so much injury as subsequently to cause his death. Poor Bubi being dreadfully scorched, sent mesengers off to Mabotsa immediately to entreat assistance, as he believed no one but a white man knew the remedy for a burn inflicted by gunpowder. But being at Chonuane at the time of their arrival, and without that which might assist their Chief, his sorrowing servants were obliged to go round again by Mabotsa, and ere they reached their master, must have travelled nearly 200 miles. About a month previous to the accident which caused his death this amiable heathen Chief visited us at Mabotsa, and when spoken to said, in his usual way of endeavouring to please, 'I love the Word of God'. . . .

After the Chief was departed who by his influence kept most of that section of Bakwains together, many of the principal people preferred escaping to Sechele to remaining with Khake, the successor of Bubi. It then became necessary for Sechele to

Sechele's character

demand the goods and dependents of those who had returned to their allegiance. The tribe being weakened it would in general have been considered a good opportunity for revenging antient wrongs, but Sechele having promised not to shed blood, on approaching the town of Khake, left the great body of his people at a distance, and nearly unattended advanced to entreat the people to return to the allegiance. Entreaty having failed Sechele told them that he refrained from the usual course on such occasions, simply because of his promise to his missionary, and only demanded the goods of those who came over to his party. With these, others took the opportunity of changing sides. But every article brought which formerly belonged to Bubi was instantly returned. Sechele then returned to Chonuane. Subsequently to this transaction an old man who had been an accomplice in the murder of Sechele's father, was concerned in instigating some of Khake's men to an assault on some of Sechele's people, and to the abuse inflicted an insulting message was added, upbraiding the latter Chief for cowardice, '*pretending*' he did not fight because of his missionary &c. We endeavoured to allay the irritation produced and hoped that as the men who were wounded and abused were of an inferior rank the affair would pass over. An expedition was planned under the appearance of an elephant hunt. And the first intimations of our disappointment we received were the sight of the wounded carried past to the town, which was soon followed by the sounds of heathenish joy mingled with the loud wailing of those who had lost their friends. These events caused us much sorrow. The Chief justified his conduct on the ground that these people were his own subjects, and the deceit he employed lest we should again have prevented his avenging the indignities done to their hereditary chief. His conduct has in no way been altered for the worse, although we were not sparing in manifesting our detestation of the crime of murder. In desire for general information and assiduity in reading he surpasses all the chiefs, except Waterboer,[1] with whom I have

---

[1] Waterboer. A Griqua chief; see *Travels*, ch. v.

Gift of bulbs and seeds

come in contact. May the Lord incline his heart to righteousness and make him a blessing to his people.

Khake, with the remaining portion of his people, came about a week ago to this station. These commotions have thus ended by the whole of these two tribes being brought into closer proximity to the Gospel. We pray that we may yet see that the plans of the Divine mercy have been carried right through the midst of all this human wickedness, and that those who now feel no compassion for each other may have mercy shewn to themselves. . . .

Believe me Dear Sir,
Yours affectionately,
DAVID LIVINGSTON.

LETTER 25

(*Original at Scottish National Memorial, Blantyre*)

To CHARLES WHISH, ESQ., 144 *New City Road, Glasgow*

Chonuane, 9th Octr. 1846.

MY DEAR FRIEND,

I am sure you have wondered again and again why your seed box has been so long in making its appearance. The reason of the delay has been the isolation to which we have for a long time been subject. Even our Kuruman friends were in ignorance of our welfare for about six months, and the transmission of the box was an impossibility. The country has been very much disturbed of late. The Caffre War has raged and rendered communication through the Colony very precarious. You must have heard of the destruction of nearly all the Mission Stations &c. throughout Caffreland. If I had sent sooner, the whole of the contents would probably have been lost by delay in the frontiers of the Colony or perhaps they might have fallen into lawless hands. I need not say more about the delay, except that in process of time it has grown from a small box to a pretty large one and contains the following articles: . . . (*Here follows a list of Karosses, curios & seeds.*)

I am sorry I have appeared lacking in the acknowledgment

line. It certainly does not arise from the want of gratitude, . . . When I heard of your projected kindness, I thought I might wait till I saw the presents. The majority of the articles sent never came. Their loss I believe was owing to their being packed in Casks, even very strong ones soon yield to the influence of the climate, the ends fall in, and a strong temptation is placed in the way of carriers. The box now sent will give you an idea of what does best for this country. If dove tailed and a feather put into the joinings, such a box is just the thing. There is another box in it wrapped up in an old bag to prevent the charcoal in which the bulbs are packed, from permeating and spoiling the Karosses. The bulbs number upward of twenty, but the varieties included may not amount to so many. The delay has brought them to the very best time of the year for conveyance. It was winter when they were taken up, and as most of them are very tenacious of life, I think you might have some satisfaction from them. They are not in general covered with earth. A little more than half ought to do, and little water will suffice. The soils of all ought to contain a considerable portion of sand. . . . You probably have some new plants, as the botany of this region has never yet been explored. If you discover a new one, it must be called—Whishii—. Mrs. Moffat took the whole to the Kuruman last month.

After a protracted search I cannot lay my hands on yours containing a list of queries. I must try and answer such as I recollect, and such as may not be answered you will place to the account of defect of memory and nothing else. Salary for an unmarried missionary in our Society is £75, for a married one £100. Our Society gives the least. The Wesleyans have considerably more. The French have £20 to £50 to be expended on improvements at the Stations, £80 being considered as a supply for the Missionary's personal wants. I cannot specify the salaries of other Societies. I have never been intimate with any except the French. They have a mechanic on each Station. Other Societies' Missionaries employ mechanics from the Colony to build etc. etc. We do all ourselves. £75 seemed a

Cost of goods and labour

large sum to me. I thought I could maintain three native teachers out of it. But it takes all my £100 now to keep my Station going. It would be impossible to do with less. I think it would be an advantage if we had less manual labour. As I write now my hands have the same aching sensation I had when spinning. My mind is often so exhausted by sympathy with the body I cannot write in the evenings, and this is the only time I have. I do not know in what I could curtail my expenses. These are great chiefly in consequence of great distance from the coast. The prices of everything are doubled or more ere they reach us. A common clasp knife worth 6d. sells for 1/3, a wretched fustian Jacket 18/- to £1, and other things in proportion. We receive our salaries in money invariably. . . . All in our Society receive alike. The majority I believe are content, and try to leave the future with God. We have a man and his wife as servants, and a girl as a nurse maid. The man is waggon driver and everything else he can do, his wife a servant of all work. These form our establishment. But these are not all we require. Grinding corn, baking, washing etc. are done by calling an assistant from the town. Mrs. L. changes these assistants as soon as they have acquired some knowledge of household duties and operations. These supernumeraries are taught reading as well as washing etc. All sleep in their own homes. . . . They are paid in beads, a variety which costs about 3/- a pound. I mention this that you may not think the three above specified all we employ. We adopted the plan of employing others besides those absolutely necessary in order to do good. Mrs. L. superintends everything domestic, and the superintendence involves her arms up to the elbows in all processes. We must be at the beginning, middle and end of everything everywhere. If not, matters invariably go wrong. Mebalwe is the only man I know who carries a piece of work right on to a termination without being looked after. We are all working clergy and no mistake. I bought ten cows for about £11 when I was married. I have the same number yet. Each when in milk gives about a mutchkin. I once had seven in milk

Honest drugs

at once, and the whole did not yield as much as one cow at home. They cost nothing for grass. . . . To have plenty of milk throughout the year, we ought to have forty cows. This would equal two or three cows in Scotland. . . . From £1 to £1:10/- is the price of a cow with the traders. Few bring them on account of the losses they sustain by lions on the way. We have no sheep. I once bought twelve goats. But whether they have increased or diminished I do not know. The man in whose charge I placed them lives so far off I have heard nothing about them for two years. I think I mentioned the price of my horse. It was captured and recaptured and I have it now. It is very useful. By sending out our man to ride down a Giraffe or Eland we get a good supply of meat. Each of these animals is very good, but the Rhinoceros is our frequent fare. Baba, a Kuruman convert was killed by one last week. Unprovoked, it rushed on him and ripped him up. Mebalwe and I galloped off when we heard of the accident. . . . We saw a form in the distance and believing it was Baba and party made towards it. We found that he had died the day before and his companion had gone on to lay his body in the dust at Mabotsa. . . .

I thank you most heartily for the medicines you sent. They are excellent. The gentleman you bought them off has acted conscientiously. There was no trash in the box. It came most opportunely. I was nearly out of some articles. I have seen boxes of medicine sent out to this country (value £10 or £12) and nothing in them of value. The price was made up by as much sulphur as would have cured all Argyleshire of the itch (and we have none of it here) and salt and senna capable of giving a black draught to all the blacks from this to Timbuctoo. But yours are most judiciously selected. I thank you most sincerely for your kindness. . . .

We have better prospects of usefulness here than at any former period. But there is not a single convert. Let us have your prayers/

Yours affectionately
DAVID LIVINGSTON

LETTER 26

(Original at Scottish National Memorial, Blantyre)
To MR. CHARLES LIVINGSTON,[1] *Hamilton*

Kuruman, 16th March 1847

MY DEAR BROTHER,

... I have had no time for correspondence during the last eight months. Have travelled and builded much. But having come out to attend a meeting of committee I have a little time to spare and will make the most of it for my distant friends. Do not expect fine composition or fine anything. I am becoming more and more a barbarian. Can read but little and yet must keep up some acquaintance with the medical and other sciences. Could not now deliver a speech in English. My sentences are Sitchuanadized by constantly expressing my ideas in that language. ...

We are very happy in our work at Chonuane. The chief, Sechele is a sensible man—now reads pretty well—is fond of his Testament and has an intense desire for everything connected with civilization. We are poor and cannot help much. But when he has no soap he washes his clothes with pipe clay. We hope his people will follow his example. He and his wives are our best scholars and afford us much satisfaction. None however are converted. This is the great desideratum. Our thoughts always alight on it. The locality we now inhabit is not good. Our water is scanty and bad, but we hope to remove to a better shortly. This will mean hard work for me, but it is all in the course of the service of a good master. So we cannot grumble. This subject brings a remark of yours to my recollection. You worked a day or two on John's farm and got knocked up for several days after. Did you wonder at it? What a physiologist you are. Suppose you had worked two hours for the first week, three for the second, and four for the third, and so on, would you have been knocked up? Your system may

[1] Charles was David's younger brother. The three sons and two daughters of Neil and Agnes Livingstone who survived them were John, David, Janet, Charles, and Agnes.

Bechuanas and the Supreme Being

not yet be all fitted for work but we cannot conclude that it never will be. You are not yet old. . . . Your questions respecting the idea of a supreme being in the Bechuana mind is rather difficult of solution. We come after missionaries have been in the country 30 years. Marimo or God or Chief is at every one's mouth. Intelligent natives say their forefathers spoke of God in the same way. A man escapes from an elephant. Now he instantly exclaims 'How good God is to me. What a heart God has to me'. A person is sick or dies. The exclamation then is 'God has no heart' i.e. He is not kind. They have parables from God. We who are better informed can gather an idea of a future state. The knowledge of some of these parables is universal and if we can believe testimony it was so of old. Here is one. God sent a cameleon to say to men, though you die you do not vanish or become annihilated. You will return again. The cameleon being a slow walker was outstripped by the little black lizard sent by another, and the latter came first to man. The black lizard said to men 'One will come after me and tell you that when you die you will not perish but will return again—this is all a message of lies. When you die, you perish as an ox'. When the cameleon came men stopped his mouth by saying 'O we know your message. It is all lies'.

There are cairns on the hills and when a traveller comes to one he throws a stone or branch of a tree to it and says with a loud voice 'Hail O king. Let it be well with me in the way I now go. Let me find game. Let it be pleasant for me among the people I may meet'. From these and other facts we can gather fragments which seem to point to a primitive faith and worship. But none of the Bechuanas in distant parts can connect these fragments together so as to form one rational idea of the subject of the Godhead or futurity. They seem at one period to have worshipped animals. A little beetle is tied on the hair and something like a prayer is sometimes made to it. If a Marolong (one of the tribes) kills a khoodoo he breaks out into a loud wail 'O I have killed my father. What shall I do, yo yo yo yo'. I asked why they do so. 'It is our custom. We saw our forefathers do so and we do the same'. They laugh at it. Have not the smallest devotional feeling unless spitting on the ground when they see the animal after which their tribe is named can be denominated such an emotion.

. . . Study thoroughly my dear brother. If you become a missionary you will have little time then. I wish I had a thorough education. If your constitution is not ruined you would be better in connexion with our Society than School keeping because you would have both summer and winter for study. If you can afford it go to some eminent physician and request his opinion on your health, also whether you may think of Missionary labour. Our Society has been trying to get agents for China and after trial of several have come to the resolution of educating sixteen expressly for that Mission. The funds are at present depressed but will come round again to success. You will know best how to act. Let us hear from you soon and often. We answer all who write us but find it beyond our temper's utmost stretch to write those who maintain a majestic silence. I thank you most heartily for the books you sent. Am sorry I cannot possibly send you any money. The reason a most cogent one—is, I have none. We got letter after letter from home breathing the most ardent aspirations for emigration. We made a great effort and sent £20 to enable them to emigrate.—Think of the acknowledgment. It runs as follows, 'John's views of emigration exactly correspond or coincide with ours. He says you may do something to a garden but old trees seldom bear transplanting well'. . . .

Yours affectionately,
D. LIVINGSTON.

LETTER 27

To REVD. ARTHUR TIDMAN

Kuruman 17th March 1847

DEAR SIR

As a considerable period has elapsed since I had an opportunity of transmitting letters to the Directors, and those which

Wild Animals

I have now brought with me seem out of date, I shall endeavour to embody their contents in a general sketch of our proceedings during the last eight months. This will include a short account of two journies in an Easterly direction, undertaken in order to attempt the removal of certain obstacles to the establishment of a native mission in one of the tribes located there; And in order that you may understand the nature of these obstacles, and the circumstances which rendered it desirable to make an effort for the settlement of at least one of our native teachers in that direction, I may mention that the country situated Eastward of our station & North of the 25° degree of South Latitude has been taken possession of by certain Dutch emigrants who consider themselves sole masters of the soil by virtue of having assisted in the expulsion of Mosilikatze; While still engaged in the erection of our dwelling at Chonuane, we recieved notes from the Commandant & Council of these emigrants, requesting an explanation of our intentions &c. as also an intimation that they had resolved to come and deprive Sechele of his fire arms. We recieved too about the same time several very friendly messages and presents from an influential chief called Mokhatla who lives about four days Eastward of the station and at last during my absence at Mabotsa he paid a visit to Chonuane and expressed satisfaction with the idea of obtaining Paul as his teacher—As soon as our house was habitable Paul and I proceeded to the Eastward

After crossing the River Marikoe our attention was attracted by villages which were scattered over the country in numbers to which we had been unaccustomed. One cannot travel far in the Bakwain Country without seeing large trees broken, bent and twisted, and other indications of the presence of Elephants and Rhinoceros. Or he may come upon herds of the Giraffe, Eilands, Buffaloes and other varieties of game. But here we found wild animals comparatively scarce and we beheld instead the more pleasant haunts of man & though travelling we had the pleasure of addressing immortals on their eternal destiny at least once every day. On reaching the town

Contact with emigrants

of Mokhatla we found him busily engaged in drawing Copper wire and manufacturing ornaments—(He works also in wood and iron with considerable dexterity which is remarkable as manufactures are not hereditary in his family) He was still of the same mind in reference to Paul but told us that the settlement must be effected with the Commandant of the emigrants as the only mode whereby peace could be secured to himself—He being no longer considered master of his paternal territory. Mokhatla is chief of a large section of the Bakhatla. He mentioned about fifteen villages who own his authority and he has a good name among all the other tribes. In the distance we saw the residence of another Bakhatla chief called Pilanie whose people are still more numerous than those we visited. Compared with these the Bakhatla to whom most of our efforts have hitherto been directed appear a mere fragment of a tribe, the people of Mokhatla had never heard the gospel before except from Paul and Mebaloe. Proceeding Eastward through his villages untill we crossed the River Ourie or Limpopo, we then came to a large tribe of Bakwains and spent the sabbath with them. The chief a most friendly man shewed me the scars on his back, of stripes which had been inflicted by those who consider themselves masters of his country. While standing in his town we counted eleven villages in the plain below all of which acknowledge him as their chief. Everywhere we were recieved with kindness and confidence as soon as we were known as missionaries, and some of the chiefs informed us that they had formed part of the train of Mosilikatze in his frequent visits to the waggon of Mr Moffat. They seem then to have acquired an idea of what teachers are—

The Commandant lived near to this tribe and being a well informed man we found no difficulty in persuading him that an attempt to disarm the Bakwains would break up our mission, and that he ought to delay the execution of the orders of Council untill I should lay the whole matter before it, this I did by letter and likewise stated my intention of introducing the gospel amongst the Eastern tribes by means of native agents

Cotton and iron workers

As soon as we arrived at Chonuane we commenced the erection of a school 50 feet by 20. Having finished this in less than two months and set systematic instruction fairly into operation under Paul & his son Isaac Mrs L. Mebaloe & self proceeded again to the Eastward. Our course was straighter than formerly and we thereby visited many villages we had not seen in our previous journey. We had resolved to call on the Commandant and Mokhatla on our way home. After spending another Sabbath with Mamogale the chief of Bakwains on the Eastern bank of the Ourie we continued our Eastern course. On our right lay a considerable tribe under Samogoe We did not visit it but proceeded to the Bamosetla a large tribe consisting of about a dozen villages grouped together on a plain—they knew nothing of missionaries but we found no difficulty in collecting them in large numbers. Six days beyond the Bamosetla we came to a cluster of tribes We could at one view behold the localities of seven and these in amount of population seemed to exceed the whole of the Batlapi and Batlaros, the natives say the population is still denser the nearer we approach the coast. They are called Bagalaka. Their dialect is somewhat different from that we use. But we were readily understood and they easily accommodated their language to ours. In appearance they resemble Matibele and the men cultivate the fields. We procured specimens of the spindle and distaff with which they spin cotton,—the plant seems to be indigenous. They smelt iron copper and Tin and in the manufacture of ornaments know how to mix the tin & copper so as to form an amalgam. Their country abounds in ores. And the Ourie or Limpopo after recieving many considerable streams becomes, as the natives call it, the 'mother of all rivers' being at least 400 yards in breadth. It is said to enter the sea a little to the North of De Lagoa Bay. The people are rich in cattle, and were never subject to Mosilikatze. They recieved us in general with fear. Indeed on approaching the town of Mankopane the chief to whose people we had promised a visit we saw the men all armed and running up the rocks at the foot of

Dutch and natives

which their town is built. This arose from the impression, that we were enemies and might make use of our fire arms. When their fears subsided we found the chief & people kind but their confidence was far from full. We preached several times but there was far more palaverish ceremoniousness than we could relish. The chief though not more than 20 years of age had 48 wives and 20 children—the latter in feature all very much resemble himself. While here we recieved a pressing invitation from another chief to visit him. And heard of another tribe which exceeds all others in manufacturing skill, '*they have never been known to kill any one*' Hearing such a character from their brethren, our desire to visit them was great But being between 2 & 300 miles from home we were obliged to defer seeing this 'lily among thorns' till some other opportunity. The state of the three tribes of Bagalaka we visited may be stated in the words 'hateful & hating one another' Crowds followed our waggon from one tribe untill we approached the next. They returned then lest as they said 'they should be killed' But though surrounded by such crowds our conversational opportunities were but few. If either Mrs L. or myself made any movement towards them a general rush backwards and treading over each other occurred. Mebaloe was better able to quiet their fears and held many conversations on revealed truth, very little can be affected in one visit

In speaking of the relations between Dutch & natives I shall confine myself chiefly to the statements of the former. They have taken possession of nearly all the fountains and the natives live in the country only by sufferance. Each chief when called upon is obliged to furnish the emigrants with as many men as any piece of work may require and except in the case of shepherds no wages are paid for labour. Labour is exacted as an equivalent for being allowed to live in the land of their forefathers—In this system of unrequited labour all the emigrants from the Commandant downwards, unanimously agree. In other ways of maltreatment they are not so unanimous. The better disposed emigrants lament the evils they witness But

Power on the side of the oppressor

the absence or laxity of law leaves the natives open to the infliction of inexpressible wrongs. A short time previous to our visit to Mañkopane a few emigrants galloped up to the herds of that chief—singled out 30 of the finest cattle & 50 of the largest sheep—and then driving them off, proceeded to act in a similar manner in an adjoining tribe. On complaining of this to the Commandant he professed entire ignorance of the transaction and promised to investigate the matter and apply the law in the case. The deed was the more galling to the natives because a son of Conrad Buys was among the marauders, and this man when his father died & left him an orphan among this people, was kindly treated and enabled to discover his relatives. A misunderstanding occurred between Melechoe chief of a large & powerful tribe and some of these emigrants, the latter ordered three tribes to assist them in an attack upon Melechoe, these formed a living bulwark in front of one hundred mounted whites. The ill fated tribe was driven back by the battle axes of their own countrymen and the whites found it an easy way of fighting to fire over the heads of their sable assistants. Melechoe held out long but by employing their allies to capture the cattle immense booty was secure—10,000 sheep and 400 captives were included in the spoils. On asking the natives why they had been so foolish as to asist in the murder of their countrymen their reply was that they feared that had they refused to go they themselves would have been attacked. An *English trader* too joined in the attack made on Melechoe. Now the emigrants invariably admit that in reference to them the Bechuanas are an honest and peaceable people. I have frequently put the question whether the Dutch ever knew Bechuanas guilty of stealing cattle from white men as the caffres near the colony have done and the uniform answer has been 'No, they are honest and peaceable towards us'. The above mentioned massacre, for such it was the natives having no fire arms, may however teach them to be neither. On the side of the oppressor there is power, the black man may yet obtain a knowledge of that power and then it may appear

Training Institution proposed

that the emigrants have industriously sowed the seeds of some future 'Caffre War' the lawless alone may now be guilty but vengeance may be wreaked on both good and bad as is now the case in the Colony. . . .

I now gratefully acknowledge the receipt of your letter some months ago in which you appear to consider that I needed to be stirred up on the subject of Native agency—In the absence of information respecting my efforts to induce the bretheren to commence the systematic training of a native agency it was quite reasonable to suppose that I had cooled down on the subject I could not however inform you of those efforts without appearing to criminate those who opposed them—I preferred silence though with the conviction that to you that silence must appear a diminution of zeal An expression in a letter from the Directors which I recieved some time previous to our first meeting of committee led me to believe that some definite plan would be promulgated in that meeting; When the business was nearly over and nothing likely to be said on the subject I put the question, What is to be done in reference to training native Teachers? and found that my impression derived from the Directors' letter had been erroneous. At our next meeting of Committee (1845) I presented a paper on the subject to the bretheren. In it I expressed my convictions on the subject of systematic training of agents & ventured to suggest that an institution for the purpose be organized at —— and —— be requested to act as tutor of the same—the clause runs verbatim thus—'While then I have no idea of superseding by any new arrangement the duty of each missionary making every effort in his own sphere for raising up suitable individuals, I earnestly entreat your serious deliberation on the suggestion that an Institution for the education of native teachers be organized at —— and that —— be requested to act as Tutor of the same' the reason why I left blanks was simply because I concieved the filling up of these would come better from the elder bretheren. Some approved of it heartily. Others assailed with such logic as 'suppose we make you professor in this college'

A Tutor for Africans

There are no individuals in the churches fit for a course of training' and it was more than insinuated that in bringing forward 'that paper I wished to appear well with the Directors' This last induced me to withdraw it—the conviction seized my mind when I witnessed the opposition of some honoured bretheren, that by bringing the subject forward myself instead of waiting till it emanated from those of higher standing, I had retarded instead of furthering this most important mode of spreading the gospel, this conviction caused me months of bitter grief,—everytime the subject arose in my mind I felt a pang—I could not possibly leave the Interior Mission to attend the meeting of committee for 1846. The fact that nothing was said at that meeting, Nor yet at this (47) untill the evening of the second day, has freed my mind from the conviction that in 1845 I acted prematurely. I waited untill we were proceeding to elect the office bearers for the ensuing year before making the motion which you will see in the minutes. Had I put it in any other form I might have been foiled by the assertion which I could not have disproved, that there is a lack of men suitable for training. As it was stated that I made the motion for 'returns' with a view to founding a motion for systematic training and employment of native agents thereupon, I fear the returns will be sought for by each according to his wishes for the success of such a motion. At present I have not very sanguine hopes of success in inducing the bretheren to cooperate in the undertaking, and unless the cooperation is hearty no good will result—I feel inclined to say though I do it with diffidence, that the probabilities of success would be greater if Mr Ashton were appointed by the Directors Tutor of all suitable individuals who can be found willing to dedicate themselves to the Divine glory among the distant heathen. I know he would most willingly enter into such a work for he has always supported the suggestion which was made and from his zeal & energy we might hope for good results. He would however require the cordial cooperation of the bretheren who have charge of churches. I hope to be able to demonstrate before another year that native

A year with the Bakwains

teachers may be placed even among very distant tribes. The objects of my present visit to this quarter have been to attend the meeting of committee and procure a supply of food

It will afford me much pleasure to furnish you with some account of the conversions of Mebaloe and Paul. I have requested the former to write it out himself, the whole will be included in my next communication His name is David Molehane, he always signs himself so—Molehane is the family name, David was given at baptism but not being partial to changing their expressive names. I have always called him by his common one Mebaloe. Paul is of the same family but as he disliked his former name viz. Father of darkness, he has always been called by his Christian one. David has been supported by the contributions of certain friends in Glasgow collected by a M^{rs} McRobert now in Islesteps near Dumfries. I intended to place Paul to the account of a certain school in Southampton but Mrs Philip informed me that £15 collected there was not intended for me but for some one under Mr Solomon.[1] Your subsequent notice that that sum was intended for the Kat River Mission convinced me I had nothing to do with it. . . .

We have now been a little more than a year with the Bakwains. No conversions have occurred, yet real progress has been made. The indications of advancement may be more interesting to myself than to any one else yet I believe it would be apparent to all who might witness it: the sabbath is observed so far that no work is done in the gardens on that day, & hunting is suspended There is a general impression among the people that we are their real friends. This is manifested in a variety of ways— When we came, the belief in rain-making was universal—they believed that as God had given the white man guns & other things whereby he excelled the black so he had conferred the knowledge of rain making on them as one thing in which they might excel the white—it availed nothing when told that their rain-medicines produced no visible effect, 'your

[1] Rev. Edward Solomon of Griqua Town, father of a family eminent for service in South Africa.

Sechele abandons rain making

medicines' said they, 'produce no visible effect either when you administer them, but they enter into the inward parts—do their work and then the cure follows many days afterwards. In like manner our rain-medicines enter into the clouds—heal them—and we have rain some time afterwards' Sechele was chief rain maker himself and had unbounded confidence in his own powers last year however proved one of unusual drought, the clouds went round & round us untill the people were saying 'these clouds make sport of us' Our house was supposed the cause why no rain came down, and we were requested to allow them to sprinkle it with medicine. To this we had no objection provided the stuff did not smell badly. Yet no rain came. The crops were lost. When I asked Sechele whether he intended to make rain this year, He replied, 'you will never see me at that work again' A rain maker came from a great distance. He asked a sheep and promised rain at a certain period but the time having arrived, and no rain, when he asked another sheep he was answered by banter & laughter—Many still fear the rain maker but formerly no one dared to laugh at him. Formerly all believed that preaching, praying, observance of the sabbath were just the customs we had derived from our ancestors and many felt jealous lest compulsion should be used to make them part with their superfluous wives, and other practices and become Makoas, or white people in customs But after some time they began to enquire, why some white men only observed the customs of their ancestors and others observed neither the sabbath nor any custom whatever, 'To be plain with you' said one, 'we should like you much better if you traded with us & then went away without for-ever boring us with preaching that word of God of yours' They were exceedingly anxious to obtain medicine which should enable them to shoot well. A Griqua came & sold a little bit of sulphur at a high price and some of it was inserted under the skin of the hand of the chief. This was shewn to me as a great acquisition. I told them they had been decieved—handed the chief a cupful of sulphur as a proof that it was not niggardliness that prevented

Obstructive colleagues

me from giving the 'gun medicine' he looked at it some time & then said, 'I wish you would decieve me too. It would be pleasanter though you cheated me out of my goods' He returned the sulphur apparently feeling that falsehood was sweeter than truth; the people in general have more curiosity than any other I have come in contact with. Most of the principal men attempt to acquire a knowledge of reading. The famine caused by the loss of the crops has however prevented many from making much progress. After attending a few days they are obliged to go to the fields in search of the roots on which they subsist, the chief having always had food has never been absent. He & his wives have therefore been our best scholars. He can read the Testament pretty well & always seems to relish explanations of what he does read. He has adopted European clothing and is most desirous of making progress in civilization. We are encouraged by these things to hope that his example will have a good effect on the people. We trust that our supporters do not cease to pray for the influence of the Holy Spirit to change their hearts. Unless they are converted, advance in civilization will be a poor reward for our toils.

You are already aware that by the advice of my brethren here and in accordance with my own previously expressed wish to carry the gospel to another tribe I left Mabotsa and proceeded Northwards to Chonuane, Messrs Ross Inglis and Edwards uproariously opposed the introduction of my reasons for leaving that station and it was voted 'informal' to accede to the requests I had made in the belief that the subject would be introduced by Mr Edwards. That being the case, I have waited for the sanction of the Directors to my new station, and that not having arrived I could not bring forward the expenses I have incurred in building a house and school. I am not aware by what process of reasoning the same individuals, viz. Ross and Inglis, could vote the introduction of my reasons 'informal' last year, and move for their production this year, I am left to conclude, from the expression oft repeated in the ears of all present

'*I have spent every farthing*'

while I was discharging a sacred duty in reference to the funds of the Society 'Wait till Livingston brings forward his expenses' that there were some feeling akin to revenge prompting the motion Mr Inglis having taken up his residence in my house at Mabotsa where certainly there is no work for two missionaries—continued to talk of a station among the Bahurutse untill actually expelled by the Bakhatla He then offered himself to the Wanketze & was rejected, Proceeded to Colesberg for supplies and now imagines that the Bahurutse will go with him to form a station at Mainaloe. As there is not the smallest probability of any movement of the sort I felt it a solemn duty to endeavour to prevent the loss of another year's salary in mere talk by recommending Mr Inglis to act according to the pointed instructions of the Directors. I might have remained at Mabotsa untill the Bakwains removed to a better locality and had I done so I should not have incurred the expenses which now press heavily on my spirits but having gone, although to a place where water is scanty and bad—been obliged to sow corn at a fountain forty miles distant—lost it all by buffaloes and Rhinoceros, yet our pleasing prospects of success prevent us from regretting the exchange; and we believe the people will soon remove to a better locality from a conviction of the advantages to be derived from European improvements, In wishing to fix Inglis to do something for his salary I am conscious of having acted from a solemn conviction of duty to Him who knows my heart; . . .

I have spent every farthing I have in the world—worked hard and fared hard—and am not ashamed to say that I am in Debt £29 for building expenses £3..8 of this sum were expended at Mabotsa, £15 or £20 more will be expended in commencing the new station and as our corn was eaten by buffaloes while I was looking out for a proper sphere for Paul nothing can come from my salary for the purpose of building. But for the assistance of the native teachers I could not have succeeded with so little expense to the society—the above is what I wish the Directors to take into consideration—the movement I have made has

South African mission staff

not been sanctioned by them yet I should not act otherwise were I in the same circumstances again. . . .

A circular from Dr Philip has lately come to hand concerning the depressed state of the funds of the Society and that the Directors had resolved to diminish the sum annually expended on our South African Missions. In this resolution I most cordially concur and my concurrence is founded on the impressions I received in passing through the Colony. I did not then communicate my convictions to the Directors that the Colony was no longer a missionary field, because I believed that from a mere novice such a broad assertion would be considered mere censorious conceit. I shall now give my reasons for believing that too much has & is being expended on South Africa and need scarcely premise that I state my impressions always with the conviction that the Directors having superior sources of information and of course better means for forming a correct judgement will take my statements only for so much as they are worth. It is easy to recommend changes but there is great responsibility connected with every change in missionary operations.

At Algoa Bay there are two missionaries connected with our Society A Wesleyan, a government school master, qualified & willing to teach all both white & black. The clergyman is I believe non evangelical the village is as like Ongar[1] in Essex as regards population & appearance as two places can be. The only exception is a small clump of native huts a little apart from the *one* street of which the village is composed. Suppose a Wesleyan Missionary—an English clergyman non-evangelical a salaried Government schoolmaster and Mr Passmore with a small clump of fingoes, alongside Mr Cecil at Ongar and you have a correct picture of one missionary field Uitenhage appears a mere village, not twice the size of Ongar yet it has an evangelical clergyman, of the Dutch Church, a Wesleyan missionary, one of our Society and a Gov^t schoolmaster Graaf Reinet has a population equal to a very small

[1] Ongar had a population of about 800 at that time.

Moving onwards

country town in England yet here we have an evangelical clergyman of the Dutch church one of the Church of England, A Wesleyan Missionary, Mr Gill[1] and M^r van Lingen[2]—Colesberg when I saw it was not equal in size to Ongar yet it too had an evangelical schoolmaster a Wesleyan and London Missionary Society's agent. Graaf Reinet has a Gov^t school master too. these are the only Colonial fields I saw and can say without the smallest personal feeling towards any of the respected bretheren who occupy these fields I wonder what our Society's agents do there. The Colonial market is literally glutted with missionaries. I do not believe that equal advantages are enjoyed by any town or village in the United Kingdom as those which are pressed on the people of Algoa Bay, Uitenhage, Graaf Reinet & Colesberg. With such an overflowing supply from Europe will the Hottentots ever bestir themselves so as to become preachers? I fear, never. I am more and more convinced that in order to the permanent settlement of the gospel in any part the natives must be taught to relinquish their reliance on Europe—An onward movement ought to be made whether men will bear or whether they will forbear. I tell my Bakwains that if spared ten years I shall move on to the regions beyond them. Now is their opportunity and if they do not learn, the guilt will rest on their own heads. If our missionaries would move onwards now to those regions I have lately visited they would in all probability prevent the natives settling into that state of determined hatred, which I fear now characterizes most of the Caffres near the Colony, to all Europeans. If natives are not elevated by contact with Europeans they are sure to be deteriorated. It is with pain I have observed that all the tribes I have lately seen are undergoing the latter process. The country is fine. It abounds in streams and has many considerable Rivers The Boors hate missionaries But by a kind & prudent course of conduct one can easily manage them, Medicines are eagerly recieved and I intend to procure a supply of Dutch tracts for

[1] Rev Joseph Gill, afterwards of Fort Beaufort.
[2] Rev Albert Van Lingen

Removal from Chonuane

distribution amongst them—the natives who have been in subjection to Mosilikatze place unbounded confidence in Missionaries. The Boors spoke disrespectfully of me to the natives as soon as my back was turned but they always came and related it with shouts of laughter. If the Boors knew this and many other things I have mentioned they would become more exasperated against them and probably shew their hatred towards myself

If in consistency with your financial plans May I be favoured with £5 or £10 of medicines? My friend Dr J. Risdon Bennet would procure them cheaper and better than any one I know. He knows too which will be most useful for me. I have spent more than £30 of salary in this way. which may be an inducement to you to accede to my request. It is necessity alone makes me trouble you But if it is not in accordance with your usual plan of operations, you have only to say No.

With Christian salutations
I am Dear Sir
Yours Affectionately
DAVID LIVINGSTON

LETTER 28

To MR. ROBERT MOFFAT Jn^r, *London*

Kolobeng. Bakwain Country 13 August
1847

MY DEAR BROTHER

We recieved your favour dated Augth/46 while at Kuruman and returned at least in quantity an equivalent. Let this large sheet be added to the former and leave quality out of the question and you will never again be able to utter your complaint about 'return letters' The circumstances in which I am at present placed and the object I have in view in writing at present are the following The water of Chonuane being scanty and bad, and it being impossible for us to raise the staff of life in that locality we felt it to be our duty to propose removal to a more

Life at Kolobeng

salubrious situation. Many of the Bakwains were opposed to it because Chonuane afforded good garden ground for native corn pumpkins &c. But Sechele declared he would cleave to us wherever we went and having fixed on the Kolobeñ. a fine stream which drains that mass of hills which lies Eastward of Kuakoe. we are now in process of removal thither. Our new station is at the point where the Kolobeñ emerges from the hills, and about 40 miles N.W. of Chonuane. I am engaged in erecting huts. Mebaloe alias David is thatcher and I am architect. Paul remains with M^{rs} L at Chonuane, the mass of the people are engaged in removing their corn & goods from stage to stage—others are engaged in building. Mary feels her situation among the ruins a little dreary & no wonder for she writes me yesterday that the lions are resuming possession & walk around our house at night. Kolobeng means the haunt of the wild bear but it seems to have been the haunt of everything wild. Hyænas abound exceedingly, buffaloes in immense herds. and Zebras quite tame in the thickly wooded country around. Elephants too have left their traces on what will we hope for the future only contain marks of the 'pleasant haunts of men' The evenings afford me a little time for writing &c. and as you express a wish to have a grammar of the language I intend in the absence of any grammar of Sitchuana deserving the name to furnish you with a few remarks and these I expect to be of more value to myself than to you, for I shall send them to Father[1] and entreat him to correct my observations at the same time hoping he will add information on those points in which I am ignorant I need scarcely remark that it is of the utmost importance to attain an idiomatic acquaintance with the channel through which we hope the streams of Divine mercy & consolation will flow to the benighted inhabitants of this region. I have heard it spoken by individuals who thought

---

[1] This letter to Livingstone's brother-in-law was sent to Robert Moffat, Sn^r., for his comments before dispatch. He appended a note: 'Kuruman 26. My dear son Robert. I forward this as received. I have not a moment for remarks. Very good as far as it goes. RM.'

The Sicuana language

they had acquired a knowledge of it yet using the English idiom they could only be understood by natives who being accustomed to Europeans knew what was intended as well as the speakers themselves. Had they come to the Bakwains or to any of the Interior tribes they would not be understood by a single individual. The English idiom here would be unintelligible gibberish. In the following remarks I shall not attempt to follow grammarians. The endeavours of some to reduce the Sicuana to the grammatical forms of Latin & Greek &c seem to me to have been complete failures. I shall attempt an analysis only and should I stick fast in the middle it will be because I lack either time or ability or both. We will begin by what we can between ourselves dignify by the name of a

Phonetic Table of the Sicuana

A is sounded as in Fāther Māmmă or Scotch way of pronouncing latin example bathu, men, mālā bowels, mālă cold, gonă there, ñāpă (verb) pinch, lithāko walls. logoră a hedge,

E as in Pear, Were, Their, ex. s*e*pha, brittle. s*e*nya (v.) destroy. H*e*ta, (v.) pass, l*e*ta (v.) wait (or watch)

E with accent as in L*e*mon, cl*e*rk. Fri*e*nd, D*e*ad, s*é*ka (v.) judge. *é*tă travel r*é*ka (v.) buy. mas*é*ka, leglets. s*é*ba (v.), backbite

I as in Scotch Latin or English dim*i*nish bel*i*eve or as seek, peep, ream. Kika a corn mortar Th*i*pa a knife. bos*i*go night Tur*i* a goat: Letsals*i* the Sun.

O as in Mole. Toad. Tlotla to honour. shotla (v.) mock, kopa (v.) beg.

O as in broad sought broth. Tlōtla strain (a liquid) Lōpa to ask

U as in c*u*shion. cuck*oo* soothe Lekuka a milk sack. Phupu a grave. ruta (v.) teach pula rain.

AE—dipthong as English I. in high lie al*i*ke Tsam*ae*a (v.) go r*ae*a say Tlatlatl*ae*a (v.) load a gun. put one thing into or on another as putting a kettle on the fire &c, b*ae*a (v.) place or put

Sh. as in di*sh* fi*sh sh*all ma*sh*i, milk se*sh*e*sh*e a blossom or flower. Shoñkoe a plant.

Kolobeng grows

C as in Italian, vocce. or as ch in church lurch, caka a battle axe, coga rise, cukuru, a rhinoceros, all pronounced as if spelled with ch.

N with the circumflex over it is the same as the Spanish ñ or English ing in coming writing but in sicuana it begins words as well as forms a frequent termination, mo lehatsiñ, in or on the earth. mo tseleñ, in or on the way or path, mo thutoñ, in teaching. mo nokeñ, in the stream. all these are pronounced as if instead of ñ they were written ng—ñoñola to mock or deride. ñoñorega, grumble, are pronounced as if written ngongola ngongorega, taking the initial from any word ending in ing but allowing the i to be silent.

G. gutteral as in Scotch Loch. gago thy ñoñorega. riga, throw down

H is always an aspirate except in combination with s as sh. Phiri, a hyæana, the p is pronounced distinctly & followed by the rough breathing Ph is never f as in English

Septr. 30 We are all at present in pretty good health—thanks to Him who bestows this blessing—Our temporary huts finished —School nearly so—Will begin watercourse in a day or two. Mary salutes you & Helen kindly & you may believe us yours Affectionately

D. LIVINGSTON

Sept. We have now got into our hut on the Kolobeng—the Town has as Dr Hamilton of Leeds would say an oppidal appearance though still in process of building. Our corner although we are attempting only temporary buildings has assumed a touch of the European style. Mebaloe, Paul, Isaac & our man Friday (Morukanelo) have for the first time in their lives got up square huts of poles & reed—the Chief without any suggestion from me determined to erect the school. I desire said he that you be at no expense whatever, I wish to build a house for God who is the defence of my town. I shall call upon all the people to cut wood &c It will be my work. You must go still farther N. or N.E. & try for yourself. There is plenty of

A stimulus to prayer

room. Itineracy is good if you have a permanent sphere—a focus. He proposed likewise that after the school was built we should have an interchange of works, he doing some work for us which required a number of men & we leaving that to him should put a square house together for his use. We were glad of the proposition for the making of a water course must be our first effort & will require aid—as the season is far advanced & we cannot well do without corn for two years everything now is of a temporary nature. The school must be so too, But we hope both chief & people will be as favourably disposed when we do need permanent buildings & this if they were converted I am sure they will be. We earnestly pray for this. Everything else goes on as well as we could wish. Indeed better than we could have expected But the immortal souls there are still in darkness & need your prayers & those of every believer in Jesus. to whom their state is known. A lady in the excess of her simplicity wrote to me requesting me to tell more of our success in order to stimulate her prayers. Poor ignoramus that I was I had told of the degradation into which so many precious immortals had sunk and that the Gospel had little or no effect in the Interior even when preached again & again. I thought this stimulus enough to any one who longed that the Glory of Jehovah should dispel the clouds of darkness & death which cover the earth. But the longer one lives the more one learns. All the success in Bechuana land belongs through the Divine favour to those who preceded me in the field. We are beyond their line & of things I have as yet seen none.

A day's work

LETTER 29

Original at Rhodes Livingstone Institute

To REV. D. G. WATT,[1] *of Benares*

Kolobeng, Bakwain Country
13 Feby. (1848)

MY DEAR WATT,

My date will shew you if you have not received my last that we are now in a different locality from that to which I suppose you have been accustomed. Hoping you have received my account of the removal and circumstances connected with it I proceed to mention that we still have some encouragement in our people. All our meetings are good compared to those we had at Mabotsa and some of them admit of no comparison whatever.... Ever since we moved we have been incessantly engaged in manual labour. We have endeavoured as far as possible to carry on systematic instruction at the same time but have felt it very hard pressure on our energies. Although I date this at Kolobeng I am now on a journey among eastern tribes one object of which is to recruit and remove the languor of body and mind which affected me before I begin the erection of a permanent dwelling. Our daily labours are in the following sort of order. We get up as soon as we can—generally with the sun in summer, then have family worship, breakfast and school and as soon as these are over we begin the manual operations needed—sawing—ploughing—smithy work and every other sort of work by turns as required. My better half is employed all morning in culinary or other work and feeling pretty well tired by dinnertime, we take about an hours rest then, but more frequently without the respite I try to secure for myself, she goes off to the infants' school and this I am happy to say is very popular with the youngsters. She sometimes has 80 but the

---

[1] David G. Watt was a friend of Livingstone in his Glasgow days. He was appointed as a missionary to Benares and arrived there in 1841. In 1847 he went to Almora with the intention of commencing a station there, but his health failed and he returned to England.

Sechele and his wives

average may be 60. My manual labours are continued till about 5 o'clock I then go into my rooms to give lessons and talk to any one who may be disposed for it. As soon as the cows are milked we have a meeting and this is followed by a prayer meeting in Sechele's house, which brings me home about $\frac{1}{2}$ past 8—generally tired enough, too fatigued to think of any mental exertions. I do not enumerate these duties by way of telling how much we do but let you know a cause of sorrow I have that so little of my time is devoted to real missionary work —I wished to come on this journey long ago but incessant occupation prevented me till December a mad sort of Scotchman having wandered past us elephant shooting lost all his cattle by the bite of a small fly—a very little larger than the common house fly, he sent us an imploring letter and instead of going eastwards we were obliged to send him all our oxen and bring him back to the side of civilization. Then our watercourse burst and detained us again. We made a start last week and our friend Sechele convoyed us about 50 miles of the way. It was gratifying to see him on his pack ox hunting for us, and endeavouring to promote our comfort in various ways. We met a large party of strangers on their way to visit our tribe, this rendered his presence at home necessary. He informed me at parting that he had intended to accompany me on the whole itinerary—then presented me with about 4 gallons of porridge; and two servants to act in his stead. He is almost the only individual who possesses distinct consistent views on the subject of our mission. He is bound by his wives. Has a curious idea— he would like to go to another country with the hope that probably his wives may have married others in the meantime. He would then return and be admitted to the Lord's supper and teach his people the knowledge he had acquired. He seems incapable of putting them away. He feels so attached to them and indeed we too feel much attached to most of them—they are our best scholars—our constant friends. We earnestly pray that they too may be enlightened by the spirit of God—On the subject of admitting a man who has more than one wife I have

Caffre war not ended

felt as you but though not clear that I ought to refuse I am glad I have not been asked to baptize a polygamist. I think I should decline because of the evil which a contrary practice to that which has been followed if now introduced would effect. . . . We heard with pain that you had been called on to part with your partner soon after your union. The time which elapses before a letter on the dead of any of our connections can reach its destination makes me afraid to say anything to those in whose losses I sympathize for fear that my letter may only have the effect of opening up the wound again. . . . I have lately been much impressed by the thought that the first Salutations of ministering Angels to the soul rushing out of its falling tenement of clay will make it feel quite at home and then the confirmation from the Lord Jesus himself will certainly wipe away all tears, sorrow and sighing will flee away. Let us live as seeing Him who is invisible. The world to come exercising a constant influence on our conduct. I hope you are favoured with health in your new sphere of labour. I addressed you Almorah. Hope you have not stopped short of it. A younger brother of mine in Ohio wishes to go to China. This is his last year at Oberlin. He wishes to be connected with our society. Have written the Directors on the subject. . . . He is 'engaged' to a descendant of the Puritans in New England and I suspect a bit of a blue for she has been educated at College but in this I may be mistaken. . . . The Caffre War is not finished yet. All the missionaries have been driven helter skelter out of the country; this I don't understand—the mission premises are burned I think I should stick by my people to the last but that you will say is the same folly as to get bitten by the king of beasts. . . . Lately we were menaced by an attack by a party on horse back. I got information of it one night and instantly went up to the town and when our invaders came all were ready. The worthies thought proper to deny that they had any bad intention but having come at a time when horses die, the loss of a portion of their horses shewed they had been baulked in their intention. They would never have risked their horses had they not

'A real friend'

expected to carry off cattle. Some of our old big-wigs said to me 'Now we understand that you are a real friend'. . . .

Yours affectionately
D. LIVINGSTON

LETTER 30

To HENRY DRUMMOND, 62 *Queen St., Glasgow*

Kolobeng, Bakwain Country,
19th June 1848.

MY DEAR FRIEND,

Your favour of 10th November 1847, informing us of some tokens of your kindness reached its destination a short time ago. Its perusal afforded us much pleasure, and as it has come a long time before the articles sent we have superadded to that of the perusal what Campbell calls 'the pleasure of hope,' and can thus afford to thank you most sincerely for your letter and for the other fruits of your friendly feelings, which we expect will in due time arrive. My better half joins with me in hearty acknowledgements for your remembrance of her wants. We shall refer to the subject again when the box comes to hand.

I am sorry my letter was detained so long, and one of my reasons for writing now is to prevent the occurrence of a similar uncertainty. If this reaches you, be kind enough to regard it as an order which will be repeated in another letter, written a month or two hence. . . . In my next I shall inform you of my having advised the Directors to pay you about £20 for what I request you to furnish. We are unable to give positive instructions as to how the one-half of the above sum should be expended. Mrs. L. will be able to state with precision what will be most suitable when she has seen the contents of the box. I have the greatest confidence in your taste, etc, and am sure she will be delighted with your selection, but my rib has not yet reached my state of assurance so I can only mention as articles of which we stand greatly in need:

Order for garments

One large piece of strong bleached calico
One piece of good flannel suitable for children's underdresses.
½ doz. strong bed-chamber candlesticks, with snuffers.
1 doz. female stockings (i.e. ½ doz. woollen & ½ doz. cotton)—middle size.
1 doz. stockings as above, woollen and cotton for child, say 4 years of age. Another dozen for child, say, 3 years of age.
Some small shawls such as cover the neck and shoulders.

We have put down candlesticks although not in your line, but hope you will take the trouble to stow them in—brass perhaps will be best, as it is stronger. Half of the snuffers may be large in size, and the bottom just broad enough to retain the drippings. My own wardrobe stands greatly in need of being replenished, and I feel inclined to try Moleskin for trowsers. The sailcloth is excellent, but washes very white and appears soiled directly, common drab moleskin, or any darker in colour, if it will stand washing. Of course the strongest you can furnish—no matter how thick and tradesman-like it looks. For jackets I should like something which my good lady calls *respectable*, and which, though I try to catch the idea, I cannot describe. We have gentlemen from India occasionally as visitors, and others, as officers of the Army come up on hunting expeditions. Now it sounds rather discordantly when we hear the title 'doctor' applied to a poor fellow in a fustian jacket. You must have seen the sort of fustian which after a shower assumed a peculiar crumpled appearance. For such stuff we have sometimes to pay three shillings per ell (27 inches) and for wretched prints we pay as much as one could procure silk gowns at home. But I am away from the 'Respectable'. A thin dark-coloured stuff, something coloured green, will do. But two of the jackets must be of Moleskin for working in—strong braces. Flannels—woven—such as sailors use. Two blue flannel shirts, do. do. Two blue cloth caps,[1] similar to those worn by officers in the

[1] This seems to show that the familiar peaked cap of the illustrations—sometimes called a consular cap—had its origin in the proved convenience

The 'consular' cap

Navy, the upper part having plenty of wadding, is the best protection from the sun I know. ½ dozen strong striped shirts. ½ doz. good white, do. with fronts. Lastly a surtout of best black cloth. This last I do not expect can be purchased by the sum to be sent, but it may be put down as for another order, which we hope to send next year. If we can manage to purchase all our clothing at home it will enable us to devote much more of our salary to the objects for which we hope to live, and in the prosecution of which we expect to die. Everything in this country is ruinously dear. I put down the above articles not as the result of my expectations of what the money ought to bring, but that you may know our wants and spend the sum in suitable proportions. We think, if it may not put you to too much trouble, that the half of the goods might, when ready, be put into one box, and the other half in another, and each be sent at different times. If one is lost the loss will not be so severely felt as if it had been the whole. It will be a favour, too, if you order the boxes to be tinned—the lid of the tin being so formed that it will be useful as such after it is unsoldered. We think the box you mention very cheap. All boxes sent ought to be dove-tailed, and feathered, even though the price should be higher than that you procured. It just occurs to me that the lid of the tin might be made with hinges and a thin slip of tin put round the seam, which slip when unsoldered would leave the lid in the state it was before being sealed up. We have so

---

of custom. The consular service in Africa did not require any special dress. The naval cap to which a gold band was afterwards added was Livingstone's own device. Other travellers also found it useful to wear a distinguishing head-dress when moving from tribe to tribe. Dr Moffat, for example, wore on occasions a French *képi* which must have looked striking above his long beard.

Artists depict Livingstone wearing a pugaree hanging over his neck round the back of the cap, but there is no warrant for it in the records or pictures with which he himself had anything to do. His profile portraits show that he had a good crop of long hair at the back of his head. In Dean Goodwin's *Memoirs of Bishop Mackenzie*, Livingstone is stated to have laughed at the white-covered broad-brimmed hat of the Bishop and the latter calls Livingstone 'a salamander' in his indifference to heat.

Conduct of Sechele

many destructive insects in this country we feel anxious to preserve our goods as well as possible. As for Sechele's present we are on the best terms with him and will have much pleasure in being able to make a suitable one. He never once treated us in an unfriendly manner—seems to take a pleasure in presenting us with food, when he has it. He lately sent us a whole zebra, and tonight the breast of a buffalo. None of his presents are made for the purpose of securing greater from us in return. He purchases soap, clothing and crockery from us when we have it, and always goes dressed and clean. He never begs now—a great virtue in an African. We are sensible of a great change in him—is very fond of reading, and explanations of what is read—has perused all our books four times over—his whole deportment is good. He always takes the side of Christianity in discussions, and when he requested us to establish a prayer-meeting in his house he told me that he prayed regularly. Polygamy is the great obstacle he has to contend with. He has not courage to part with his wives, and we can sympathise with him for his wives are certainly the most amiable females in the town. He earnestly entreated me to send him to England, or some other country for three or four years in order that he might be instructed without any of the hindrances which distract his mind in his occupation as Chief, and that his wives might in the meantime forsake him and take other husbands. When he returned he hoped he might be allowed to partake of the Lord's Supper. There are others of whom we have hope, but we do not encourage a hasty profession. We should greatly prefer a few consistent members, as a nucleus, to a number of uninformed, unsteady professors. The people in this country who have not been favoured with the visits of missionaries require a long course of instruction. We have need of patience, and you must remember us and our people before the Throne of Grace. We are highly favoured in the Bakwains, all treat us with great respect, and there seems to be a general belief that we are their real friends. Their kind conduct makes us doubly anxious that they may be turned to the Lord. You think it

The dark North

possible we may yet see our native land. I often, in reading some of the periodicals which reach us, afar from the din of war and strife of tongues, exult in the glorious prospects which God is working out for our world in this 19th century. But never yet has a wish crossed my mind to return homewards. All my desires tend forwards, to the North, and that the Bakwains receive the message of mercy. Why we have a world before us here. We have no missionary beyond this—all is dark. You live amongst a war of opinions and no doubt are sometimes pained by the strife around you, but it is worse in the regions to the North of this. No conflict there between truth and error, there are no beams of the former penetrating the mass of the latter. They live without God and die without hope. We have, however, a little to the North of this a fly, very like the common house fly, which seems a sort of barrier. Its bite is certainly fatal to cattle, sheep and dogs, although harmless to goats and men. But God will open a way. A Scotchman passed us last year elephant shooting. We had to send after him and bring him out after 30 oxen, 15 horses and 18 dogs had perished. Yet he passed us again a few weeks ago on the same errand. We shall not, we hope, be outdone by a man of the world.

I must now give you my measure, and for the jackets and surtout I give you the dimensions of an old one. It fitted me well when I left England, and does so still. From the collar seam to the waist (behind) $16\frac{1}{2}$ inches, do. do. to the bottom of the skirt 36 inches, from centre of back to elbow 21 inches, from the elbow to end of sleeve 12 inches. Size round the breast, under the coat, 3 ft 2 inches. Size round the waist, under the coat, 2 ft $9\frac{1}{4}$ inches. From the centre of the collar seam behind, to bottom of waistcoat in front $22\frac{1}{2}$ inches. For trowsers, inner or leg seam, 2 ft 10 inches, waist 2 ft $9\frac{1}{4}$. Knee 16, whole length of trowsers 3 ft. 9 inches. Head 22 inches in circumference.

Sechele desired me to write for two pairs of moleskin trowsers for him. He would have me enclose a much larger order

Poor goods from traders

for him but he only now sends out ivory to Kuruman to get money and I cannot afford to spend a larger sum of what I shall send this year than will purchase the two pairs. His measure is, inside seam 3 ft. Waist 3 ft 2 inches, knee 20 inches. Whole length 3 ft 11 inches—strong, whatever colour they may be. You must please use your judgement in the selection of the articles. It may perhaps be better to let the surtout stand this year and send chiefly the stronger articles, some neckerchiefs also.

We enclose a little bit of the stuff we wish the jackets of. We use it on Sabbaths, although green. One or two pairs of trowsers may be something of the same sort, the trowsers open front, without pockets, except one in the same situation as a watch pocket. The jackets single-breasted, the collar made like that of a soldier's jacket in form, but to lie down on the shoulders and not quite so broad—pockets inside. If we could afford to purchase beforehand we could exchange clothing for food among the people, for many are anxious for clothing, but the expenses of removals, buildings, and want of corn have prevented us spending any of the salary for their benefit. We are more than 200 miles from the nearest trader, and every time we are compelled to go near his vile shop we feel as if going to get the marrow sucked out of our bones. His goods are enough to put the natives entirely out of conceit with European clothing. A railway would be a blessing. It would take ten weeks constant travelling for me to reach the Cape.

I will conclude this hurried epistle by wishing you every blessing. Mrs. L. joins me,

Affectionately yours,
D. Livingston.

LETTER 31

To the Revd Arthur Tidman

Kolobeng, 1st November 1848

Dear Sir

No portion of our lives ever seemed to glide more swiftly past

Change in Sechele

than the year which has elapsed since our location on the Kolobeng. Our operations have been characterized by a pleasant variety, but, of necessity, chiefly confined to our own people. The results though considerable compared with nothing, are trifling indeed when contrasted with what remains to be done. Many discussions & incidents have occurred to cheer us in our solitude and an interest has been imparted which often lightened the manual labour on which during the intervals of service, it was necessary constantly to engage. Circumstances have also developed considerable opposition but it has been of a kind which afforded much encouragement, for our most bitter opponents seemed to entertain no personal animosity and never alluded to their enmity to the gospel in our presence unless specially invited to state their objections. An event which excited more open enmity than any other was the profession of faith and subsequent reception of the chief into the church. As the circumstances which led us to recieve his confession as genuine are somewhat peculiar I may be allowed to mention a few particulars in order that the Directors may form an opinion as to the propriety of the step we have taken. The state of the Bakwains about three years ago was very unlike that of the tribes adjacent to the Kuruman, among whom the gospel had been in silent operation for nearly a quarter of a century previous to their obtaining the present ample supply. I have never been able to contemplate the condition especially of the old without a painful foreboding that our entreaties & warnings would only render their doom the more terrible. They generally resist an invitation or if they listen to our message, it is with the firm persuasion that they have been preserved to old age by some medicine or other and it would be folly to think of another saviour now. Sechele though generally intelligent had imbibed largely of the prevailing superstition and in addition to being the chief rain-doctor of the tribe, we have had evidence that he was reckless of human life Indeed although he had the reputation among other tribes of being addicted to witchcraft, he thought it highly meritorious to put

Sechele baptized

all suspected witches to death. From the first day of residence with the Bakwains he attended school & all our services with unvarying regularity. The first indication of deep feeling observed in him was when sitting together under our waggon during the heat of the day, I endeavoured to describe the 'great white throne' 'Judgement seat'. &c. He said 'these words shake all my bones, my strength is gone' & the existence of our Lord previous to his appearance among men & Divine nature surprised him greatly. We have often during the three years in which we have been with the tribe witnessed that the word of God was with power and as his knowledge increased, he professed among his own people firm belief in divine truth and great thankfulness because the Gospel had been sent to him while so many were left in darkness—a poor scoffer from one of the southern tribes having visited him we felt anxious lest his taunts should have an injurious effect but were relieved when we ascertained that while Sechele treated his visitor with the deference due to his station in his own tribe, instead of argument, generally sat down by his side & read four or five chapters of the testament to .him. His taunts are very bitter said he 'but I fear only for my people lest they too should believe as he does' The greatest sacrifice he had to make was the renuntiation of polygamy. Of all other sins, they had possessed the idea that they were wrong but this practice had never been imagined as possessed of moral turpitude. . . .

On the morning after it was known that Sechele had renounced his wives on account of the gospel a general consternation seemed to surge both young & old—the town was as quiet as if it had been Sunday. Not a single woman was seen going to her garden. Pichos were held during the night in order to intimidate him and make him renounce his purpose. But after being tried in various ways for two months we proceeded to administer the ordnance of baptism. Many of the spectators were in tears but these were in general tears of sorrow for the loss of their rain-maker or of grief at seeing some of the ties of relationship to him completely broken. . . .

Basuto-land teachers repelled

We have erected a substantial house 50 ft by 20. and a workshop of smaller dimensions. This work prevented us from proceeding with the settlement of Paul with Mokhatla's people so soon as we intended. We went in order to erect a small hut as a commencement but the opposition of the Boers or emigrants was such we felt assured they would burn it in our absence: we contented ourselves by providing the materials and will return in two months with his family. I hope then to be able to remain two months more on the spot, & build a small school & think that our presence will prevent any actual outburst of hostility. The French missionaries in the Basuto country lately sent 5 native teachers to one of the tribes in that direction. The commandant of the Boors tore their letter of introduction & threw it into the fire & sent them back with scorn. Apprehension of a similar treatment for Paul is the reason why I prefer going with him and acting in what may appear to you an over cautious manner. We shall now have more time to devote to the Eastern tribes and they form a most interesting field for missionary labour. If we cannot furnish native teachers soon the field will in all probability be lost in as far as our mission is concerned.

The infant school under the care of Mrs L. afforded us much encouragement—the attendance during the past year may be stated as from 60 to 80. The failure of the native crops has lately had considerable effect on the regularity of their attendance for the children have been obliged to go great distances in search of locusts and roots on which to subsist. M^{rs} L must also soon discontinue it for a season but it will be resumed after her confinement . . .

A vote of disapprobation with the mode in which the Directors favoured me with £30 for building expenses at Chonuane, makes it necessary that I allude to the circumstances in which I applied for it in a manner more minute than I should otherwise have done. I have in spending my salary always acted on the conviction that it was wrong to go to the Colony merely because there we could obtain supplies much cheaper than

'Has he starved her?'

from the traders who occasionally visit us. By a journey to Graham's town or Algoa Bay I could have saved more than £30 of each year's salary, but it would have been at a loss of from six to nine months, each time, to the mission I have bought from traders often at a price double sometime three times more than I should have done at Algoa Bay—the salary was sufficient for all I wished but when it became necessary to remove to Chonuane the expenses of removal, building house & school having been superadded to ordinary outlay reduced our resources to nothing. We endured for a while using a wretched infusion of native corn for coffee but when our corn was done we were fairly obliged to go to Kuruman for supplies I can bear what other Europeans would consider hunger and thirst without any inconvenience but when we arrived to hear the old women who had seen my wife depart about two years before exclaiming before the door. Bless me! how lean she is! Has he starved her? Is there no food in the country to which she has been? &c. this was more than I could well bear. I went to the meeting of Committee with the full persuasion that the building expenses would be given so that I should be able to procure supplies for my return. But before I had stated the case Mr Helmore brought forward a motion expressive of disapprobation at my leaving Mabotsa and withdrew it. another & another followed exhibiting a spirit which prevented me from making known my necessities. I then returned to the Kuruman to muse over my position. I had come for supplies & had not a penny in the world to buy them with—the bretheren of the Committee would not probably be more willing to sanction the new mission on another occasion more than this. Mr Moffat willingly advanced the money but then no one likes to be in debt so thinking that now was the time in which I really ought to make known the case & ask the aid of the Directors and I did so and believe I acted properly though all the world should disapprove. Mr Hughs mentioned in Committee that he had recieved £30 through Dr Philip for his project on the Vaal River. It is surprising he did not see that that was equally

Gift from Carr's Lane

an irregularity with mine & being then on the point of starting for the Colony he might have had a little consideration in his motion for those who do not go thither. Colonial journies are in general serious drawbacks to the mission. Mabotsa will again be left desolate for six or eight months. I have often thought of bringing the subject under the consideration of the Committee but my motives will now be suspected and I am not sure but they would be justly so. Man is a complex being & we greatly need our motives to be purified from all that is evil.

We have purchased a bell. & it was with joy we mounted it It relieves us from the task of going through the town with a small hand bell. I made an application to the committee on the subject as also on the subject of expenses for building on the new station. but they seem to have thought only on the £30 which they had no power to refuse. I shall apply again by letter, for I do not feel it my duty to go out this year merely to attend its sittings

I shall feel obliged if the Directors will forward the sum of £20. to Mr Henry Drummond 62 Queen St Glasgow to defray the expense of clothing which I have ordered from him. I shall advise Mr Rutherfoord of Cape Town of the amount to be deducted from the salary. Mr Drummond will apply for information as to the conveyance to Algoa Bay. We have sustained considerable loss from the boxes having been broken open there & do not know who is now the society's agent there. Friends unknown to us send boxes without invoices & we do not know who to thank or blame. The ladies connected with Carr's lane chapel Birmingham sent two chairs to Sechele. They came safely and arrived just two days before that on which we had resolved to baptize him—they were to him highly interesting as tokens of love from those he had never seen.

Yours affectionately
DAVID LIVINGSTON

The Climate of South Africa

LETTER 32

To MR. CHARLES LIVINGSTONE, 46 *Almada St., Hamilton*[1]

Kolobeng, 16th May 1849.

MY DEAR BROTHER CHARLES,

Yours of Sept. 30th/48 reached me yesterday. I had previously resolved to write you but the sight of your *pucella dulcissima's* hair sent the steam up, and here I am at it. My Mary and the little dears have gone to Kuruman in search of vegetables and rest. We have had an intensely hot and dry season. Only four inches of rain have fallen, and the season is past. Our potatoes were burned off, and nearly all my trees killed, the Kolobeng nearly dry and the winter beginning. If we do not get lots of locusts we shall have many deaths from starvation. We had good supplies last season, they are better than shrimps but that is not saying much in their favour. A man came here last week saying he was God, and would—if the women paid him well—bring them locusts. The chief told him he would pay him with that which Solomon says is for the backs of fools, if his godship did not take himself off next morning. The women would have divested themselves of their ornaments for this imposter had they been allowed. We are hard up Charles. We cannot help the poor people, and to make bad worse, another tribe called the Bakaa attracted by the report that Sechele had secured the good word has come to live here. They 'come to enjoy sleep', and so long as the Bakwains have anything it will be freely shared. We have had scanty harvests ever since we came to this tribe and this year it is a complete failure. We can do nothing without irrigation. Have but little rain, and a climate intensely dry, I ought to say atmosphere. Sulphuric Acid is used at home for absorbing moisture from certain products which require it in setting a galvanic battery into operation. I used about two ounces of this concentrated acid to two pints of water. When set aside

[1] See letter No. 34 to William Thompson (Aug. 1850). Charles is there stated to be settled in Livingstone County, New York.

On breaking an engagement

in this house, the whole of the water evaporated, and left pure acid. If concentrated acid is left uncovered at home, it soon becomes weak by absorbing water from the air. It is a fine climate, however. There are no lung diseases, and cases of consumption near the coast have become well when brought up to the Kuruman. . . . My dear brother, I think you are not quite clear upon the indications of Providence. I dont think we ought to wait for them. Our duty is to go forward and look for the indications. . . . But in general I have observed that people who have sat waiting, have sat long enough before they saw any indication to go. . . .

As to breaking your engagement, you break brotherhood with me on the day you do. Are the old folks Christians? If they are parting with their daughter for such an object it would add ten years to each of their lives. It would act like marriage—you perhaps know that that adds about 10 years to a man's life as proved by statistics. It would be quite a new thing in the world if they should cut their sticks in the way their good daughter fears. A single case has never occurred in England. Try if you can find one in America. The old man and lady too will come down to New York with you. The latter will buy a pair of new spectacles in order to make new pinafores for her grandchildren. Die by the shock!! My dear fellow it will renew their youth like the eagle's. . . . I think however the old people are not fairly dealt with. Trying them, would be what I call going forward. Lay the case before them in unmistakable vernacular. Lay the responsibility of refusal on their consciences. We dont know how bad some people are untill they are tried nor how good others are untill put to the test. Getting the opinion of Medical men on your suitability would be something like going forward too. And so would applying to a Society. There have not been Missionaries enough in China to elicit the statement that four years is the average of a female life. That may have been the average with a number but we must stick a *non sequitur* on all inferences that might follow. Vital statistics require some thousands to pro-

The children in 1849

duce an average which can be depended on. In Medicine 84 are required in 100 before we can speak with the certainty you do. Is she merely weakly in appearance? or has she any symptoms of organic disease? Marriage makes an improvement if the stamina is good. I speak to you freely and know that you will take my remarks all in a kindly spirit. Life is very precious and it is encouraging to know that our times are in his hand whose heart is full of pity. Commit it all to Him he will guide you safely and surely. You ought to have some medical knowledge before you go anywhere. Take particular care of your person in respect to sudden vicissitudes of temperature, damp etc. . . . You ask what the people think of us. They are very sagacious. Have much of the old Scotch farmers in them. Selfishness is ingrained into their very core & they judge of other people by themselves. They have unfortunately had some bad examples sufficient to induce them to think all Missionaries are actuated by the same feelings as themselves. Very like Napoleon they can divine what people in general will do in particular circumstances and like him they are nonplussed by a thoroughly honest course of conduct. A man once brought a piece of work to be done at the forge, I was otherwise engaged and while waiting he fell into conversation with me, and told me in reference to the subject under discussion that I was a deciever and a liar. I immediately left the work in which I was engaged and did his and when done I told him I was happy in assisting him and should do the very same again although he thought so badly of me. He went home and sent a servant with 12 shillings requesting me to take it for the little job I had done. He appeared quite distressed when I refused. The work I did was not worth 6^d. . . .

On their manners and customs, I could almost write a book, so I wont begin here, for I must say something of my family. Mary has very little time for anything but household matters. She had an infant school which was very well attended, but the appearance of Thomas Steele, our third, made her give up that. Three children and domestic matters engross most of her time so you need not expect to hear much from her. We have so many things to attend to I can scarcely spare an hour for correspondence, and except in winter, I am in general quite exhausted by the evening and how it is with her you may guess. Robert is just beginning to understand matters, a great imitator. When just beginning to walk he was fond of doctoring the natives, and himself. Butter is his great remedy. After having the rod applied to his tail, he applies a piece, and thinks all right. Any one with a wound coming past may get it mollified if Robert sees it. He shewed his faith in butter long before he could speak. He speaks the native language well, but feels much at a loss in English. Never addresses us in it, and as we wish him to know the English we prefer to hear it though we lose much of his prattle for want of words. He is excessively obstinate at times. Never saw one so very determined at his age. He often causes us sorrow. Nannee is all fun and frolic, perpetually wanting new modes of merriment. She gabbles what she can in pure Sitchuana. As for Thomas he is a strong fellow but as he was but five weeks old when they left I must end the juvenile chapter. Mary speaks the language like a native, without knowing so much of it as your servant.—I have a foreign accent—a heelenman.—The native children are fond of her and may be so am I. Robert has hair a shade lighter than your lady's, Nannee's a shade or two darker. Both have black eyes. I am darker than either. . . . There is a new Josephus by Isaac Taylor. Have you seen it? It was begun by another. I lived near Mr. Taylor and formed such an opinion of his ability for the translation etc., I have sent for it, or rather told a friend who will buy it for me, that I should like to have it. He Mr. T. wrote me a long letter lately inviting me to become a contributor to a new Missionary Periodical. . . . Blessings on you Charles. May the Lord guide you. Mary, if here, would send much love. . . .

        Ever affectionately Yours,
          D. LIVINGSTON

Lessons of the Bechuana Mission
LETTER 33

To REV. J. J. FREEMAN, *London*

Kolobeng,
24th August 1850.

MY DEAR FRIEND,

I have to acknowledge the receipt of two letters from you, one a circular relating to Mr. Thompson, and the other dated 23rd May in answer to one you had received from me before you left the Cape. The belief that in one or two points in the letter I ought to try and effect your conversion, induces me to trouble you with another letter. I hope you will kindly excuse the infliction.

You object to the 'idea of giving the people a trial with the Gospel for a certain number of years, on the ground that in nearly all cases where Christian Societies are now reaping success, a considerable time elapsed before there were indications of that success.' And you allege that 'had there been any precipitate removal of the Missions under the impression that it was useless and hopeless to give them a longer trial, then humanly speaking all the present success had been lost.' I agree with you entirely in reference to the time which has usually elapsed before success became visible. But the history of the Bechuana Mission forbids assent to the inference you draw. At least that is my conviction, and if you will only review that history I have strong hopes that you will view the matter in the same light. The Bechuana Mission began at the Kuruman, and the attention of the missionaries was directed chiefly to the Batlapi. No visible success attended their labours, but the tribe got a fair *trial* and instead of the missionaries removing at the conclusion of the trial, the experiment was performed for our instruction in the opposite way. The Batlapi left the missionaries, the tribe divided into several fragments soon after leaving, and without following their wanderings we may just note their positions—those under Motheebe at Lekatlong, Lingopeng and Borigelong, those under Mahura and Motlabani and Tlaganyane at Taong, Mamusa and Lathako. You will remember that Mr. Moffat in his work[1] mentions

---
[1] *Missionary Labours and Scenes in Southern Africa* (1842).

Progress without a missionary

that the first success they subsequently had at Kuruman was among a small tribe of Balala called Bachaine (of which Paul and Mebaloe here are members) and a lot of refugees from the interior. But the seed had been sown in the hearts of the Batlapi too. The *trial* had been made and the results were as follows.— When the party which settled down at Lekatlong had got a little time for reflection they actually sent a deputation of their number to the nearest Mission station, Griqua Town, to beg instruction. And the bretheren there being unable to supply them with a missionary, the people sent individuals statedly to Griqua Town to receive a little instruction, and while they returned to Lekatlong to impart that little, others were sent to receive a fresh supply. This system went on till many were fit for fellowship, and when the missionaries went for the first time they were surprised and delighted with the progress they had made. The visits of the bretheren ever afterwards were for the purpose of examining candidates and receiving them into fellowship. Before a European missionary came to settle among them there were upwards of one hundred in the Church, and when I visited Lekatlong a short time after Mr. Helmore's settlement there, religious profession was rather too fashionable. He found it necessary rather to restrain than urge to a confession of Christ. As we are reviewing the subject privately no one's feelings will be hurt by supposing we think little of his labours, but I think you will agree with me in thinking that *up to the period* of Mr. Helmore's settlement, the fruits were those of the *trial* made at Kuruman. Mr. Wright did not, so far as I recollect, look upon the work in any other light.

The distance has always prevented the Kuruman bretheren from visiting with any regularity the next division of Motheebe's people settled at Barigelong. But the seed was sown before they left that station. The native teacher was sent after a wish had been expressed by the people, and when he went his position was totally different from that to Sebube among the Wanketse, the Gospel having been deposited, the influences of the Holy Spirit soon caused the fruits to appear, and the result

Power of the Chief

of the trial has been especially satisfactory, for we have had a Church planted in the midst of a mass of heathenism, and every year there has been what Dr. Chalmers called 'an excavation' going on. This experiment clearly proves that a respectable Church may result from such a trial as I advocate, and that Church be anything but a feeble standstill one, though it does not receive a European missionary as its pastor. Lingopeng is a twin experiment and equally satisfactory. The future will determine which will furnish the healthiest children—those who have received little or much nursing.

The division under Mahura, including the Bamaeris and Tlaganyane, exhibits another important feature in the Bechuana Mission. Let the Chief of any locality exhibit determined opposition to the Gospel, few or none of his people ever profess their faith in Christ till he alters his conduct or is removed by death. Mahura altered his conduct in order to increase his town by drawing a number of believers from other parts. Had he not done so it would have been a mere waste of life for a European to have lived with him. Tlaganyane never altered his conduct and he had no believers under him. Mochuara, who with his Barolongs enjoyed the ministrations of Lemue and Langa for a great many years, acted on the principle of getting all the temporal good out of the missionaries he could, while fully determined never to believe the Gospel, and not a single individual under him ever attempted to profess Christ. Mochuara even sent an advice to the above effect to Mosielele at Mabotsa when we removed thither. In the cases of Mahura Tlaganyane and the Bamoeris we have no fruits from the trial apparent, *up to the period* of Mr. Ross's settlement. But no one will deny the existence of a preparedness, and not even that appeared in the Barolongs of Mochuara, although Mr. Lemue and Langa spent half a lifetime upon them. As it is with the Bechuana mission in its private development I am most familiar, I can only point you to its history and request you to say whether it warrants the inference that the removal of a Mission would cause an ultimate loss of success. To me those who

Generous Oswell

never heard the Gospel are greater objects of compassion than those who have heard it for seven years and rejected it. The plan of trial would perhaps tend to the more rapid extension of the knowledge of Christ in the world. The full persuasion that this is the great desire of your heart makes me presume to give you this long lecture, and if I fail to effect your conversion you will not take the *trial* amiss.

I have had thoughts of writing on paper on the above subject for one of the periodicals, but people have got so much into the habit of laying everything to the account of the Directors I have had fears lest my heresies should implicate them. . . .

The Directors Manifesto has not yet come to hand. I have mentioned to Mr. Tidman my reasons for proceeding again to the Lake. Having only one establishment to support, the expense was less, but we lost eleven oxen by pitfalls, lions, etc. The sum you thought of, if sanctioned, would be amply sufficient. Mrs. L. promises me a twelvemonths leave next time. We met Oswell[1] on our return—brought supplies for us from the Colony and returned a bill of £40, which was to be spent in purchasing them—seemed very anxious to get me to promise to allow him to accompany me next trip. . . . I shall not involve the Society in any expense till I have the sanction of the Directors. If I go down to the Colony to get my uvula excised I should procure supplies by drawing a year in advance. . . . I begin to fear we have established a branch of what Sidney Smith called 'the great Irish manufactory.' Mrs. L. got a daughter seven days after we reached Kolobeng. Sechele sends you many salutations. The Boers are more than ever troublesome,—waylaying travellers between Sentube's and the Moloso in order to rob them—the rebel Pretorious sent an order lately to him to stop all English travellers and traders, and many other indications of a coming storm present themselves. I have but small hope for the stability of the station—in the present posture of affairs it would be impossible for Sechele to leave. I

---

[1] William Cotton Oswell the hunter and explorer; always a generous friend to Livingstone.

Gift of gun to a Chief

never have had a wish even to return to England, but what you suggest would answer extremely well. Sechele does not make any progress in English. This is rather surprising for he is a first rate speaker in his own tongue and comprehends most subjects readily.

Wilson (and Mr. Edwards's son) went in (company) this year and got nothing but a terrible squeeze from the king of terrors. We found him in high fever—gave him some medicine which relieved him. He again exposed himself—had a relapse and sent after us for more medicine, before that reached him he had been lying two days insensible. Large bed sores formed, &c., &c., and he is not yet perfectly recovered. The Batauna Chief[1] would not give him guides, although he offered anything he chose to ask as wages. The same Chief took a great liking to a beautiful gun I received as a present from Lieutenant Arkwright, after setting his collar bone, and also the broken thigh of one of his servants. It must have cost him £25. When I asked guides to Sebitoane, he promised meat for my family during my absence, guides, &c., &c., adding, if I only knew him I would have no hesitation in trusting him anent both family and *gun*. I handed it to him at once, an act of entire confidence goes a great way with these people, for instead of refusal, as in the case of Wilson, he was ready to do everything for me, and but for the fever I should have been more than paid for my gun.

Your beautiful telescope shews the satellites of Jupiter well, and were it not that my plague watch is dead again I could observe an occultation by the moon's dark limb sufficiently well for the Longitude.

May I ask you to pay Mr. Snow £10 out of the salary of 1851 for books I now order.

Of the Anti-rhinocerists you saw at Blomfontein, Rider[2] the young artist, died of fever. Rider took some views of the Lake.

[1] Lechulatebe; see Blaikie, p. 87.
[2] Rider. The drawing of the discovery of Lake Ngami which appears opposite page 66 of *Travels* is ascribed to 'the late Alfred Ryder Esq.' See also *Travels*, p. 75.

Grave of a Bushman

Harris, who now has them in his possession, never went down to see it.

With kind salutations from Mrs. L. and self,
Believe me
Yours affectionately,
DAVID LIVINGSTON.

¶ On the same day (August 24, 1850) Livingstone wrote to Tidman giving an account of his second journey to Lake Ngami. Mrs. Livingstone, her three children, and Mebalwe went with him. The party crossed the river Zouga and ascended the northern bank where Livingstone

'stumbled on a native grave, for the first time since I came into the country', it was that of a Bushman. An old tortoise shell which they use as a dish, a stick used in digging roots, some grass and bushes were placed above it, and a fire had been made on the edge of an old pitfall which the relatives had used to save themselves the trouble of digging a grave.

'On enquiry, the Bakhola informed us that the Bushmen in burying their dead address them in reference to these articles, thus. "Go away to your God and let us eat what we can get here".

'A little farther on we came upon an old man quite naked and hopelessly diseased. He informed us that he had been deserted a few days before by his daughters, that he suffered much from thirst, for though lying under the large trees which line the banks of the river he could not crawl down for water. Having supplied him with a covering and some food, we offered to carry him to the next village. "O," said he, "if they saw me they would flee from me." Socialism has but sorry fruits among those unsophisticated specimens of humanity.'

The expedition was to have travelled to Sebituane's country, but the fever & tsetse fly compelled a return to Kolobeng. Two of the children had fever, and there was some suffering from thirst on the homeward journey. These troubles are not given prominence in the letter to Tidman but he wrote

'That which inspires more fear than anything else in the Lake Country is mosquitoes. They are dreadful. Their bite is more venomous than anywhere else, at least so said those who had been in India. New South Wales & Brazil. They are really painful and the pain continues for several days—sleep is out of the question when you come to a den of them. I could not touch a square half-inch on the bodies of the children unbitten after a single night's exposure.'[1]

LETTER 34

To The REVD. WM. THOMPSON, *Cape Town*

Kolobeng,
27th August 1850

MY DEAR SIR,

I received a few days ago the circular announcing your appointment to the Agency at Cape Town,[2] and to which your kind note of 3rd July was appended. I now beg leave to accept of your offer of service in reference to the transmission of letters to and from America. My brother Charles[3] is settled as Pastor of a Church in Lakeville, Livingstone County, New York. He was educated at Oberlin and Andover—indeed he is a naturalized citizen of the United States. I have another brother settled in Lanark Canada West. My parents are also in that country, and having so many relatives there I begin to feel anxious to have a more direct means of communication than that which I have hitherto availed myself of, viz, by way of

---

[1] See Blaikie, p. 91.

[2] Rev. John Philip, D.D., had retired and Thompson, formerly of Bellary, South India, succeeded him. Philip died in 1851.

[3] See letters no. 26 and 32. The other brother in Canada was John. 'My parents are also in that country.' Their emigration had been considered but evidently they did not go to the colony. The argument in letter 26, 'Old trees seldom transplant well', seems to have prevailed.

The need for books

England. Both brothers would like to send me books, periodicals, &c., but the expense by way of the Mission House we found to be so enormous we were obliged to forbid them sending. That which I shall be much obliged if you can do for me conveniently is to enquire of the United States Consul — Chase, Esq., if he acts as agent in such matters. If not, is there any American house which does. And what is the firm in New York to which, in the event of Mr. Chase or another American gentleman acting as agent, my brother ought to address letters and parcels. Also what is likely to be the cost of agency in reference to letters, parcels of books, etc. I am quite willing to pay any reasonable amount that may be thought proper. If you obtain a satisfactory answer from Mr. Chase will you state in a note the name of the firm in New York to which my brother ought to send, and address it to Revd. Charles Livingston, Lakeville, Livingstone County, State of New York. Perhaps a mere slip inserted into a letter, which I now send him addressed to your care, would be sufficient, as I explain to him in the body of it that I intend applying for the assistance of Mr. Chase.

So it seems we not only met at Mrs. Sewell's.[1] but we shall yet meet up in the interior of Africa, perhaps on the banks of the Lake. You will never think of turning round in your visitations without seeing us all, and you will be sure of a welcome if you come our length. We lately returned from another visit to the Lake country. Were compelled by Fever and Fly to return without going any farther than last year. Met Mr. Oswel on our return and do not know where he is now. . . .

In the last statement of accounts from Mr. Rutherfoord, a balance of £10.15.6 was stated to be overdrawn. This sum ought to have been put down as £5. 5. 6. I explained the

---

[1] Mrs. Sewell's boarding house in Aldersgate St., London. They must have met there in 1840, when Thompson returned to England to be married. Thompson had again been to London in 1849, and Livingstone appends a note to this letter: 'You might have told me how our old friend Mrs. Sewell looked.'

Livingstone's salary

reason to Mr. Freeman when here. As we have four children the salary may be put down as:

```
        £120
deduct     6 in order to have even money
        ___
         114  amount of salary
         125  amount drawn for 1850
        ___
        £ 11  overdrawn and due by me to the Society.
```

I mention it before you can have found it out by the appearance of bills, for I have no apprehension that you will catch your fellow servant by the throat saying 'Pay me that thou owest'. I have still to draw £12 for a native teacher, and may perhaps be obliged to run a little more into the Society's debt, for in my late trip I lost a great many oxen. I do not however advise you that I certainly will do so.

Shall write you more at length soon. This is by an opportunity I should not expect, which I embrace to write the Directors, &c. By excusing this and attending to my request, you will very much oblige

Yours affectionately,
D. LIVINGSTON.

LETTER 35

To MR. BENJAMIN PYNE, *Wildingtree, Ongar*

Kuruman,
4th December 1850

MY DEAR FRIENDS,

The date of this will show you we have come to visit our friends. We are all sick and out of supplies and our mother came to our assistance and we have accompanied her out. I can only write a few lines to you now. Mrs. Livingston had a paralytic attack a short time after her confinement—the right side of the face becoming motionless. The motor power has been restored, but the pain continually recurs and affects the right side and leg. Our little Elizabeth Pyne[1] took the sickness

---
[1] Elizabeth was their fourth child.

Death of Elizabeth

which was prevailing amongst the Bakwains, and after bearing up under it for a fortnight was taken away to see the King in His beauty and the blessed land. We hope to follow her thither. It is wonderful how soon the affections twine round a little stranger. We felt quite desolate without her—she was very beautiful, had fine blue eyes and was very strong. The complaint was very fatal amongst the natives. All our children had it but the others recovered.

She was buried in a grove of mimosa trees and a board marks the spot. Here is the first grave marked as such in the country.

ELIZABETH P. LIVINGSTON

(*Here follows a Sechuana inscription meaning*: When men die they are not annihilated. Jesus will raise and judge all.)

The children were all very thin and ill afterwards. So we have come to rusticate a little. We shall return in about six weeks hence.

I put a few seeds in the corner of this of the kind of hibiscus, of which I spoke in my last, but was prevented enclosing. The natives make nets of the plant.

Mr. Moffat is busy translating the whole Bible. It is a great work and will in future be splendidly useful. We saw a man belonging to the tribe which has the odd custom of knocking out the front upper teeth of both men and women. Ask Mary how she would like that custom. He had come down with Sebitoane's people to visit us in Kolobeng.

The Royal Geographical Society has decreed, or awarded me twenty-five guineas for the discovery of the Lake[1] (Ngami) I think they must have left out a cypher (250) by mistake, but unfortunately it was written in words. It is from the Queen! I shall try and render her twenty-five guineas' worth of loyalty.

I have not heard from you for a considerable time, but do not blame you. I have been so negligent myself I am ashamed to scold anyone. My negligence has, I must say, not been optional. What would Mrs. Pyne think of oxen which stand

---

[1] The Council of the R.G.S. 'request that he will accept the sum of twenty-five guineas (one half of the Royal Donation of the year) as a small encouragement toward further efforts'.

Large ox horns

as high as the highest horse—the point of the horns are bent ten feet apart. I brought one for Mr. Moffat from Lake. We unite in kind regards to you all. This is not enough, saith my wife, who is looking on. So you must please receive her love as a bundle by itself. May God bless you according to your need. Excuse me for I have five other letters to write today on business. Believe me,

Yours affectionately,
D. LIVINGSTON.

¶ A certain playfulness appears at times in Livingstone's letters, but it is not usually sustained for long. The most deliberate effort of this kind was a letter from Kuruman (Jan. 10, 1856) to his friend D. G. Watt, who had by that time returned from India owing to ill health.

Incidentally it illustrates Livingstone's perpetual hunger for letters and news of his friends. He begins:

'Dauede Watte Maister of Airts, I commende me vnto you and Albeit I haue not receyud the letters qhuilk manyfestlie yo dyde not wryte; I hereby advertyse and command ye sayde Maister Dauede Watte instantly to repayre to his wryting box & use his pen, or, as the boards used to say 'Beware of Crow toes & spring guns and being prosecuted to the utmost rigour of the law'

In September of the same year he wrote again to Watt

'I was glad to receive your letter in this distant corner, read it three times over, not because of its intrinsic value, don't think that now, but because I had nothing better from home

'Your calculations of the number of words etc did not please me. However true they may be, facts & figures don't please so well as a little blarney would

'You ought to have told me how much better my letters were than yours, how deeply interesting etc. That would have gone down sweetly

'You don't know human nature yet I see—Hope you are not too old to learn'

Delays in post

LETTER 36

To the REVEREND Dʀ TIDMAN   Boatlanama 30ᵗʰ April 1851

MY DEAR SIR

After a silence prolonged since 1849 I had the pleasure of again hearing from you on the 19ᵗʰ currt. But being then engaged in putting our provisions &c. into the waggons I defered answering your favour till some leizure hour should occur on the journey—that opportunity has occurred while the people are drawing water for the cattle out of the deep wells of Boatlanama and one of the Bakalahari will take this back to Sechele. Your letter is dated 5ᵗʰ August 1850 nearly ten months ago. and I am sorry to learn that my letter from the Zonga 3ʳᵈ September /49 was quite as long on its way to you. One reason I had for writing there, was that you might have the information before any of my friends should. And it was dispatched to the colony a few days after I reached Kolobeng. Letters sent direct to Colesberg seldom remain longer on the way than five months. I have recieved them at Kolobeng in a little more than four from the date of their leaving England But if sent to the care of any one at the Cape, much longer time is required and nothing is gained in either expense or safety Be so kind therefore as to address letters & Newspapers when sent to the care of Mʳ David Arnot, Colesberg—South Africa. But parcels. periodicals &c. may come in the usual manner. I beg to call your attention particularly to this as all the letters &c. except your own to which you refer as leaving in the same ship reached me in November last. nearly seven months ago. In consequence of not knowing that you had recieved the sum awarded by the Royal Geographical Society till many months after the letter of the President arrived, I requested my friend Captain Steel[1] to purchase a watch with it suitable for observing

---

[1] Captain Steele of the Coldstream Guards (aide-de-camp to the Governor of Madras), later General Sir Thomas Steele.

Watch from the Geographical Society

occultations of stars by the moon in order thereby to find the longitude. Mr Maclear the astronomer at the Cape having publicly invited any one to make observations on certain stars, engaged to observe them simultaneously and make the calculations. As it would not require much time and a small telescope kindly presented me by Mr Freeman with my own sextant are all that are required besides the watch I felt anxious to comply with Mr Maclear's invitation, And as the watch might have an inscription. it would serve as a memorial of the occasion on which the money was given, As I am not sure whether Captain Steel is in England or whether it may be convenient for him to attend to my request in consequence of having met with an accident. I am unable to say anything more about the money, except that if he applies for it you have my authority for furnishing it to him

In my last I gave you an account of our unsuccessful attempt to reach Sebitoane. We were driven back by fever. We are now on our way to try again and should we find a suitable people and locality will commence a station. You are aware that the Bakwains have for successive years suffered either partial or entire failure of crops. The want of corn has been contemporaneous with the possession of the Gospel, and as some of the ajacent tribes who have shewn considerable opposition to the 'Word of God' have been favoured with years of plenty. many of the people associate teaching and hunger as inseparable. the dearth caused by repeated droughts has operated most injuriously on our success for those who were willing to be taught, and these were not a few, have always been compelled to leave the school for the purpose of obtaining food by hunting &c. The Boers too by perpetual meddling have distracted the mind of the tribe, and to crown all the Kolobeng which for the first year after our settlement was a fine large stream capable of irrigating land enough for the subsistance of the whole tribe, has gradually dried up, and renders a removal to a new locality absolutely necessary. All the streams & fountains in the tract of country inhabited by the

Country drying up

Bakwains & Bangwaketse have been subjected to the same cause of desiccation. the chief of the Bangwaketse lately shewed me nine streams which were perennial when Mr Moffat visited Makabba, but now during the greater portion of the year they present the spectacle of dry watercourses. The only course left for the Bakwains is removal to some other part of their country equally destitute of flowing water with the Kolobeng, but where native corn may be raised. They propose to go about 10 miles higher up its course to a part called Limaoe. We quite approve of the step. But with the prospects God has opened up for us in the North we cannot see it to be our duty to incur the expense and undergo the toil of building in that locality. There is no probability that they will remain there permanently, and it is quite certain we cannot raise the necessaries of life in the spot. And under existing circumstances we have little real missionary work among them. Not more than a native teacher could effect. On the other hand, the Bakwains have increased in knowledge since our residence among them, they have uniformly treated us with respect and kindness and though the numbers willing to be taught both of adults & children are small compared with what might be. the Bakhatla & Bahurutse combined do not furnish so many. We know them now too, and we love them—the attachment is reciprocal and I have a strong impression they will yet in numbers turn to the Lord and be blessed—the seed sown will not be lost. But we have an immense region before us thousands live and die without God & without hope though the command went forth of old Go ye into all the world and preach the gospel to every creature. It is a venture to take wife & children into a country where fever—African fever prevails. But who that believes in Jesus would refuse to make a venture for such a Captain. A parent's heart alone can feel as I do when I look at my little ones & ask shall I return with this or that one alive. However we are His and wish to have no interests apart from those of His kingdom and glory. May He bless us and make us blessings even unto death the country around Sebitoane is described as

—since did not furnish so many. We know them now too, and we love them. The attachment is reciprocal and I have a strong impression they will yet in numbers turn to the Lord and be saved. The seed sown will not be lost. But we have an immense region before us thousands live and die without God & without hope though his comrades went forth & go up & go up into all the world and preach the gospel to every creature. It is a venture to take wife & children into a country whose however African fever prevails. But relief that believes in Jesus would refuse to make a venture for our "Captain". A parent's heart alone can feel as I do when I look at my little ones &

Part of a letter from Boatlanama, to Dr. Tidman, dated April 30th, 1851
(see letter No. 36)

Salary insufficient

quite a network of large rivers 'Linoknoka' river upon river. We may require to go beyond him for an elevated locality. We shall seek such though the people may not be very numerous. the Bakoba carry intelligence far and may be instrumental in assisting us in various ways. We feel the necessity of making a venture at once as so much time is consumed in the weary 600 miles beyond Kolobeng before we reach the Lake country. Mr Oswel is on his way in too. We are separated at present by want of water. He is unwearied in his kindness for all which may God bless him.

On the subject of expenses I may mention to the Directors that these have been considerable. Two spans or teams of oxen alone cost £40. Tear & wear of waggons, extra wages, &c are considerable. But the Leed's Luminaries[1] might advert to the twentyfive guineas I have got so I beg to refer you to the opinion of Mr Freeman on the point. I have overdrawn the salary for this year considerably. I shall feel obliged if you pay on demand to Mr Pyne £10. for female clothing which we order by the same post & £10 to my father part payment for clothing, already sent by Mr Drummond. These £20 to be put to the account of salary for 1852. I shall advise Mr Thompson of the sum. If as successful as we hope we shall not return before the beginning of /52

As I cannot possibly write the secretary of the Geographical Society at present I shall feel much obliged if you communicate the following corrections which I have made on a map sent by Mr Arrowsmith for the purpose: and in which Mr Oswel fully concurs. He paid considerable attention to the course of the River, during last years trip and naturally feels anxious that three or four mistakes which we made in our first visit should be corrected by ourselves rather than by any one else

The river is highest in the end of August and lowest in

---

[1] 'Leeds luminaries', a reference to a special independent committee of which J. S. Miall of Bradford was secretary. It met in 1849 to consider certain criticism of the Society. See Lovett's *History of the London Missionary Society*, vol. ii, p. 679.

Corrections to Map

January March & April. At the end of April the flow has fairly begun all along its course. this is the reverse of what we stated and led to the second error for supposing the river to be at its lowest when we saw it in August /49. Mr O. calculated that when full it must in some parts be 500 yards broad. But as the result of longer & more accurate observation he is convinced it does not exceed 300 yards anywhere. It does not actually flow farther to the Eastward than the Bakurutse villages and only so far when the small Lake called Kumadow is filled by the river & overflows There was water in the bed of the river at the farthest or Most Easterly Bakurutse village when we first struck it on the 4th July 1849, but none in 1850 the Kumadow is about 5 miles broad and 15 long. It is opposite the Hill Kiria

the Lake Ngami itself we believe on the report of intelligent natives to be seventy or seventy five miles in circumference Mr Oswel has no doubt from observations made during his second visit but that the Lake receves the Teogé or Teophé and the Kunyeri. He was shewn the mouth of the latter. We have both concurred in these corrections and indicated on Mr Arrowsmith's map what we concieve ought to be published as correct. But we did not apply the measurement according to the scale furnished on account of being in the act of departing. there is a correction too on the bend of the river. We feel anxious that these corrections should not be published by Mr Arrowsmith while the secretary of the Royal Geographical Society is unaware whence the corrections have proceeded. He will feel an interest in them besides[1]

LETTER 37

To REV^D ARTHUR TIDMAN

Banks of Zouga 1st October 1851

DEAR SIR

Availing myself of the kindness of a party of Griquas who leave this river tomorrow and proceed direct to Philipolis,

[1] The remainder of the letter is missing. It may not have been completed.

Chobe reached

I hope you will recieve this letter at least as soon as any of my friends can obtain information respecting the movement of which I informed you from Boatlanama. We left our old route at 'NChokotsa and proceeding nearly due North crossed the bed of the Zouga and certain saltpans remarkable for their extent. One called 'Ntwétwé was about 15 miles broad and probably 100 long. Beyond these we passed through a hard flat country covered with Mopané trees and containing a great number of springs in limestone rock. A considerable number of bushmen live in the vicinity and they seem to have abundance of food Leaving this district of springs and guided by a bushman[1] we crossed an excessively dry and difficult tract of country and struck a small river called Mababi. Visiting a party of Bushmen and another of Banajoa we after some days reached the Chobe in 18° 20'. S. the river on which Sebitoane lived. the Tsetse abounded on the Southern bank and as the depth is from 12 to 15 feet we could not cross with the waggons. the cattle were taken over to an island and Mr Oswel and I proceeded about 30 miles down the River in a canoe. It was propelled by five rare good rowers and to us who are accustomed to Bullock waggons, The speed seemed like that of boat races at home. Sebitoané recieved us kindly, and offered to replace our cattle which were all believed to have been bitten by Tsétsé. He returned to the waggons[2] with us and subsequently fell sick and to our great sorrow died.[3] He formed one of the party of Mautatees repulsed by the Griquas at old Lattakoo and since then he has almost constantly been fighting. An elderly man his almost constant companion was the individual who killed

---

[1] Shobo. See *Travels*, p. 79.

[2] 'He returned to the waggons with us.' The chief had evidently not seen wagons. Before he went to look at them he had proposed that they should be taken across the river in canoes.

[3] The death of Sebituane from pneumonia so soon after their meeting, deeply moved Livingstone as a study of the more detailed narratives in *Travels* (pp. 89, 90) and Blackie (p. 93) will show. In a letter to D. G. Watt (Sept. 29, 1851) Livingstone says Sebituane was a 'thin, wiry, cool collected man of about 50'. 'Poor Sebituane, my heart is sore for him.'

Death of Sebitoane

Makablea of the Wauketze. He several times lost all his cattle but being a man of great ability managed to keep his people together and ended his days richer in cattle and with many more people under his sway than any other chief we know in Africa. He had long wished to open up intercourse with Europeans and obtain the weapons he saw used with such fatal effect at Lattakoo but when he had reached the summit of his wishes in seeing a path made into his country He was compelled to lie down and die. A doctor who attended him interrupted with rudeness when I attempted to speak about death, and his people took him away from the island when not far from his end. M^r O and I went over to condole with his people soon after the news of his death came and they seemed to take our remarks thankfully We remained two months with them. they are by far the most savage race of people we have seen. But they treated us with uniform kindness and would have been delighted had we been able to remain with them permanently. Such was my intention when I left Kolobeng and having understood that there were high lands in that region, to avoid the loss of time which would occur in returning for my family I resolved that they should accompany me. The deep rivers among which they now live are a defence to them against the Matibele. To have removed them to the highlands would have been rendering them defenceless. And the country itself was so totally different from anything I knew or could have fancied. I felt convinced that two years alone in it, are required for the successful commencement of a mission. To say it is one vast swamp for hundreds of miles with patches of hard ground covered with date Palmyra and other trees, conveys but a poor idea of it. It is for hundreds of miles intersected with numerous rivers and branches of rivers coming out of these & returning into them again. these are flanked with large reedy boggy tracts of country. Where trees abound if not on an island the Tsetse exists. Indeed we seem to have reached the limits of waggon travelling. the intention of our kind friend Mr Oswel were to proceed down one of the rivers

Victoria Falls reported

perhaps to the sea, while we remained at our settlement But the Tsetse and country presented insuperable barriers. We proceeded on horseback about 100 miles farther than the place where the waggons stood to see the Sesheke or river of the Barotse It is from 300 to 500 yards broad and at the end of a remarkably dry season had a very large volume of water in it. The waves lifted the canoes and made them roll beautifully and brought back old scenes to my remembrance—the town of Sesheke is on the opposite shore—the river itself as near as we could ascertain by both instruments 17° 28′ South. It overflows the country periodically for 15 miles out. Contains a waterfall[1] called (smoke sounds) Mosiatunya, the spray of which can be seen 10 or 15 miles off. There are rapids in it, situated 8 days up the river, between Sesheke and the chief town of Sebitoane's daughter who is now in power It is a large river so far as they know it and its general direction from Sesheke up may be gathered from the Native expression. When you look up the river the sun rises on one chief & sets on the other. the River of the Bashukolompo is about 80 yards wide and when it falls into the Sesheke it is called Zambesi. there are numerous rivers reported to connect the two. And all along the rivers there exists a dense population of a strong black race. their country abounds in corn and honey and they shew much more ingenuity in iron work basket work and pottery than any of the people south of them We have indicated in the map the positions of the principal towns of these dark races but these do not comprise all from whom Sebitoane recieved tribute

That which claims particular attention is the fact that the slave trade only began in this region during 1856. A party of people called Mambari from the West came to Sebitoane bearing a large quantity of English printed and striped cotton clothing. Red green and blue baize of English manufacture[2] and with these, bought from the different towns about 200 boys.

[1] Mosiatunya, subsequently named Victoria Falls.
[2] And a few old muskets—For these commodities 'they refused everything except boys of about fourteen years of age'.

Wishes to send children home

they had chains & rivets in abundance, and invited the people of Sebitoane to go on a marauding expedition against the Bashukolompo by saying you may take all the cattle we will only take the prisoners On that expedition they met with some Portuguese and these gave them three English guns, recieving in return at least 30 slaves. These Portuguese promised to return during this winter. the people confessed that they felt a repugnance to the traffic but they (the Mambari & Portuguese) refused cattle for their clothing and guns It seems to me that English manufactures might come up the Zambesi during the months of June July & August or September by the hands of Englishmen & for legitimate purposes as well as by these slave dealers for their unlawful ends There is no danger from fever If people come after May & leave before September. . . .

You will see by the accompanying sketch what an immense region God has in his Providence opened up. if we can enter in and form a settlement we shall be able in the course of a very few years to put a stop to the slave trade in that quarter. It is probable that the mere supply of English manufactures in Sebitoane's part will effect this for they did not like it and promised to abstain. I think it will be impossible to make a fair commencement unless I can secure two years devoid of family cares. I shall be obliged to go southwards perhaps to the Cape in order to have my uvula excised and my arm mended. (the latter if it can be done only) It has occurred to me that as we must send our children to England soon, it would be no great additional expense to send them now along with their mother. this arrangement would enable me to proceed alone and devote about two or perhaps three years to this new region. But I must beg your sanction and if you please let it be given or withheld as soon as you conveniently can so that it might meet me at the Cape. To orphanize my children, will be like tearing out my bowels but when I can find time to write you fully you will percieve it is the only way except giving up the region altogether Kuruman will not answer as a residence nor yet the Colony. If I were to follow my own inclinations they

Sending home map

would lead me to settle down quietly with the Bakwains or some other small tribe and devote some of my time to my children But Providence seems to call me to the regions beyond. and if I have them anywhere in this country it will be to let them become heathens If you think it right to support them I believe my parents in Scotland would attend to them otherwise

I send you the map but you must please to understand it was constructed entirely for my own use and many points are put down merely for future enquiry. I have not put down all the rich towns from which Sebitoane gets tribute, but what I have put down will give you an idea of the population. the rivers only which we have seen are likely to be correct the others were drawn by natives on the ground or on paper. And as they were drawn by many and different individuals and all gave the same general outline we hope the sketch may assist future observers Please to hand a copy to Captain Steele & another to the Royal Geographical Society I shall write the latter soon.

The Griqua who takes this is waiting here—his waggon about 12 miles down the river I cannot detain him longer and therefore beg leave to remain Affectionately yours

DAVID LIVINGSTON

LETTER 38

To DR TIDMAN

Banks of the Zouga 17th October 1851.

DEAR SIR

I wrote you a note on the 2^d currt[1] and inclosing a rough sketch of what we believe to be the main branch of the river Zambesi, sent them forward by a party of Griquas from Philipolis and I shall now endeavour to give you a fuller and more connected account of our visit to the country of Sebitoane than it was then possible for me to furnish. the objects I had in view in proceeding thither were not simply those of discovery. Conversation with the people Sebitoane sent out to Kolobeng last

[1] Letter 37. It is actually dated 1st Oct.

The country of Sebitoane

year, led me to the conclusion, that I ought immediately to form a settlement in a hilly part of their country, & To the important ends, which I still hope to see accomplished, I shall in a subsequent part of this letter more particularly refer— Having been rather sanguine in my hopes of effecting a settlement, I resolved to obviate the necessity of a wearisome journey back for my family by taking my whole establishment with me, & though now obliged to return to a certain extent unsuccessful I think I erred on the right side in attempting, much. Those who may view it as a mere journey of exploration, ought perhaps to remember that we bring to view a large section of the human family, and others who have tried to discover only rivers &c &c have not accomplished so much, though quite unencumbered with 'impedimenta'. the people too whom we visited were wonderfully well pleased with the children,[1] and the presence of the little ones playing merrily among them, was of itself sufficient to dissolve all suspicion. . . .

Sebitoane was one of the Mantatee horde which was butchered by the Griquas in 1824 near old Lattakoo.[2] An old man by whose hand old Makabba fell, very soon after our salutations were over asked me why we Makoa (white men) had attacked & killed so many of them then. I replied by asking him if he had not seen a white man inviting them to come to a parley. He answered, 'We saw three men on horseback capering about in front of the others' & on my explaining their object he added, 'then we killed ourselves not knowing what they wanted'. . . . Sebitoane having promised to take us to see his country. And particularly a large river of which we had heard as the Sesheke, we proposed to his people after his death to take us thither. But to this they would not consent till orders came from Mamochisane, (Sebitoane's daughter and his successor in the chieftianship) to treat us exactly as if the old man were still

[1] There were four children—Robert, Agnes, Thomas, and Oswell, the last named being a month old, William C. Oswell equipped and accompanied the party.

[2] The affair is described by Moffat, *Missionary Labour and Scenes in Southern Africa*, ch. xxii.

Demand for British goods

alive. We then proceeded on horseback about one hundred miles from the waggons and were gratified exceedingly by a sight of the largest river either of us had ever seen. At the end of a remarkably dry season the water was from 300 to 500 yards broad. And though the banks are from 16 to 20 feet in height, we saw evidence of its annual flow extending fifteen miles beyond. When the wind blows, waves of considerable size rise on its surface and accidents frequently occur in crossing in consequence of the broadside of the canoe being kept to the wind. It was quite calm when I went over to hold a service in the town in the morning, but as the time for taking an altitude of the sun approached, the waves were running so high, it was only by great persuasion I could induce the people to paddle me back again We found the Latitude to be about 17° 28' South. . . . The price of a boy was one old Portuguese musket or about 9 yards of cotton or Baize When we reached Sebitoane's people we were much pleased to see so many wearing European articles of clothing. And since our country's manufactures are so highly valued in the very middle of Africa It is a pity the market cannot be supplied by legitimate commerce. there seems to be a large demand. Many tribes were mentioned to us as possessing an abundant supply. the Makololo purchased eagerly and though they promised to refrain from traffic in slaves, the only effectual means of stopping the trade would be by supplying the market with English goods in exchange for the produce of the country. That christian merchants who may have enterprise enough to commence a trade in these parts would be no losers in the end may be inferred from what has taken place on this river (the Zouga) since its discovery. There being formerly no market we saw many instances of ivory lying rotting in the sun. the people called the tusks 'Marapo hela' (bones only), and they shared the fate of other bones. Indeed they were much more anxious to sell a tusk worth in Graham's town 4/6 per lb. than to part with a goat for a larger price, the whole value of which was not more than 2/6. We know of 900 elephants having been killed on its banks since that period.

Sale of ivory, &c.

And independently of quantities of ivory which have found their way to the Colony by other channels A merchant at Kuruman took 23,000 lbs of that article thither during the present year and the greater portion of it came from this river alone. If one river tends to swell the amount of the commerce of the colony. What may not be expected from the numerous rivers all much more densely populated than the Zouga the supply of this one article cannot be expected to continue always so large but the natives readily acquire the habit of keeping articles (in expectation of the return of the traders) which at present are allowed to run to waste. The only use the ivory found on the rivers indicated in the map is turned to is the formation of armlets and half an inch is lost in the formation of each—the saw employed being $\frac{1}{4}$ of an inch in diameter. they would all prefer brass wire to ivory for armlets: Honey abounds but the wax is always thrown away and the only use hitherto made of ostrich feathers is to adorn the head in dancing The return of the slave dealer is never longed for by the poorer classes, but all classes are glad to recieve the visits of the English trader. Since it is found profitable for those engaged in the coast trade, to pass along picking up ivory, bees wax &c &c would it not be much more advantageous to come up the Zambesi and recieve those articles from the producers themselves I venture to put this forth though entirely ignorant of the commerce on the coast. But I feel assured if our merchants could establish a legitimate commerce on the Zambesi, they would soon drive the slave dealer from the market and be besides great gainers in the end. . . . Would the Government supply this information to those engaged in the coast trade? Or would it be better to wait until I can point out by my own residence in, & knowledge of the country & climate a spot of known healthiness & easy of access by the Sesheke, to which commercial men might be invited to carry their enterprise? The Portuguese have a sanatorium far in the Interior and Tete is reported comparatively healthy. the history of our stations renders it doubtful whether the rearing of

A populous country

such is the best way of propagating Christianity—comfortable establishments presenting such strong temptations to remain though the tribes for which they were reared have departed, and though I have undergone much fatigue & manual labour in rearing three such, I would cheerfully undergo much more if it should prove a sanatorium for more unhealthy districts. Let it once be found that Christian missionaries and Christian merchants can remain throughout the year in the Interior of the continent & in ten years the slave dealer will be driven out of the market. . . .

The Lobale whether river or lake is always spoken of as the source of all the water, and both it the Moeng or Moenge, Masoma &c &c have numerous tribes on their banks And all are well supplied with guns & clothing from the West or North West. Seunturu formerly sent people up to the Lobale to barter for crockery, cloth &c. All the rivers indicated in the sketch are navigable by canoes. They are inhabited by a black race. they are deep chested and their muscular system is largely developed. the Bechuana who live among them appear a puny sickly set. And indeed those who came in with Sebitoane are fast dying out. In our ride to Sesheke we saw more people moving about in one day than we should have seen in ten in any part of the Bechuana country as yet supplied with missionaries. I have noted only a portion of the towns and these only the large and rich ones. More might have been added for some we saw contained a larger population than any of our chief missionary stations. This black race speak a language quite distinct from that of the Bechuana. There are many dialects of it and if I may judge by a comparision of 300 words collected from the Bayeiye or Bakoba and about an equal number from each of the following tribes Bashubea, Barotsé Batōka Banyeñko Bamaponda and Balojazé it sustains the same relation to Sitchuana as the Latin does to the English. The different dialects differ from each other as much as Provincial English does from broad Scotch. Sebitoane has done good service by introducing the Sitchuana. His people being a mixed multitude

Extensive drought

of Basuto Bakwains. Bamangwato & the Black races, we found people who could readily understand us every where. It is probable a good expressive language will spring out of the materials he has brought together

The Black race designate the supreme Being by the name Nyampi or Reza. the latter is identical with the Oreeja of the Bayeiye. If a person dies they say 'He is "lifted" by Nyampi" or by the Lord' It is remarkable that of those who were found about 30 years ago destitute of the knowledge of God & futurity, no specimen now occurs. But they are degraded low enough in the scale of humanity and no one more than the African needs the humanizing influence of the gospel of Christ. . . . You will by this time be able to understand the course matters took We could not cross the Chobe at first, and before any plan could be proposed Sebitoane fell sick and died. We waited for Mamochisané the queen but she having been in child bed could not come. All the people were pleased with the prospect of our remaining with them. they even promised to plant for us—and they will do it too. The chief next in power was sent down to us to act in her behalf. But we ascertained that the hilly part to which they were willing to go was without defence from the Matibele. And Mosilikatse constantly sends expeditions against them. Their deep reedy rivers are a protection It would have been wrong in me to remove them thither merely for my safety. then the rainy season was at hand and should the Chobe fill so would the Sonta behind us. The Chobe rises 8 or 10 feet in perpendicular height and should the Sonta rise three we should be brought to a stand still on its banks and every ox would be bitten by the Tsetse. The Chobe ought to have filled during our stay and that it did not was ascribed by the people to the death of Sebitoane. The drought which has prevailed over the whole country probably extended to the sources of the river. Then would it be right to expose my family on swamps of an extent such as we never dreamed. The whole country is one vast level intersected by numerous rivers. And when these fill as they do periodically All the country we

The Tsetse fly

saw must present the appearance of an immense marsh with numerous islands scattered over its surface. The highest land is raised above the surrounding low annually flooded country by only a few feet. We saw earthen dykes for catching fish about a mile beyond where our waggons stood. And though both Mrs L. and myself did and do still regret leaving so soon had we remained till another moon should enable us to travel through the Tsete by night. this would have been no protection for we were informed that as soon as the nights became warm the insect bites by night as well as by day. We seem to have reached the limits of waggon travelling at least of such heavy vehicles as this country furnishes. Mr Oswel would have proceeded along one of the numerous rivers had it been possible but bogs and Tsetse presented insuperable barriers. I regret this more as I had hopes that he would find a passage for us down to the coast while I was prosecuting my mission among the Makololo. We returned as we had hitherto travelled together. He assisting us in every possible way. May God reward him. The route through Shobo's country being now impracticable we came down the Tamunakle and crossing it wend our way along its Southern bank.

I need not say anything about the importance of immediate action in reference to this highway into the Interior. Considering the immense distance we have to traverse before we reach the country of the Zambesi. the existence of the African fever (one child has been attacked by it three times on this river in our progress down) The nature of the country—All swampy except where Mosilikatse extends his forays. And beyond the Barotse, it seems as if it only remained for us to make an effort for a settlement in the latter direction. Less than two years absence and entire freedom from domestic care will not suffice for even a feasible effort. The tokens of Divine care which have been already bestowed and a full conviction that I am in the path of duty, induce me to offer myself for the service. There are considerations for and others against my doing so. I shall mention some of the latter first. Some of the bretheren do not

Mrs. Livingstone paralysed

hesitate to tell the natives that my object is to obtain the applause of men. This bothers me for I sometimes suspect my own motives. Then after our return last year Mrs L. was delivered of a daughter. An epidemic was raging in the town at the time, the child was seized by it and cut off at the age of six weeks. The mother had an attack of paralysis of the right side of the face, one eyelid was motionless and the mouth was drawn to the opposite side. As the uvula was unaffected I was of opinion that it was the result of inflammation spreading along the bone from some carious teeth producing pressure on the nerves as they issue from their faramina & that rest counter irritation & tonics were the proper treatment. We went to Kuruman and the complaint was partially removed. I postponed my own wants & did not proceed to the Cape in order to have my uvula excised in order to allow her rest. The death of the child and complaint of the mother have both been charged to my account and I have been asked if the 'loss of one child &c &c was not enough to satisfy me' this & other Severe expressions have been used even by those whom I esteem. Then again my predilections are for a quiet life, I love the Bakwains and believe the affection is reciprocal.—We never had a disagreement—and I should prefer to attend to the instruction of my own children, to sending them away from me. There is also the consideration that as you cannot very well realize the distances I have to travel before I reach the field I may appear more as a traveller than a missionary.

On the other hand I am conscious that though there is much impurity in my motives, they are in the main for the glory of Him to whom I have dedicated my all. I never anticipated fame from the discovery of the Lake. I cared very little about it but the sight of the Tamunakle and the report of other large rivers beyond all densely populated awakened many and enthusiastic feelings—the loss or rather removal of the child was a sore trial to me. It was the first death in our family, but was just as likely to happen had we remained at home. And we have now one of our number in Heaven.

Leaving Kolobeng

Providence has not favoured our settlement at Kolobeng the necessaries of life cannot be raised there by either ourselves or people. The Kolobeng has dried up and it is absolutely necessary that the people remove somewhere else. I cannot attach one particle of blame to them for moving up the river But then the important question comes before me. Am I to build again for them? If there had been abundance of food for the Bakwains at Kolobeng they would not have removed and I should have remained with them. But the want of food has compelled them to remove a few miles off and as there is just as little probability of their obtaining a subsistence there, it would be labour in vain for me to build another house. In all probability they will be compelled to move again—The Bakwains promised fairly and I by no means give up the hope that they will receive the gospel but they have been so pinched by hunger and badgered by the Boers they could not or rather they had too good an excuse for not attending to instruction

Then again when we consider the multitudes which in the Providence of God have been brought to light in the country of Sebitoane—the probability that in our efforts to evangelize we shall put a stop to the slave trade in a large region and by means of the highway into the North which we have discovered bring unknown nations under the sympathies of the Christian world. If I were to choose my lot it would be to reduce this new language translate the Bible into it, and be the means of forming a small church. Let this be accomplished I think I could then lie down and die contented.

Two years absence will be necessary. Kuruman is unsuitable as a residence for my family. It is too near. The reports made & circulated by the natives would render my wife miserable. She is again threatened by symptoms of paralysis but now they extend down the whole side even to the toes. . . . And as the children must go home for education I believe it would be the best policy for her to take them to England herself. this step would give me time for the important service referred to above, and the voyage would probably restore her to her former

The Bamangwato as travellers

strength. Nothing but a strong conviction that the step will tend to the Glory of Christ would make me orphanize my children. Even now my bowels yearn over them—they will forget me. But I hope when the day of trial comes I shall not be found a more sorry soldier than those who serve an earthly sovreign. Should you not feel yourselves justified in incurring the expense of their support in England, I shall feel called upon to renounce the hope of carrying the gospel into that country and labour among those who live in a more healthy country viz. the Bakwains. But stay, I am not sure, so powerfully convinced am I that it is the will of our Lord I should, I will go no matter who opposes. But from you I expect nothing but encouragement. I know you wish as ardently as I can that all the world may be filled with the glory of God. I feel relieved when I lay the whole case before you.

As it is probable some alterations will take place in our colonial missions, could a stout young man from one of the older stations not be spared to take the burden of printing off Mr Ashton's hands and allow him to occupy a new station say at the Bamangwato. This tribe is very numerous. I counted 900 huts in passing and there are two considerable villages close by. There are at least 6000 souls in the locality. Numbers of these are Makalaka who have fled from the tyranny of Mosilikatse. Should they ever return to their own country they would carry the knowledge of Christ with them. The Bamangwato have the custom of spreading themselves through the whole Bakalihari country, and living for months among that people. We found a number of them among the Bushmen at Shobo's place. It seems a most desirable point for diffusing the knowledge of the Gospel. It is a healthy country too, and if taken up would form a link between me and the world, untill we have found a path down to the coast The proposal is somewhat selfish, but I have often thought that large mass of people had claims on our sympathy. Mr Ashton would be immediately useful in consequence of knowing the language. And any young missionary could be immediately useful at Kuruman in consequence

The great Seseheke River

of the printing being easy of acquisition. Sekhomi[1] the chief has a bad name, but scarcely deserves it. He has always behaved to me with extreme kindness Mr Ashton might be persuaded to go if the persuasion came from you. . . .

Bamangwato,
14 Nov.

I beg leave to acknowledge the receipt of your letter dated 1st March /51 and thank you unfeignedly for the encouragement it affords to proceed in the path to which I concieved I was called by Providence. It affords me no ordinary satisfaction to find you entertain the same views as actual observation and comparison of the claims of the Southern & Northern regions have led me to adopt. The map sent was not intended for you The large sprawling things put down as rivers were for the eyes of natives who in being questioned understand a great sea serpent looking thing better than an ordinary drawn river. The Seseheke is however a magnificent river. I think we are under rather than over the mark in calling it 500 yards broad. I shall write the Royal Geographical Society before I reach Kolobeng. I shall acknowledge Captain Steele's present too. I wish you had proposed the Dictionary[2] of Sitchuana sooner. I collected

---

[1] Sekhomi was the father of the enlightened Khama paramount Chief of the Bamangwato for fifty years. He died in 1923. See *Khama, A great African Chief*, by John C. Harris.

[2] A resolution of the Board of Directors urged him to prepare a dictionary if it would not withdraw his attention from 'more necessary labours'.

After the receipt of this letter Secretary Tidman wrote to Livingstone promising to meet the expenses of the journey of the family to England. He also forwarded another resolution of the Board, i.e. 'It is indispensable that Dr. Livingston should be accompanied by a suitable coadjutor, if possible a missionary, in his further journey into the interior of Africa and recommend him to adopt measures in concert with his brethren of the Bechuana Mission for that purpose.' William Ashton's name was mentioned as a possible companion.

There was a postscript pointing out the advantages of keeping a journal the contents of which might be of more value than the 'vague and general impressions conveyed in a hastily written letter'. Livingstone had already provided himself with a big journal with a lock on it. It was to be a private and personal affair. He began to write it when he started from Sekeletu's for St. Paul de Loanda, Nov. 11, 1853. It might have been thought that

some materials for such a work many years ago but not being aware whether I should be able to procure funds for the printing of it, other objects engrossed my attention & induced me to lay it aside. If I should be prevented from entering the new region I shall recommence it with pleasure. If honoured to commence a work on the Zambesi, the new language will engross all my energies, but you will hear from me again on this point.

I have been advised of £20 paid by Sir Culling Eardley Eardley, to my account, and return thanks. I ordered £10 worth of books from Mr Snow & requested him to apply to you for the money. Will you be kind enough to request Mr Snow to send me out this year's /51 'British Banner' bound in cloth and continue to send ½ yearly volumes of the same along with the missionary publications.

(*Remainder missing*)

LETTER 39

To the REVEREND DR TIDMAN

Cape Town 17th March 1852

MY DEAR SIR

The following statement was penned with the intention of transmitting it to our departed friend the Revd J. J. Freeman.[1] He was intimately acquainted with our pecuniary circumstances in this country and recommended me to draw £25 or £30 annually more than the usual salary to meet the extra expenses which our peculiar position involves, and as Mrs Livingstone[2] & family would come into his department while in England, a full statement for his information & guidance seemed necessary. . . .

Separation from my family had become absolutely necessary,

Livingstone's ordinary letters were as definite and particular as other men's journals.

[1] Freeman, who had visited the South African stations and served as a colleague with Tidman, died Sept. 8, 1851.

[2] This is the first example in this correspondence of the spelling 'Livingstone', with the 'e', but it will be seen that the writer himself signs 'ton'.

Separation from family

for though I may be justified in risking my own life in the service of our Master, I may not use the same freedom with the lives of my wife and children. As much less expense will be incurred in procuring education for the children in England than there would be in Cape Town the propriety of deciding for the former will appear evident. . . . time also will be given to me to form a mission in some healthy locality in the Barotse country or beyond. I hope in that time too to be able to solve some interesting problems in relation to the slave trade, my full conviction being that this nefarious traffic will be abolished by the influence of Christian Missions and that the London Missionary Society may hold as prominent a place as it did in the emancipation of the Hottentots. We have been six months in travelling from Sebitoane's country to the Cape—the whole of our stoppages not amounting to so many weeks. The weary way between either that country and the Kuruman or the same country & the Cape presents few inducements for me to trudge it over again after only a few months sojourn there. If I am spared for two years I may be permitted to establish a mission and also find a way to the sea on either the East or West coast. If so far favoured by Him on whose Providence all depends the long irksome land journey would be avoided & much time saved The act of orphanizing my children which now becomes painfully near will be like tearing out my bowels for they will all forget me. But I feel it is a duty to Him who did much more for us than that. His command is Go ye into all the world & preach the gospel to every creature. Forbid it, that we should ever consider the holding a commission from the King of Kings a sacrifice so long as men esteem the same from an earthly sovreign an honour.

I thought at one time that the family might proceed to Scotland at once in order to be under the care of my parents but they have been subjected to so much heat of late, I believe the first winter must be spent in the South of England. The thermometer stood on the Zouga at 104° in the coolest part we could find in & under the waggon. Thomas had the Fever

Expenditure and gifts

three times in coming down that river. Agnes has since been ill from malaria inhaled on its banks. If I could support them in England I would not request an additional allowance for the purpose. I have no stock on hand and though a Scotchman I have not yet availed myself of our lamented friend's suggestion, except in the way of overdrawing in order to defray extra expenses incurred in travelling. With the exception of a few books & some clothing from home every farthing of the salary has been spent economically in the prosecution of my work. And besides the extra expenses all of which some charge to the Society as 'travelling expenses' we have large losses in oxen by the 'Tsetse'. Indeed so far from having anything to meet the present emergency but for the disinterested kindness of Mr Oswel we could not have come down to the Cape. He presented supplies for last years journey worth £40. For that to Sebitoane upwards of £20. Also a waggon worth £55. I recieved also from a chief a present of three elephant tusks worth £18. But one waggon was worn out and I was obliged to purchase another for £80. and for oxen to go to Sebitoane's I paid £47. New waggon sails £10. these are torn to tatters by each trip—I have paid off nearly all our cows to extra drivers, leaders &c. Most of our own are dead. And but for Mr O. presenting a number worth about £60 we could not have come down to the Cape. In consequence of being obliged to have fresh oxen & other unavoidable expenses we have gnawed into the salary of 1853 a gap of £57. The whole of the present years salary had been previously drawn for oxen, waggon & repairs—wages, &c. &c. The whole of the salary for 1852 was previously spent. The expenses incurred in Cape Town will leave nothing remaining of the salary of 1853. I have now to crave your indulgence with respect to this overdrawing. I cannot possibly pay my people and go back with supplies of meal tea & coffee unless I draw the salaries of /53 & /54. We have used no delicacies of any kind besides the above I have been a teetotaller for 20 years.[1] We think all the money drawn has been well

[1] He never learned to smoke tobacco.

Dr. Moffat's health

spent, when we could procure the articles we needed from Colesberg though to the cost price we had to add land carriage for 500 miles. It has been with very great reluctance I have been compelled to foredraw and I should consider it a favour to be allowed time only to make it up. But the question will force itself on the mind How is it that a mission in the paltry village of Colesberg, already supplied with a Wesleyan & a Gospel Propagation Society's missionary and a Dutch Reformed minister, is allowed to draw on an average more than twice as much as a mission 500 miles beyond the same market This question stirs up our Scotch propensities amazingly for we know that that mission does not include $\frac{1}{25}$ part of the population of one of the Interior tribes There is no itineracy. There is not even the tear and wear of body involved in tying a few letters together for the bretheren beyond. We have to pay an agent both at Algoa Bay and at Colesberg to recieve all our letters & parcels. In the former place Mr Robson[1] informed me eleven years ago that he had given standing orders to the Postwoman first to forward all missionary letters—the only benefit which has arisen through all these years in letters being addressed to his care has been an additional fourpence on each. But such thoughts I strive to drive from the mind. I may however mention to you that Mr Moffat is suffering from an affection of the head which I fear will eventually lay him aside. My opinion expressed to him with sufficient earnestness was that he ought to lay aside his translation and seek the reestablishment of his health in total relaxation on the sea coast but I fear his finances being in the same state as my own has prevented compliance with my suggestions. Some of the knowing ones believe him to be rich because he once recieved some money from the sale of his book but that is all long since spent, and my private opinion which I express to you in confidence is that there is some probability of a valuable life being lost through the *injustice* of the London Missionary Society. Observe the word I use, '*injustice*' & please to remember that I love the Society and sympathize

[1] Rev. Adam Robson of Port Elizabeth.

Distribution of energy

with the Executive on the difficulties which the stingy spirit out of doors throws in its way. But what but out & out injustice could induce you to charge the expense of the voyage of his son John to his account while the same item would have been put to the general expenses of the Society had he been the son of Mr Christie or M^r anyone else. A number of other items I know press heavily on his spirits. And we have published documents shewing that none of these would plague us if we took up our residence at the petty villages of Colesberg or Somerset or Uitenhage or Bethelsdorp. Who in England would believe that the average expenses of Bethelsdorp should be £224. Of Colesberg £211. Of Uitenhage £251. While the 'Apostle of the Bechuana' draws on an average not much over £100. My Dear Dr Tidman do look into this subject. Compare Colesberg & Kuruman and if possible prevent the character of the Society being damaged by the knowledge of such inequality oozing out. The missionaries beyond the Colony who make triennial visits to Colesberg & Grahamstown must be distinguished from such as do not. the profit made by the place is equal to 9 months pay though an equal number of months are lost to the Society.

The expenses of outfit have been borne by a friend.[1] It amounted to £70. We were a queer looking set when we came to Cape Town. Clothes eleven years out of the fashion. We all needed being clad anew. The expenses of the voyage must be defrayed by you. We shall write by next steamer and inform you by what ship M^{rs} L and family will come. I return as soon as they are shipped Affectionately yours

DAVID LIVINGSTON

LETTER 40

To REV^D DR TIDMAN

Cape Town 26th April 1852

MY DEAR SIR

The chief object of this letter is to advise you of the departure[2] of Mrs Livingston and four children on board the 'Trafalgar'

[1] William C. Oswell.
[2] Tidman's reply said they arrived safely about June 23. Mrs. Living-

Departure of family

Captain D. Robertson, bound for London. She sailed on the 23ᵈ Currt. And as this goes by the Royal Mail Steamer which will sail on the first of May, you will in all probability recieve this before Mʳˢ Livingston's arrival

In thus committing my family to your care I may state that nothing but the fullest convictions of duty would have led me to adopt this step, but having already addressed you twice on this subject, and by full and explicit statements endeavoured to furnish data on which to form your own Judgement, I feel the less inclined to advert to the subject again. Your silence however makes me fear that my letters may have miscarried, and I shall add that our children have claims on those by whom we are sent. It is well known that the laws of God avenge themselves on those by whom they are contemned. they resemble two-edged swords when caught by the blades. the emigrant boers who dispise the law of benevolence enuntiated in the declaration that God hath made of one blood all the nations of the earth are themselves becoming as degraded as the natives whom they despise. A slave population everywhere works the ruin and degradation of the free class which employs it. Tyranny and every other form of vice reproduce themselves and the moral contagion spreads like leaves by means of the children. It is but just that such contagion should infect those who fear not the vengeance of the divine laws or of Him who is their author. But missionaries expose their children to a contamination which they have had no hand in producing. We expose them and ourselves for a time in order to elevate those sad captives of sin and Satan who are the victims of the degradation of ages. None of those who complain about missionaries sending their children home ever descend to this. . . . In regard to even the vestige of a home my children are absolutely vagabonds 'When shall we return to Kolobeng'? 'When

stone's health had already undergone a decided improvement. Within a month she went to Scotland. The Directors had made two grants after hearing of Livingstone's money troubles. One of £120 a year for the support of Mrs. Livingstone and the children while in Britain, and another of £150 to meet Livingstone's own unavoidable expenditure in excess of salary.

to Kuruman? *Never* The mark of Cain is on your foreheads. your father is a missionary.' Our children ought to have both the sympathies and prayers of those at whose bidding we become strangers for life. . . .

Believe me
Affectionately Yours
DAVID LIVINGSTON

¶ On the same day as the foregoing letter was written Livingstone dispatched a second note to Tidman, chiefly concerned with the suitability of his brethren in South Africa for the post of travelling companion.

There were good reasons against all the names which suggested themselves. On this question he concludes

'I consider that when in the habit of constantly looking to the Divine hand for guidance in all our movements, when no one possessed of a small measure of suitability and willingness makes his appearance, we ought to conclude to go alone I am not given to despondency or lowness of spirits I enjoy a perpetual flow of good spirits I felt more perplexity in reference to parting with my family and about my pecuniary affairs concerning which I lately wrote you than I ever did in my life before Had Mr Oswel not presented us with about £170 since we came here, I should have been in a fix He clothed M^{rs} L and family in a style we never anticipated. This I state in confidence to you, it would offend him to make it public'

LETTER 41

To REVD. W. THOMPSON, *Cape Town*

Paarl, 9th June, 1852.

MY DEAR SIR,

I reached this yesterday evening without falling into mischief once although I had no one to take care of me! Have remained with Mr. Barker[1] through the day and gave an address in the

[1] Rev. George Barker of Paarl.

evening, which shows how very firmly I can hold to my resolutions of not speaking again till I got back to my own country, but I am done with it now till I come to Griqua Town, and I can easily refuse Mr. Hughs. Don't despise my weakness, 'Ye that are strong, &c. &c.' I found Mr. Barker must sell his horse, and that the hire of horses and the waggon would amount to £3. I resolved to buy it and now I can proceed without an attendant. I go to-morrow morning (Thursday) and will reach it on Saturday. You will receive a bill of £12 from Mr. Barker in the ordinary way (as salary). It is just possible that George[1] may not be gone when this comes to hand, if so will you tell him to bring a breed of Malay fowls with him for Sebitoané. I forgot them till my own waggon went, and then again when George was getting ready. But if he has gone do not trouble yourself as we can pick up a pair or two of some kind among the Boers.

I am sure you must be glad to get rid of me and my bothering intrusions which were always about my own affairs. Accept of my hearty and most sincere thanks for your multifarious kind offices and good wishes. May God reward you. I hope a sense of gratitude for your disinterested friendship will never be effaced from my heart. Many thanks to Miss Thompson for her kind attentions to a poor forlorn widower from the Sesheke —and love to all the children.

Believe me yours very affectionately,
DAVID LIVINGSTON.

LETTER 42

To REV. WM THOMPSON, *Cape Town*

Skeit Fontein.
[No date—probably June–July 1852]

MY DEAR SIR,

Herein you will receive the fulmination of the Commandant Potgeiter,[2] who, I believe, has gone to a tribunal at which

[1] Fleming: the black trader who was to accompany Livingstone for a time under the patronage of Mr. Rutherfoord of Cape Town.
[2] Hendrick Potgeiter: see *Travels*, p. 37.

Potgeiter's threat

nothing but truth will be told. It is a copy sent from the Committee, by the then Secretary, Mr. Ashton. The answer which they sent me at the same time, is, I find, not by me, but it must be at Kolobeng, and as soon as I can lay hands upon it I shall forward it. A re-perusal of the document brought some circumstances to my mind which had nearly vanished from my memory. One was, that when the Bakwains heard of the intentions of the Boers to molest me they instantly called a Peecho[1] and resolved unanimously to defend their missionary with their blood. On my objecting to their exposing their lives on my account, they replied it was on their own account, for whatever was done to me was done to them.... Had Potgeiter come he would have met a very different reception from any he ever had before. The Tribes he has attacked never could do him or his party on horseback, any harm. His fighting has been a series of cold-blooded murders.... Well, when I saw the Bakwain were determined to doctor the Boers I thought it right to send my family out of the way.... The Kurumanites pressed upon us the propriety of sending the family out there—and I did so about four months after the threats of the Boers had vanished into thin air. A short time after they left for Kuruman I departed for the Lake—the first time.... I destroyed about 350 letters before going—and many of these I regret, but felt unwilling anything should fall into their hands of which they could make bad use.

I am here in the house of Mr. Alheit of Skeit Fontein, and may inform you how we have succeeded hitherto. We have come but slowly. My oxen were lean but quite fresh. I used them only, and by buying some and exchanging others as they became tired, for fresh ones, giving about 10/- on each for the extra flesh on the new ones, I succeeded pretty well. I shall soon be at the River, and thence will get on well. The oxen I have now are in good condition and will carry me thither quickly. The waggon however, is enormously heavy. This loading is one of those things I shall do but once in my life. We had to

[1] Peecho: the tribal Parliament.

Preparing a dictionary

pass through a bad defile and hired a span from a Boer to take us through. He took us into it but his large fat oxen could not move it farther. I inspanned our meagre beasts and they walked out with it at once. The Boer then left us in disgust, and when we had got fairly through wanted payment, but this I declined. I shall feel glad when I deliver the articles to their owners. The wood work of the wheels cracks from the enormous strain. There now take a lesson by my folly. Of George I have seen nothing though I have travelled so slowly. I gave him two men so as they do not make their appearance he must be on his way after us either by the road we have come or by some other. We shall be sure to meet at Kuruman.

I have been quite busy all the way with the Dictionary. I did not know I had so many words in my head as I have put down, but every time I sit down there is no end to them. They are hooked together by strange associations. I have not begun anything else. The waggon is most inconvenient for writing. I can write only on my side and must doff & trek on my 'inexpressibles' only when lying flat on my back. I must be getting old and ill-natured now for the constrained positions of my waggon life rather makes me crusty than gentle. The longer one lives the more one learns—is however true.

I have been reading the tour of the Bishop, he is quite an angel compared to me. Don't you see the effects of the Puseyite partial belief in salvation by works? He is quite in earnest—no doubt of it.—He and the Archdeacon tramping it on foot. Well done my hearties! If I had £800, or even £400 a year travelling expenses as you my Lord, and your venerableness the Archdeacon have I would not be so self-denying. No not I, I would sport good oxen in my waggon and good horses in my cart, and should now be somewhere beyond your Lordship's diocese—perhaps sitting at supper with the Bishop of Kuruman, aye! with the Apostle of the Bechuanas. . . .

Mr. Alheit is a fine friendly man. He does not believe in baptismal regeneration as do some of his bretheren. At least I believe so, for when I said that the bishop liked him because

Collapse of wagon

of holding similar views on baptism, he laughed and said, 'But we don't all believe in that doctrine.' He seems a great admirer of Luther. He has been successful here. Has 80 communicants, but is plagued by the surrounding Boers badgering his people. Intends to remove to the Orange River with his people, but the present war prevents his getting the necessary permission from Government.

Please present kind regards to your sister, Ralph, Jessie, and my worthy friend Willie. May God bless you all and help you who are in the forefront of the strife to be valiant for the truth and righteousness.

I lost my horse about a week ago, a great affliction, he ran away. A trader called Bredencamp going back may find him, and if he writes I shall know how to do with the beast. He was an excellent traveller but like many other travellers became disgusted with the way and went back. Malatsi, my man, spent a week in search of him.

Believe me ever yours,
DAVID LIVINGSTON.

LETTER 43

To REVD. W. THOMPSON.

Kuruman, 6th September, 1852.

MY DEAR SIR,

Having by means of a sound constitution survived a tedious travel through the Colony, I crossed the Orange River at Priestcar—a spot which has been selected for a mission station by Mr. Alheit of Skeit Fontein—the enormous weight on my waggon soon after that told on one of the wheels and down came the elegant Dutch vehicle, the African coach and ten, on to its marrow bones. Mr. Hughs[1] kindly lent a wheel, and by the assistance of himself and some of my old patients I managed to crawl to this place about ten days ago. I was sometimes vexed with myself for having loaded up so much but when

[1] Isaac Hughes: an artisan missionary.

Arrival of George Fleming

I reached the places where I could off-load it gave me sincere pleasure to hand the goods to the owner. I was disposed to blame myself most when we had to offload at the bottom of acclivities and carry the boxes up ourselves. I am now detained here getting my wheel mended.

I had written another letter to you and mentioned a number of conjectures respecting George, but his arrival at Kuruman to-day renders my surmisings as valuable as conjectures usually are. I could not understand what should have prevented him coming up to me on the way, and after waiting here a week I began to suspect he had got into mischief by going to Beaufort. He has been at more expense than I have, and I had to spend upwards of £50 on the way. We shall now help him on. I waited for him as soon as I got a spot which possessed forage, but when he did not turn out I concluded he must have taken another road. I came here ten days before him.

Now that I can calmly look back to my sojourn among the natives who live in a hollow under Table Mountain, and who daily and nightly inhale effluvia known only to the initiated in the mysteries of Sanitary reform, I do remember them with feelings of compassion—Poor creatures, living in a state of utter respectability—exchanging their how-dye-do's—their noddings, curtseys, and ministerial breakfasts, and all the while the carnivori, the cannibals, I may say of the Law and State and Puseyite Church, ready to spring upon them and devour them. They are obliged to live and walk as circumspectly as Elephants among well covered pitfalls. I do pity you from my heart. I could not breathe freely till I got over the Orange River.

Well, that is a fine letter from his Riverence Calderwood.[1] I look upon it with mingled feelings of scorn and shame. With scorn when I think of an English Professor of Christianity so unutterably mean as to join in the hue and cry against a poor Hottentot, and so dead to the shame of infamy as to confess at

---

[1] Henry Calderwood, Pastor of the United Secession Presbyterian Church at Kendal, was appointed to Kafirland in 1838. In 1846 he took a Government appointment as Commissioner to the Gaika tribes in Kafirland.

Comment on Calderwood

the same time that it has been his practice to act the part of a common informer—A salaried Government spy.—I blush up to the ears when I read his confession (after spending years in the service of our Society) that he does not know the language sufficiently well to know exactly the statement of a native without an interpreter. Is it not disgraceful to find the Gospel of Christ proclaimed in a *patois* called 'school Caffre'? We must not lose sight of this confession. It is good that he makes it, though that and other statements ought to cover him with lasting infamy. A man who could write as he has done will do more. This is not his last letter nor his last stab at the cause of truth and righteousness. You see how the Government officials feel towards the defence of Botha. In Scotland counsel is provided for the most depraved criminals at the expense of the state. This Reverend Commissioner would have us believe that such defence 'tends to break down important social distinctions' that its tendency is to cause the whole of Scottish Society to be suspected, for we have criminals there out of every class—From commissioners who can play the fool for £600 per annum with the Bible in one hand and the sambok in the other, Good Lord deliver us!

. . . Mr. Moffat's head is still affected. Nothing he has tried has the least effect upon it. The translation goes on briskly notwithstanding. Edwards has left his station and the people of Mabotsa have come over to Sechele. The Boers are reported by an individual who came here two days ago to be encamped at Mabotsa. They contemplate rooting out Sechele and wait only till two or three of their party return from the Lake. They fear if an attack is made now that Sechele's people, fleeing Northwards, would meet their friends, and of course—treat them as they now hope to do the Bakwains—they may find it more difficult to subdue Sechele than they dream of. But their plan is to secure the whole country to themselves and prevent traders and travellers from going beyond them. . . .

Kind love to your sister, Ralph, and Jessie. I won't mention Willie because he did not come to help me. I tried your plan on one ox, and he became a beauty and so tame. All the Boers wanted to exchange him, and poor fellow he was drowned in the Orange River. Three fell into a muddy place on a Saturday evening. We all worked the whole night trying to get them out of the sloughy bank and as the morning dawned the finest of the whole lot expired. You may guess how eagerly we toiled when I mention that when daylight appeared I thought it was only about twelve o'clock.

I have not yet begun to write, but have not lost sight of the project. I have not been idle. A correct and lucid analysis of the language engages my attention and has taken up all my spare time. I have devoted a whole evening to you. Your notes were good but very short. You will some day write a longer, I hope. Poor Botha![1] The sentence is terrible. This is worse than death. Poor fellow!—The wicked shall not always triumph.—By same post I send a letter for my brother containing Sandillah's speech to Renton, to be printed in America. All we learn of the Caffre here is one-sided. We must hear both sides. It is well Sandillah speaks out so nobly. Bringing out converts to assist the English is infamous. We must either preach passive resistance or fighting for one's own countrymen.

D. LIVINGSTON.

20th. You will see by Mr. Moffat's[2] to you the doings of Dr. Robertson's dearly beloved bretheren. I mourn over my books and medicines, instruments. Please say nothing about my losses or some good Samaritan will forthwith send me odd numbers of the 'Evangelical Magazine' the pictures extracted— 'Alleines Alarm' without the title page. And odd volume Charnock's sermons, &c, &c.

---

[1] Andries Botha, an elderly Field cornet of the Kat River Settlement condemned to death for high treason after forty years of loyal service. The proceedings of the court were reprinted under the title *Trial of Andries Botha* (Cape Town, 1852), with a preface by William Thompson.

[2] Moffat's letter told of the destruction of the Kolobeng station by Boers on Aug. 27. The affair is described in *Travels*, p. 39, Blaikie, 111, and in Campbell. The last-named includes the most precise statement addressed to Lieut.-Gov. Darling.

Destruction of Kolobeng

Many thanks for the Psalter and other books. Doubly precious now. I send Sandillah's speech to be printed in America. Please notice if it comes to you: also two letters for Mrs. L.

LETTER 44

To REVD. W. THOMPSON.

Kuruman, 30th September 1852.

MY DEAR SIR,

Enclosed you will perceive a letter which I have ventured to address to the Lieutenant Governor.[1] I have endeavoured to give a plain outline of the facts and merely hinted at the probable consequences; and now if the Government goes on heedlessly, the blame will rest on its own shoulders. I enclose it to you because I understand you are expected to be our go-between in all matters pertaining to the Government. The reason which I feel the chief one in my mind for troubling you is that you may exercise your judgment on it whether it ought to be delivered at all. From it, and Mr. Moffat's letter, you will have a pretty clear idea of the doings of Dr. Robertson's converts. . . . They went the whole hog, attended Church on Sunday hearing Mabaloe preach, and then made the parson flee for his life on Monday. He ran the gauntlet—some of them calling out when they saw him with clothes on, 'Here is the chief,' and then the bullets whistled over behind and before him. He seems to have become terrified—ran through the midst of the Boers and so fast that his feet were dreadfully bruized. He has lost all he had, viz, 27 head of cattle, and his

---

[1] The report to the Lieut.-Governor of the destruction of the Kolobeng station is reprinted in full in Campbell, p. 95. It is of interest to read the story from the Boers' point of view. It is given in *The Memoirs of Paul Kruger*, told by himself, 1902, 2 vols. In vol. i, ch. ii, the author took part in the Commando under Chief Commandant Scholtz which went to punish Sechele. He was twice in danger. First a ball from a Boer gun rebounded from a rock and made Kruger unconscious for a time. He was hit also by a bullet from the Bakwain side which struck him on the chest and tore his jacket in two.

Hottentot Rebellion

furniture, &c. His house was burned by the *Christians*. He it was who stood by me when bitten by the lion and got bit himself. He has been with me ever since I came into the country, but I fear this will be a settler for him. He is now on his way out here. Some fine young men whom I knew and loved, have fallen. My heart is sore when I think of them. Sechele had two bullets through his hat and a third through his coat sleeve. The Boers have lost one of their principal men. I don't know his name. The chief with whom Inglis lives is heart and soul with the Boers. . . . You may wonder what will be the end of all this, and you may perhaps wonder still more if I venture to say that I see nothing in it all unfavourable to the progress of the kingdom of Christ. There is evidently a process in operation in the whole of South Africa, and there soon will appear another wonderful developement of His Providence Who is wonderful in counsel and excellent in working. In every district of the country the process tends the same way. We 'poor renegades from the anvil and loom' long insisted that the Hottentots had souls and our statements were looked upon as the blarney of silly enthusiasm. A few hundreds of them however, take it into their monkey heads to rebel and they actually kick the ossa coccyzes of our dragoons and minié rifle men. No wonder that great was the wrath of the Government officials—Hottentot rebellion! what next! We may expect our cats to have a strike 'cause Missis don't give us the silver forks to eat with'. If we had hinted at a Hottentot rebellion I believe they would have believed that a cow could handle a musket as well as they. The Rebellion is however a great fact, and the condemnation of Botha has sown seed which will yet vegetate. But I am away from my text. Everywhere there is a strong feeling of independence springing up. The English, as a nation have lost character and honour. The destruction of my property is a fortunate thing for me. There is not a native in the country but knows now for certain on whose side I am. The Boers in plundering my house often expressed great regret that they had not got a hold of me. 'But we shall yet catch him,' said they.

Losses of Bakwains

How good God's providence is to me! I was detained in Cape Town till I fretted, and then again in the way up. But now I can plainly see that had I got my own way I should have been in the very thick of the fight, for I always intended to spend a fortnight or so with the Bakwains. I grieve over the losses they have sustained, but there is another point of view in which the matter may (be) considered. The majority of the Bakwains have heard the Gospel repeatedly but have not received it. They treated me uniformly with respect, but when Sechele professed faith in Christ they persecuted him bitterly. The Bakhatla have not only long refused to listen even, but treated Mr. Edwards with great disrespect. Nearly £1000 has been spent on them in vain, indeed their professed principles were to get all out of the missionary they could, but never receive his message. The same may be said of the Bahurutse, and though the two stations are broken up it is no cause for sorrow. The Bakwains, I am informed, attended both school and church better after I left for the Cape than for a long time previously. Average of the school 80. Sechele's children are out here living with Mrs Moffat. they are well-behaved, the son resembles his father in manners. They give much less trouble than was expected. I think the seed sown will yet spring up among the Bakwains, though I may not live to see it. . . . I have just been drawn away from my writing by the Chief Mahura. He is here on a visit—a great rogue. He made a remark worth noting. 'Sebube and Paul and you were taken out of the way of being killed. If either of you had been there you would certainly have been in the midst of the affair and been killed. God helped you by sending you out of the way.' Sebube and Paul are gone North. Sebube is a very brave fellow, native teacher to the Wanketse. He has lost all. Though Mahura is a heathen he has imbibed some Christian knowledge. I have been thinking that I might draw £12 for Mebaloe. I have drawn nothing for some time for either him or Paul. Our operations have been interrupted, but as it is a matter of business I shall write you if I do. No word from my better half yet.

Sechele falls back

Will you be kind enough to acquaint Mr. Rutherfoord with any of the particulars of our hindrance which may interest him, also George's wife[1] if you happen to see her.

Excuse this long ramble, my mind is troubled by the afflictions of others. Poor people, when will they learn wisdom!

Believe me yours of course
D. LIVINGSTON.

LETTER 45

To REVD. W. THOMPSON

Kuruman, 12th October 1852.

MY DEAR SIR,

... I mentioned to you that after three years consistent conduct and profession of faith in Christ I baptized Sechele on the first Sabbath of October 1848. In March or April 1849 it was discovered that he had had connection with one of his former wives whom in consequence of having a young child and no parents he had found impossible to send away with the others. He at once confessed his sin and added as an excuse that having been accustomed to her he had not for the time felt as if he were sinning by going to another man's wife. He professed much penitence entreating me not to cast him off 'as he hoped to stand along with me before the throne of Jesus'. I cut him off from fellowship and as he entreated to be allowed to remain as a spectator only at the ordinance, and I felt that I must not count him as an enemy, I acceded to his request. He sat back from the spot where the few believers communicated, on two or three occasions which occurred subsequently to this fall, and his manner being no ways changed from what it had been previously, I indulged the hope that if he continued to walk uprightly for two or three years we might again receive him. Immediately after his fall I wrote to the Directors about it knowing that they would sympathise with me in my sorrow.

---

[1] Mrs. Fleming.

Teachers fail

And I mentioned to them subsequently the fact of his walking consistently. I thought this was sufficient unless I had restored him again. But as soon as I heard of his conduct in the case of Mr. Moyle,[1] as it seemed widely different from consistency I wrote to the Directors a detailed account of the circumstances and stated that I now considered him an entire backslider though not an apostate. I was the more careful to give the facts of his case because they had in some speeches made reference to his conversion, and some, who did not of course, know what I had written, thought that I must still be holding up Sechele to the Board as a convert. Well, eight to ten months after Sechele was cut off a worse affair came to light amongst the young people belonging to the families of the two native teachers Mebaloe and Paul, viz, excessive impurity, and when I began to make enquiry I found out that the teachers must have known of it and kept me in ignorance. . . . The wives of the teachers too had been using enchantments. I felt very much vexed to think I had been administering the ordinance to them as consistent believers, and the whole town knowing all the while what their conduct had been. Their number being only seven I cut the whole off having had no ordinance at all since. None of them even asked why they were kept so. They seemed determined to act as if they had never been guilty, or as if they believed that I knew nothing about it. Paul's family being notoriously bad I requested him to leave, but he did not go. Mebaloe however, confessed to me before I went to the Cape that they had done great harm to the cause, in fact, said he, we have spoiled the teaching at Kolobeng. The Boers now have cleared out the whole of them. I did not pay them anything from the time I discovered their inconsistency, but Mebaloe having confessed his sin and also carried on the school up to the time of the Boers' attack, I may perhaps without impropriety draw a year's salary for him. I have not yet however, made up my mind. There are always two sides to a

[1] Moyle was an Englishman who was thought to be responsible for the death of one of Sechele's people and was therefore plundered.

Troubled by ill-health

story.... Tell me some of your trials and how you manage to overcome. It is something to overcome oneself.... I cannot help believing that you possess a great deal more prudence than I ever did or ever will get hold of. In proof of want of prudence I intend to begin tomorrow another spell for the British Quarterly on the Caffre war. It is high time that we speak out. We must pitch into them. It is infamous to see our Cape Government scraping and bowing to the Mobocracy of that cesspool called Graham's Town.

I have sketched out a grammar but done nothing else except collecting words and making notes. (a very few on natural history) When I think of it it grows on me and seems a work of a life time, and I suspect mine will not be a long one. I cannot get over the idea that complaining of one's ailments is old-wifish, yet a pain in my chest I never felt before, when I exert myself to speak as loudly as I used to do in preaching, warns me that my days are few. In preaching in Sechuana, which I do occasionally, I feel at home and speak much more loudly and quickly than when gasping for words as much as for breath and voice in Union Chapel. Will you present my kind remembrances to Dr. Abercrombie, and ask him what he would recommend for a pain apparently confined to the middle and upper lobes of the left lung. I feel it only when I preach loudly. It continues half a day afterwards. I use sponging the whole body, the chest in particular, with cold water, but have not much inclination to use medicines unless recommended by a judicious old practitioner as he. The throat, I am sorry to say, is not so much benefitted as I expected. There is no symptom of any disease whatever in the lung. I feel nothing but the pain and a feeling of weakness....

Yet that you may not think me entirely destitute of prudence I may mention that I have remained here more than a month after my wheel was repaired waiting till the Boers have got out of my way. They intend, it is reported, as soon as they hear of my passing, to send a party on horseback after me, and if

I will not come back they must kill me. I intend to lighten the waggons of as much food as possible and everything else except bare necessaries, and then we shall have a run. . . . Tell Ralph that the miserable white pony is become fat again and carries me about finely—he would not know it now.

. . . Last Sunday I preached 3 times and did not feel the pain I have had for some time so you need not think anything more about it. Ludorf is at Motïto having fled from his people. They too are flying. Griquas are said to be stabbing each other, through brandy of course. I shall write to Directors by next opportunity.

Ever yours,
D. LIVINGSTON.

LETTER 46

To REV^D DR TIDMAN

Kuruman 2^d November
1852

DEAR SIR

With feelings of unfeigned gratitude I acknowledge Your letter of July last, containing information respecting the safe arrival of Mrs Livingston and family in England, and I hereby tender my fervent thanks to the Directors for the various arrangements by which my mind is relieved from anxiety and I am constrained to dedicate anew my whole being to the service of our Lord and Master.

I have especial reason for gratitude in the kind consideration shewn towards the case of Mr Moffat.[1] Every variety of treatment which we have either seen, heard or read of, has been tried but hitherto without the smallest effect on the complaint. Sudden pressure on one side of the head having been observed to make some little difference in the constant loud ringing sound within. I recommended iodine on the supposition that

---

[1] Robert Moffat made three trips to Matebeleland after this date and lived till 1883.

Moffat's translation work

the symptoms might have been caused by hypertrophy of one of the cerebral membranes, but there is not as yet the slightest benefit from its employment. The thorough manner in which he applies himself to the translation involves a large amount of mental toil. Incessant attempts to make the Sichuana harmonize with the Hebrew, render the undertaking nearly the same as learning the latter language and translating too. The various uses of each Hebrew word are ascertained and uniformity in the use of the Sichuana attempted. Assistance in this is drawn from the Dutch, German, French & English translations and also from a number of commentaries. Complete cessation from this severe toil is almost the only means which remain to be tried for his recovery. And the fact that Mrs Livingston began to amend as soon as she came within the influence of the sea air makes me think favourably of a visit to the coast. Mr Moffats own inclination, if he could tear himself away from translation, would perhaps lead him to visit his old friend Mosilikatse—that chief having lately sent him a pressing invitation. . . .

I am sorry to find that my remarks on the relative expenditure in the Colony and countries beyond, have appeared to imply a charge of maladministration on the part of the Directors. These remarks were founded on data published in the Colony, shewing the average expenditure for a series of years and though it is quite true that 'a missionary looking to an object from an isolated point of view is very liable to misinterpret the measures of the Directors when applied in a wide scale' it is not quite so obvious that the relative or numerical value of these data can be affected by our mode of viewing them Having full reliance on the purity of motive which influences and controuls the general administration of the Directors I imagined that their attention might be drawn to certain inequalities without impugning their integrity, and even now if we push aside for a little the very laudable touchiness on the subject of management my remarks may be viewed as implying no more than want of faith in their omniscience.

State of the district

In pages 42-43 of the printed 'letter of instructions' I am enjoined to present from time to time, statements respecting the circumstances and necessities of the ajacent country'—and of the course of events and opinions bearing on the interests of christianity' I have refrained from the performance of this duty during the last eight years I have been deterred, from furnishing information concerning events which were notorious to the whole Bechuana country as hindering the gospel of Christ, by the fear that my judgement might be biassed by the 'difference' to which you refer. During those eight years of silence on my part, it was notorious that the Bakhatla had repeatedly by public proclamation rejected the Gospel. Not one individual of the tribe was permitted to attend either school or church and consequently £800 of the Society's funds were spent on two or three families who had come to Mabotsa for the sake of better gardens Mr Inglis spent one of his first four years in formally holding school for Mr Edwards with the children of these highly favoured families. The contemptuous treatment of Sebubi the native teacher among the Wanketse by Mr Edwards The railing accusations of Mr Inglis against Sechele during the period of the consistent walk and conversation of that chief. On these events & opinions formed on these events I refrained from remark. There is no reference to them in my letters during the last seven years But when winding up my connection with that part of the country it seemed natural and proper to obey the positive injunctions of the Directors and give a general view of the causes of the failure of the mission in the Kolobeng district. Between this view and a quarrel which took place eight years ago a connection is instantly established. And Mr Moffat is lugged into it too. As he was not engaged in that quarrel, I begin to suspect that the '*connection*' was suggested by some member of the South African Committee who had been seven years out of office. I can scarcely believe that the Directors are totally oblivious of the fact that for the sake of peace I yielded up a splendid station and good prospects for a new people and a locality which did not afford a promise of the necessaries of

Attack on Kolobeng missed

life—and yielded it up too though cooly informed by Mr Edwards 'that had he known of my desires he would have waived the whole quarrel'. I was convinced that I could not work in connection with him afterwards, and did what ministers in England do—viz. maintain perfect silence. Had I done what some better men do to Dr Campbell, evince my hostility by a perpetual stroke there would have been some ground on which discernment of motive might tread. But having carried out my desires to carry the gospel to another tribe irrespective of Mr Edwards's furious attacks on my character in order to secure Mabotsa to himself, I am almost as much startled at the exhumation of the old quarrel as if I had met a resurrectionist. I feel sorry that any of my remarks have conveyed a charge so different from what I intended and beg leave to withdraw whatever may after the above explanation appear offensive

I reached Kuruman about three months ago. I was longer on the way from Cape Town than the distance required, and all the other hindrances which occurred were at last crowned by the complete breaking down of a wheel near this place. As soon as this was ready I prepared to leave but the news of the horrid deeds of the Boers arrived and I then percieved that a kind Providence had been detaining me that I might not fall into the hands of the marauders. Had I been able to travel as quickly as my desires dictated I should have been at Kolobeng at the very time of the attack. And as the commandant repeatedly expressed sorrow at not having caught me and also his determination to cut off my head. I feel certain that they would at least have taken all the property I now have and rendered my present enterprise abortive. They are much exasperated against me because Sechele cut off about thirty of their number and resolutely refuses to block up the path to the North for Englishmen—they have attacked and dispersed eight tribes since I came into the country and though great numbers of the natives have fallen not a drop of Boerish blood has been spilled. The Wanketse and Bakhatla followed the usual course of tribes in that quarter. They fled without attempting to strike

Farmers and Chiefs

a blow on those who were wantonly killing them. But Sechele fought a whole day, therefore say the Boers 'that horrid doctor must have taught them to fight'. . . . It is necessary to distinguish between the Colonial farmers of Dutch extraction who are usually called Boers and those in the Interior of the same name whose independence has been lately acknowledged by the Government. The latter are the dregs of the Colonial population and if we do not bear in mind the general belief they entertain that black people are soulless, it is difficult to believe the records of their barbarity and callousness in shedding the blood of the coloured people. I can declare most positively that the Bakwains have given no offence to these Boers during the last eight years, and the only reason they themselves could urge for attacking them were that Sechele refused to become their vassal and prevent English traders and others from passing him towards the countries beyond. . . . The plea of preventing the English from dealing in arms and ammunition among the natives is a mere subterfuge as it is notorious that they deal largely in these articles themselves—their determination makes me more resolved than ever to open up a new way to the Interior and the experience of that kind providence which prevented me falling into the hands of those who would have at least sadly crippled my efforts, encourages me to hope that God graciously intends to make some further use of me. I have received friendly assurances of welcome from the principal men of the Makololo by means of native traders who have lately returned from that country. And though the present delay is the more difficult to endure inasmuch as it is consuming the time in which I am unencumbered, It may be that I am thus prevented from falling a victim to the fever—the losses we have sustained amount to upwards of £300. We shall move the more lightly now that we can put all our goods into one waggon. Cannot say I take joyfully the spoiling of my goods. If they had made any use of my books and medicines I could have forgiven them—but tearing smashing and burning them was beyond measure galling

Church and State

The notice taken of Mr Oswel by the Directors has been highly gratifying to my feelings. By a letter from Mrs L. I find that he is still anxious to befriend us.

I am Dear Sir Yours
Affectionately
DAVID LIVINGSTON

Nov 12th I am preparing to start for the North during this week—or the beginning of the week following.

LETTER 47

To REV. W. THOMPSON, *Cape Town*

Kuruman, November 24th 1852.

MY DEAR MR. THOMPSON,

Am very sorry to say I am still here in durance vile, but matters are in a fair way now. . . . I have made arrangements with two Hottentots and I think I shall be off positively before the next moon. The delays which have occurred have prevented me falling into Boerish hands, so I am thankful, and indulge the hope that God has still some little work for me to do. The belief that my hindrances from the Cape off to the Kuruman, are providential makes me submit with a good grace.

Fine fellows you Cape worthies are. Mr. Fairbairn tells his contemporaries that the connection of the Dutch Church with the State is very slender, and you believe it, of course! They get £200 per annum and the State appoints the ministers, or has all the patronage in its hands. Our connection with the Society is half as slight again, for we only get £100. He, of course, knows what sort of people he is speaking to. Humph! Sir George C. tells the Caffres that they may receive the Gaiki warriors into their houses; receipt of stolen goods is no crime in his eyes. Its 'for any sake take them away, I can't bear them'. Bochoo O thou mighty man of valour. That's 'extermination' 'driving over the Kei' and 'unconditional submission' 'complete subjugation—and £500 for Uitaalders' head too. I intend to offer £5000 for the Lion's Head which looks down at Church Square. Said Lion's Head to be delivered at

Manochisane gives up

Lattakoo, and I give you the first offer. What unutterable meanness that Sir George Gilbert Cathcart can be guilty of, and a Scotchman too! Did I not tell you we Scotchmen are a bad set? I don't understand your question about responsibility. The Superintendent will get all the blame of everything bad if he allows the Committees to do wrong. I think the Directors will do so. In Africa we all blame each other and we are blamed by everybody else. Make them all independant. That's my advice.

D. LIVINGSTON.

Please inform your sister that the fish and bracelets were punctually delivered to Manochisane, who expressed herself pleased with the gift. She gave over the chieftainship to her brother, and that too, gracefully. She had no taste for ruling, preferring to be married and rear a family. She seems a very affectionate mother—sending every now and then during our interview to see if her child were awake and hurrying off to it quicker than ladies in this part usually do, when informed that she was needed. The fish was an object of great attraction among the Barotse. Many disputes took place as to its genus, and the scales being removed, whether it were roasted or only prepared for roasting. They made a little song about it.

As I don't wish to be guilty of plagiarism I have to ask your permission to adopt the following flourish[1] which though similar is not identical with yours.

DAVID ZAMBEZI
His mark X

Unto the Right Reverend & venerable William Capeton with *greeting*. (Scoticé)
I have sent a paper on the Caffre war to the B. Quart. If this is blabbed by the D^r I shall not write any more for him
    We have a new claim out for the discovery of the Lake, viz.

---

[1] This appropriate 'flourish' is followed by a rough sketch showing the writer 'cocking a snook' at Thompson. Against the sketch Livingstone wrote: 'Not for everyone's eye of course.' He was addressing a friend not at the moment as a representative of the Society but in private playfulness.

A reputed discoverer

Mr. Wilson,[1] a trader who asked and obtained permission from me to accompany us as such. Oswel and Murray were not pleased with me for giving permission. His opinion was never on any occasion asked never spoke a word in any emergency, paid nothing to the guides, was fed and otherwise assisted and got a fine load of ivory for next to nothing. Yet some of his friends in order to detract as much as may be from my honours set up his claims as the true discoverer of the Lake. He, it seems, says we should all have turned back but for him. Now the question of turning was never mooted except by Sekhomi's messenger. My answer was, 'They must put me in my grave first'. Mr. Oswel asked what I had said and when I told him he replied, 'I am very glad to hear *you* say so'. Murray may have spoken to Wilson about turning, but the idea never entered my head I know. On the single word 'turn' hang all Mr. Wilson's claims. I perhaps ought to give him the medal on such serious grounds. But turn we didn't, so to us belongs the discovery.

The information I have given is scantier than I should like you to have got, but time is awaiting,

Farewell Dear Brother.

P.S. By this post I send 10 letters addressed to your care, and Post paid as far as Cape Town. There is no use in attempting to pay beyond that. You must open an account against me and put down Postage, Forage, and all other monies expended on my behalf. I enclose a letter to Mr. Macgibbon of the Botanic gardens, and if you can spare time to glance over it you may oblige me in one of your walks next winter by putting him in remembrance. Macgibbon's letter contains seeds—2 of the above named letters are for yourself. I say 'put down all monies &c.' What hypocrisy! if honest I would say you may either put it down or not, I see no prospect of ever paying you. If I live to come back to Cape Town I shall get a share of Mr. Holt's parlour in the house by the jetty, or a lodging in the Union

---

[1] Wilson was mentioned in letter 33. He was an enterprising trader stationed at Kolobeng.

workhouse. Please request Mr. Pococke to get a supply of vaccine virus from the Institution for me. I forgot it. If you are acquainted with the officer he will do it better and send it post-free. I shall probably draw £12 for Mebaloe. This is all the business I have to transact or trouble you with.

One of the letters is for America through Captain Holmes and you will perhaps be good enough to present my kind remembrances to him. As the post is not going for an hour or two I may have time to write another letter, which will be eleven to your care.

I heartily approve of your conduct in the case of Sechele. He entertained the project for many years but always received my decided veto on it. Again and again have I said, 'Your duty lies among your own countrymen and not to be stared at as a wild beast, or as the children of strange towns do to me'. When I met him at Kuruman he had made up his mind to go with others. All I could say was, you need not think of the governor, he is gone to punish Moshesh. 'But I will go to the Queen'. I could say nothing about her, and as he appeared to be going at the expense of others did not feel at liberty to object farther than by telling him the difficulty I had in getting ammunition. He was perfectly aware of my sentiments about going to England. I have always been opposed to exhibiting real or supposed converts prize cattle fashion. Whatever he may be now, I have not the shadow of a doubt that during the $2\frac{3}{4}$ years before his admission he was sincere and most consistent. If those who blame you want him now, let them come down with the dust and send for him.

LETTER 48

(*Original at Scottish National Memorial, Blantyre*)

To REV. CHARLES LIVINGSTON, *Plympton, Massachusetts*

MY DEAR CHARLES, February 6th, 1853.

As I am not far from the country[1] in which I expect to have but few opportunities of sending letters, and it is just

[1] The letter was written on a journey in the Makololo country. Living-

American books

possible I may meet one of Sekhome's people among these Matlomaganyana,[1] I write you a few words, and indeed I ought to write you for I have been enjoying a rare feast all the way from Kuruman through your princely generosity in the matter of books. I remember you with feeling of grateful affection every new volume I read, and as I have still a good stock untouched, my emotions will not want occasions of being stirred up for some time to come. The *Bibliotheca Sacra* and *New Englander* and some other Theological works have given me a high idea of Yankee attainments in that Science. They seem ahead of the British in several departments, and I am proud to think I have a brother capable of standing among such giants as a companion in arms, and I pray he may prove throughout a good soldier of Jesus Christ. Yet I dont very well understand what they see to praise in the works lately published by Dr. Chalmers. His private notes, for instance, are to me very poor, and many of what he calls *notabilia* are just what everybody knows And then when he comes to a difficult passage, he slips over it, saying a great deal on other parts which might have been left alone. I have seen the three volumes of it, and could not manage to wade through them, it was so 'wersh'. I suspect some critics just take up the 'spoor' (trail) as we call it here, of others. In coming across the desert, we had a good deal of difficulty in consequence of our oxen running away and leaving us at a spot far from water.... remained there three days withstone had been in the desert. His journal is full of suggestive thoughts about this time.

'*28th September 1852*.—Am I on my way to die in Sebituane's country? Have I seen the end of my wife and children?

'*23rd January 1853*.—I think much of my poor children.

'*4th February 1853*.—I am spared in health while all my company have been attacked by fever. If God has accepted my service then my life is charmed till my work is done. And though I pass through many dangers unscathed while working the work given me to do, when that is finished, some simple thing will give me my quietus.

'*22nd May*.—I will place no value on anything I have or may possess, except in relation to the Kingdom of Christ—' (Blaikie, pp. 115, 116.)

[1] Matlomaganyana = The Links, a place with a chain of never-failing springs.

Mr. Macabe's Journey

out water. I dug an old well and found very little water at the bottom. We got an eland at the time. It was quite fat and good. They seem most abundant when water is scarce. A Mr. Macabe crossed the desert this year and found abundance of melons in the driest part of the Kalihari country. His oxen subsisted on melons for 20 days. The people always told me before the discovery of the Lake that if a wet year occurred melons enough would grow to support the oxen while going to the Lake. Last year was unusually favoured with rain, hence Mr. Macabe's success. He however made no discovery of importance. He went to the Lake and went round it, as did also another party, the latter say its circumference is 130 miles, the former 90. We from the reports of the natives conjectured it to be about 75. The Teoge, a large river runs into it from the northwest. Some gentlemen went up the Teoge 120 miles in a straight line and lost all their cattle and horses by the bite of the Tsetse. The only parts of much interest in a religious or a commercial view have been left untouched. Macabe is fond of travelling and many others who went in were burning for the fame of discovery, and all of them went to Sebituane's country for ivory and while there were within two days of the large Waterfall, yet it is left for me. I feel thankful to God who, in permitting me to labour in his work, bestows tokens of the appreciation of my fellow men by throwing discoveries in my way. I never need to go much or at all out of my way to make them. Two of the persons above referred to, set off on horseback to see the Falls but were prevented. The only point of interest, last year's batch of travellers settled, was that the bite of the Tsetse does not act as the inoculation for smallpox does, for a horse which was bitten and recovered last year died from having received a greater number of bites this year. Mr. Moffat goes on laboriously with his translation of the Bible into Sechuana. In his hands, it is something like translating and learning Hebrew at the same time, for he is so anxious to make the Sechuana and Hebrew harmonize; he examines every word in the latter language. He writes a neat hand, yet his translation in manu-

The Sechuana Bible

script is covered over with references and the various exercises of his mind on different words. I proposed to him to offer his manuscript of the whole Bible in Sechuana to the Library of the Amhurst College, and he seemed pleased with the proposition. Would the authorities there value the gift. I was induced to think of it by seeing that that Library possesses a collection of the Bible in various languages. Will you make enquiry and write either him or me on the subject. We could send a Testament now and the whole Bible when printed. . . . You are not restricted to Amhurst. What I should prefer would be where it would be valued most. In my opinion, it is a curiosity of great interest. We could send too, copies of Bunyan's Pilgrim in Sechuana. If you find it convenient to write on these points soon, address to Rev. R. Moffat, Kuruman. It will be sure to find him. I am standing under a Moana or Baobab tree at present composed of six branches rising from one root and joined together till about five feet from the ground. At three feet from the ground it is 85 feet in circumference. It is at least 60 feet high. The redish colour makes it look more like a mass of red granite than a tree. The branches high above look like what I have hitherto called large trees. The wood is quite soft and spongy, and though such a giant in size I suspect he is a mere baby compared to some of the historical Yews and Oaks of England.

It is a poor country after all. The frequent drought, the cattle stealing and children stealing and murders make the heart sick. But its future is in the hands of God, and he will cover it with his glory. The dwellers in the wilderness shall bow down before him and all nations shall serve him. When at Sechele's town I took down the names of 124 children who had been stolen from that tribe alone. Many of them I could identify as having been in the Mission School. The Boers now want peace from Sechele because the Barolongs commenced stealing their cattle immediately after their attack on Sechele. This is the first instance in which Bechuanas here have been known to steal cattle from white men. Sechele replied to their

Lost children of Kolobeng

application, 'can we talk of peace so long as you retain my child in slavery'. They immediately sought out one of his children who had been captured and restored him. I was present when amidst the tears of a crowd of mothers whose children are still in bonds, Khari was restored to his mother. They have of course 123 children still in their possession, and leaving out of view the men and women murdered, the cattle stolen, the provisions, clothing and property destroyed in burning the town they think they have done enough for securing peace by restoring one child. This is portentous impudence. The Bakwains have not yet learned to fight, but fight they will and then the Boers will leave the feud to be settled by the English. Sechele has gone south in order to implore the English to assist him to regain his children. I believe he might as well have remained at home. He abstained from all acts of retaliation lest the English should be offended. He has a high idea of our benevolence, and his ideas collected from the conduct of Missionaries would I am certain not be confirmed by a journey to the camp of the Governor. . . . I have written four papers for the British Quarterly, and now hold up. I had important ends in view in each, and now that I have accomplished as much as I could for those ends . . . my thoughts run on a book of travels, but when I reflect on what is necessary for such an undertaking, I give up in despair. I think it will perhaps be my wisest course to keep in the shade and among the *Hoi Polloi* who gazed at trees, birds and beasts centuries ago, and now sleep beneath the plains over which I now wander. . . .

18th March. I am, I may say, in Sebituane's country but not at their towns. We have been detained by fever for some time past The whole party is down except myself and a Mokwain. I have six patients on my hands. We came to a number of ponds containing rain water nearly dried up. Thermometer 100 degrees in the shade. My driver took it first then George's driver and leader, then my two leaders and a bushman guide. It is a great mercy my Bakwain lad was spared, for I could not manage the cattle alone. But we are protected by a kind father,

A plum pudding appears

and He will provide. Rains are falling which reduce the temperature, and will I hope cover decayed vegetation. One of the people went about 50 yards from the waggon last night, fell down in a swoon, and remained so the whole night. The rain poured down on him and he felt nothing. In searching for him this morning my driver himself ill, came on him and thought him dead. You may be sure I felt glad when I roused him from his protracted swoon. As soon as we can muster as many as will suffice to catch the oxen, we shall go on. Perhaps we shall come to a more salubrious spot. Since writing the above, I have been amused by George[1] who is an American or perhaps was for he calls himself a West Indian, for there, freedom was proclaimed to the slave, and I suspect he was once one. He is quite black and goes with me on a trading speculation. He thinks his forte lies in cookery. He has been lying very ill, but a permission I gave him to use some Kuruman raisins seemed to have worked wonders. He has been bustling about ever since he got up about eleven o'clock, and when dinner was served, behold a plum pudding was produced. The very idea of it seems to have fused new life into him. I only fear a descent to our usual fare of game and meat will produce a relapse. We have had Zebra for some time back. It smells just as a horse does, and is not nice till one gets used to it, and even then though we get to like it, we dont prefer it. Other kinds of flesh may be eaten after they are green and maggotty but this when rancid is very nasty. They are more easily got than other game as they often turn round to stare. I shot three the other day. A lot of Bushmen who were with us soon eat them up. The hunting must now be done by me, as well as other people. I dont like it and never turn to it except when compelled. . . . The loss of the oxen is very trying as they run a long way. The Mokwain is a good fellow and will follow on their trail till he finds them or falls down. I have known Bakwains run off at night with the oxen at full gallop, and one or two lions chasing them. Tearing through bush and brake with bare legs wherever the terrified

[1] Fleming the trader.

Sechele's brother and a lion

beasts went, and when they got well away from the lions, make to the front, stop the oxen, make a fire and lie down and sleep till the morning. They have done this though they might have remained by the fire at the waggon in safety, but though sound asleep when the oxen have been attacked, up they jump and away with them. In 1852 a lion caught a brother of Sechele by the arm, he having run up to it in order to rescue a man who was under it. Afraid to fire lest he should shoot the man, he called for a spear. The lion turned round upon him. The other people rushing forward came to him just as he was caught, some seized the lion others the man. Fancy, if you can, a lot of black fellows pulling one way by the man, the lion holding the arm in his mouth, and others holding the lion, so that he could not move. When spears were brought they soon finished him. This is a jumbling account of it, but no white man ever showed more bravery than some of these people do.

I have now no hope of sending this back, and must just close it, and send it with another, when I can. My love to your good lady and 'sma' family. May God grant you every blessing. I have never had a touch of the fever. I am with Sebituane's people. 7th June. I shall tell you all in another letter. In the meantime, rest with assurance of unabated love,

D. LIVINGSTON

LETTER 49

To REV. W. THOMPSON, *Cape Town*

Sekeletu's Town 17th September 1853.

MY DEAR MAN,

Your letters are 'necessarily brief' so you say, and I am bound to believe the Right Reverend Father William Capeton seeing he hath received two students from Hankey into his ghostly care. Ah! mine are necessarily long, long winded or flatulent, as a follower of Esculapius expresseth it. The reason whereof lieth in an immense sheet of paper which must be filled, for Nature abhorreth a vacuum, and want of time to shorten them.

Directors' instructions

The Directors and you are wonderful men. The former decline to write concerning certain minutes of committee though informed that no meeting will take place till such writing has been received. And they at the same time cooly tell me that they hope I shall derive counsel, assistance, &c, &c, from the committee of which no meeting can take place. Then you, if I recollect aright, twitted me about our committee being defunct and yet presume the matter of a companion will come before it. But who will go? I am gone. No matter my companion can follow. The Directors requested Ashton to leave the Kuruman and settle with a tribe as I had done. He refused. Subsequently Mr. Freeman proposed in committee held at Kuruman that Ashton should go to Barigelong. He refused by saying 'It would be like taking Mrs Ashton to her grave'. 'Then you must take the entire charge of the printing press (Mr. Moffat had till then done the press work) and leave Mr. M. to devote his entire time to translation'. This, you will perceive, settled him at Kuruman. Mr. M. is the only man willing to go, but would it be advisable for him to do so? No certainly. But here I am after my 8th attack of fever. The last very severe being accompanied with large discharges of blood. It has made me quite thin, but as I am becoming old and skinny per process of time that doesn't matter much. I never laid by, but vertigo from exhaustion compelled me to give up some of my sedentary work. By the way it now glances across my mind that the Daguerro-type portraits entrusted to Mrs. De Smit had not in November last been delivered. I blame myself severely for entrusting them to a young man through his mother. She, of course, good woman, wished to oblige, but what thousands of gracious mothers have striven to make their sons appear obliging; everyone else understanding it as merely efforts to make silk purses out of sow's ears. Though too much given to jesting to-night I am really very sorry for the loss I fear Mrs. L. has sustained. She feels it very keenly and I cannot repair the loss. Please retain the medal[1] in Cape Town till you hear from

[1] From the Paris Geographical Society. See letter 51.

Hampered by fever

me. It is not likely I shall ever come your way again. Here one of your questions holds up its phiz at me, 'Unless you discover a good way to the sea either to the East or West how are we in future to send men to the region of the Lake or to the parts beyond? For Lobale?' 'In future', the dear man! How many has he sent in time past? 'Unless you discover a good' &c. An indifferent one will do for those who have any pluck in them, and for those who have none, the old overland route may be safely recommended, for they will discover some important and very large field of labour a long way South of the Orange River in which they will be associated with a Wesleyan, a Church of England clergyman, a Dutch Predicant, and a Government schoolmaster, each of whom considers the 10 shanties and 8 shopkeepers' houses as his 'sphere of labour' involving the most excrutiating responsibility.

I was delayed long at Kuruman by the Boers and want of people, for all feared to go North. But having got over these difficulties we made very good progress till we came into Lat. 190.16 South. There all my people, were knocked down by fever except one Bakwain lad. I managed the hospital and he the oxen, and by God's mercy none were cut off. When we were able to move Northwards the poor Bakwain lad took it too. I had to drive and cut a path too for keeping more to the Eastward in order to avoid the Tsetse we travelled through a densely wooded country in which the axe was in constant operation. But for two Bushmen who managed the loose oxen, and otherwise assisted, we could not have moved. Some were still so weak we had to lift them out, and into the waggon. When we came near the Chobe the adjacent country was flooded for 15 miles out. Vallies appeared like large deep rivers, with hippopotami in them. We tried long, in vain, to get a ford through one large river called Sanshureh. Our bushmen decamped too. So I took a small pontoon kindly presented by Messrs Webb and Codrington, and the strongest of my weak crew, crossed the Sanshureh—$\frac{1}{2}$ a mile wide and went North to find the Chobe and people. We waded among reed and

Welcomed by Makololo

high grass for three days trying to obtain a passage in to the Chobe through the dense masses of reed, &c. which line its banks. On the fourth day we obtained our object, launched the pontoon, and after passing along about 20 miles we reached a Makololo village. In their figurative language they said I 'had come upon them as if I had dropped out of a cloud yet I came riding on the back of a hippopotamus'. A rumour had reached the Makololo previously, and two parties had been sent out in search of us. All our difficulties were now at an end. Canoes were soon sent down by the Chief, our waggons, etc, were transported across the country and river, and after proceeding North in order to avoid the flooded lands on the other side, we turned S.W. and reached the town. Our reception was far more flattering than I could have anticipated. The Chief, just over 18 years of age, said he rejoiced to obtain another father instead of Sebituane, and repeatedly requested me to name whatever I wished and he would show his affection by giving it; cattle, ivory, &c, &c, and he seemed distressed when I refused to name anything. He is not equal in appearance or abilities to his father, but there is nothing weak or childish in his conduct or conversation, and several executions which have taken place on account of conspiracy shew that he is not destitute of Sebituane's energy. He is afraid to learn to read at present 'lest it should change his heart and make him content with one wife' as in the case of Sechele. I like a frank objection—one cannot get a hold on a 'Ya Mynheer' they are too oily. I have just returned from a nine weeks tour through the country in search of a suitable location for a mission. Went up the Barotse River, or as it is universally called by the Makalaka—the aboriginal inhabitants, the black race of whom I spoke—the Leeamby, or 'The River' reached the confluence of the Loeti, with its light coloured water, also that of the Leeba or Lonta. Londa is the proper name because it comes from Londa, the capital of a large state. The confluence of the Londa and Leeamby is in 14° 11' South. This is a point of great importance for the Leeamby turns thence away to the East N.

A land of rivers

East. The Londa about 150 yards wide (the Leeamby 250 beyond it) the Londa coming from the N & by W. or N.N.W. is, I dream, yet to form part of our way West. Conveyance by water is of great importance. With 6 paddlers we went 44 miles of Latitude in one day of $10\frac{1}{2}$ hours and taking into account the windings of the river, and our course being what sailors term a $2\frac{1}{2}$ point one, the actual distance must have been upwards of 50 geographical miles. The river is one of very great beauty and breadth. It is often more than a mile broad, with islands 3 or 4 miles long in it. These are covered with sylvan vegetation, the rounded masses of which seem to recline on the bosom of the water. The Tsetse spoils the most beautiful and healthful spots. I must reserve details, but after a laborious search have not found a spot I could pronounce salubrious. We must brave the fever. It is God, not the devil that rules our destiny. Surely we may, when slave traders do. . . . Nine weeks intimate intercourse—hearing their conversation, anecdotes, quarrelling, roaring, dancing, singing, and murdering, have imparted a greater disgust at heathenism than I ever had before. And in comparison with Southern tribes a firm belief that missionaries effect a great deal more than they are aware of, even when there are no conversions.

I am sorry you cannot be furnished with a correct sketch of the country which I have seen. I have used the last bit of tracing paper for the Directors. 2 letters for America per Captain Holmes, a packet for Dr. Tidman, 4 English, and 1 Canadian letter.

[*Signature omitted—paper full.*]

LETTER 50

To The REVEREND DOCTOR TIDMAN

Town of Sekeletu, Linyanti
Sept 24th 1853

MY DEAR SIR

When the obstacles which caused our detention at Kuruman were removed we passed quickly towards the country of Sebi-

Gift of ivory

tuane until within one degree of Latitude from this town. All the people were then laid prostrate by fever, except one lad and myself. This caused a further loss of time, but through the goodness of God all recovered. On reaching this, the Southern capital of the Makololo we were received with all the demonstrations of welcome which they are accustomed to bestow on their chiefs. The idea seemed universal that with a missionary, some great indefinite good had arrived. Many expected at once to be elevated to a condition equal to that of the Bakwains and inhabitants of Kuruman, of which they had received very exaggerated accounts: others imagined that they would very soon be transformed into civilized men, possessing the clothing, horses, arms, waggons, etc, of Europeans. 'Jesus had not loved their forefathers, hence their present degradation. He had loved the white men and given them all the wonderful things they now possess. And as I had come to teach them to pray to Jesus, and to pray for them, their wants would soon be all supplied'. A very great deal was expected too from medicines and my liberality in giving things I have not in my possession. Patient industry and perseverance in learning were never thought of. The Chief, not yet 19 years of age, frequently pressed me to name something I wished, so that he might by presenting it shew his affection, and I suspected, induce me forthwith to commence the work of metamorphosis by means of enchantments. But when I steadily refused to mention any object I desired more than to secure their temporal and spiritual welfare by means of the Gospel, he seemed to test my sincerity by presenting 4 small & 8 large elephant's tusks. I had not an opportunity of refusing them, as they were brought and laid down by the waggon during my absence. And then the Chief came and begged me so earnestly to accept them I felt at a loss how to act. In other circumstances I should have felt no hesitation in appropriating them to defray expenses, incurred entirely on account of this people. But as it was, though I had no direct evidence that the Chief's object was such as I have described, the mere suspicion led me when departing from the

Sekeletu's doubts

Barotse country, to request him to leave orders that if any traders came, my ivory must be used as well as his own. By this means no offence was given which might have been the case had I at once sent them back. Some months were spent here for though I soon proposed to examine the country in order to discover a suitable locality for a Mission, Sekeletu objected first that he had not yet had a satisfactory look at me. He must see me longer. Then he could not think of allowing me to go alone. He must accompany me and see that no evil befel me. This required considerable preparations, during which I offered to teach the people to read. Long and profound were the deliberations over this. They are never in a hurry in Africa. And reading seems so supernatural: it cannot be explained to those who know nothing of letters. At last the Chief told me that he was 'afraid that learning to read might change his heart, and make him content with one wife only, as in the case of Sechele'. It was in vain to urge that the altered state of mind contemplated would be as voluntary as the present. No underhand means would be employed to convert—all the means employed being open teaching—there is no compulsion —the truth is taught respecting God's will and the belief or unbelief of the instructed is left as an affair between their Judge and themselves. It was just as I have felt in my early years in contemplating that everlasting preaching, praying and singing prolonged into Heaven—quite failing to realize the altered state of mind which produces a relish for such service it seemed as if celestial joys might be endured, rather than be consigned to the other quarter. As I was then subjected to repeated attacks of the Fever, I did not press the subject long. But when we returned from the Barotse an experiment of which I have reason to be satisfied was set on foot. Sekeletu's father-in-law and step-father were appointed to learn to read, in order that their experience may serve as a beacon to others. Although the plan exhibits the extreme of African caution, they applied themselves so vigorously they and several others mastered the alphabet perfectly in one day. But teaching to read being less

Description of Barotse land

my object in this journey than preaching the Gospel of peace—while endeavouring to discover a salubrious locality for a Mission, I shall proceed to relate our visit to the Barotse country.

Two sketches are enclosed, one long and large is just as I put it down as we went along, the other small—reduced to the Latitudes & Longitudes, according to observations taken as opportunities occurred. The large is sent in order that you may see several remarks which my pen is not fine enough to insert in the reduced scale, and in order that if necessary a more correct reduction may be made. We embarked on the river, called everywhere Leeambye at the village of Sekhosi, our fleet consisting of 33 canoes, and our Company of about 160 men. From the bend at Katima-molelo up to the commencement of the Barotse valley the country is covered by forest and Tsetse. The country otherwise seemed well adapted for a residence. Many villages of Banyeti, a poor but industrious people, are situated on both banks. They are expert as hunters of hippopotami & other animals, they cultivate grain too, extensively. At the bend above named commences the rocky bottom which forms cataracts and rapids all the way up to the Barotse—the river is of very great beauty and breadth—in the Northern confines of Latitude 16, the high banks seem to leave the river and stretch away to the N.N.E. and N.N.W. until between 20 and 30 miles apart—the intervening space is the Barotse country and is annually inundated as Lower Egypt is by the Nile. The valley is covered with coarse succulent grasses which are the pasturage of large herds of cattle during a portion of the year. There are many villages of Makololo in the valley. I have not put down all that I visited and many were seen in the distance. But there are no large towns—the reasons are the mounds on which alone towns and villages are built are all small, and the people require to be separate on account of being rich in cattle. Nariele ·does not contain 1000 inhabitants—. The ridges are thickly strewed with villages. The people, Banyeti and Barotse, are not rich in cattle, but they require to live apart on account of cultivating large gardens of

Going Northward

sugar cane, sweet potatoes, manioc, yams, millet, maize, etc., The exhalations which arise from a valley 20 miles broad and about 100 long produce Fever, which is very fatal even among natives. It prevails most virulently when the waters of inundation are retiring. We went North till we came to the junction of the Leeba or Londa with the main stream, Leeambye in 14°. 11′ South Latitude, and found the country presenting the same characteristics as I have described. On returning towards Nariele I went to the Eastern ridge in order to examine that, and see the establishment of a Merchant from the farthest inland station of the Portuguese opposite Benguela—a stockade had been erected, and a flagstaff for the Portuguese banner planted. The houses of the merchant and some bastards, were in the West African style the owner, whom I had previously seen at Linyanti was absent, but his servants did their utmost to shew me kindness. When my boatmen prepared my bed outside, they insisted on my occupying their Master's couch, and I never felt so grateful in my life for a warm shelter, for I was in the cold stage of one of the intermittents which continue to plague me after the Fever—. I thought of going westward in company with this merchant but the sight of gangs of poor wretches in chains at the stockade induced me to resolve to proceed alone. I have not, I am sorry to confess, discovered a healthy locality—the whole of the country of Sebituane is unhealthy. The current of the river is rapid as far as we went, and shewed we must have been on an elevated table-land yet the inundations cause the fever to prevail very extensively. I am at a loss what to do but will not give up the case as hopeless. Shame upon us if we are to be outdone by slave traders. I met Arabs from Zanzibar, subjects of the Imaum of Muscat, who had been quite across the Continent. They wrote Arabic readily in my notebook and boldly avowed that Mahomet was the greatest of all the prophets—. In pursuance of a nobler object then theirs I have determined to try and fulfil the second part of my enterprise, viz. open up a way to the Coast. I give the West the preference because it is nearer. If my calculations

Nearing the West

are right, the Longitudes of the map of last year are all wrong—the waggon stand for instance, instead of being in 26° is in 23°. 48′. or 50′ I have repeated the calculation of Lunar distances again and again and always with the same result. But I do not wish this error published untill I hear from the Astronomer at the Cape to whom I have submitted the observations and also some occultations by which to test them. But for the destruction of my Celestial map by the Boers, I might have determined the Longitudes by occultations alone, they being much more to be depended on than the common method of Lunar distances. If then I am right, we are nearer the West than the East Coast. Nariele is in 23° East and the confluence of the Leeba or Londa not much more. I have not had time to work out the Longitude of that point, but the river Leeba comes from the capital of a powerful state whose Chief is reported to be friendly to foreigners. If I am permitted to return by this chieftain it will be water carriage for perhaps two-thirds of the way, and should a Mission be established there in time it will be all the better. I intend to try for Loanda because though farther, many English live there. I go on horseback—waggon travelling being reported impossible on account of forests and numerous rivers. The Portuguese are carried in hammocks hung on poles. Two slaves carry a man—it does not look well. The Portuguese maps are all constructed from native reports, so no dependance can be placed on them. Many tribes inhabit the country, all more or less accustomed to the visits of strangers. The greatest difficulty I apprehend is that of making our objects understood. Their languages bear a close affinity to the Barotse dialect, but this I was compelled to give up reducing.

I never had a touch of the fever till my employment became sedentary here. I have had eight attacks since. The last when going north of Nariele was very severe, being accompanied with large loss of florid blood. It thinned me much. But on no occasion did I lay by. Fits of vertigo probably from exhaustion troubled me for some time. Everything seemed to rush to the

Native remedies

left and I had to lay hold on something to prevent a fall. These induced me to give up collecting Barotse words and other materials for a Dictionary. Though still thin the intermittents have left and I am only waiting for the rains to commence to start for the West—they begin next month. It will be seen that Mrs Livingstone had better not come to the Cape to meet me at the time appointed. If I reach Loanda in February, I must return with the people again and will be here instead of at the Cape. The time unavoidably lost by Boers and Fever renders a little extension of my furlough necessary. Then if the Directors sanction a permanent station or any other form of labour for this miserable interior some other mode of travelling in from the west must be arranged. A few kind words to Mrs L. from you will, I think, make her willing to prolong her stay in Scotland. Although the prospect seems dark for the Interior it may not be quite as gloomy as I have drawn it. The natives describe the mortality as very great and that attacks of fever are excessively frequent and severe. I have given you their ideas. But my own except at times are not so sombre. I tried native remedies in some of the attacks to which I was subjected in order to discover if they had any valuable means of cure, but after being stewed in vapour baths, and smoked over fires of green plants in hot potsherds etc. I find that our own medicines are more efficacious and safer. I have not lost a single patient by fever, and if I had been able to regulate my diet I should not have been subjected to so many attacks. As it was we were frequently compelled to eat on the principle of laying in a stock for the next day. My own people being too weak to go with me and the Makololo cook only in the evenings when travelling. Then if I left the canoe in order to visit a village, there are so many branches of the river intersecting the valley everywhere I was always wet up to the middle. I fear to give you either a too encouraging or discouraging report. I am afraid to incur the responsibility of inducing you to regard the case as hopeless. The American missionaries report the Gaboon station as not warranting the long established belief

Slavers depart

that Europeans could not live there, and my firm conviction is that even the Interior of Africa merits a fair trial. Such with the help of God and your sanction I am determined to give it.

The slave trade was prohibited here, and a large party of Mambari who were here endeavouring in vain to renew it, fled precipitately as soon as they heard that I had crossed the Chobe. The Makololo remonstrated with them but they asserted that I would take all their goods from them because they dealt in slaves. A Portuguese came from the West, but he, finding no market, remained only three days and returned. It was different in the Barotse or Northern division of the country. Another Portuguese merchant came thither and by means of an underchief who had some pretensions to the Chieftainship obtained free access to all the Banyeti, Batoka, & Bashukulompo villages East of the Leeambye. There the stockade which gave great offence to the Makololo was erected without the knowledge or permission of the Chief. They would have commenced hostilities at once in order to drive the whole slave trading party out of the country but a variety of considerations induced me to intercede for them, and by that intercession they will be allowed to depart in peace. Probably deceived by the assurances of the disaffected underchief they seem to have had no idea of the risk they were running. But when the conspirator came down with the intention of cutting off Sekeletu, he was instantly seized and killed. His father and several others were cut off in the most cold-blooded manner and when I remonstrated against the shedding of human blood the councillors quietly remarked 'You see we are still Boers, we are not yet taught'. But for this unfortunate affair no trading in slaves would have been allowed. In this they have the precedent of the former Chief of the Barotse who refused to grant the Mambari permission to visit his country as slave traders. A cannon of small calibre was found in the possession (of the) underchief mentioned.

The country in the direction of Mosioatunya has high mountains, and the Batoka country is a high tableland without trees except along the rivers. Healthy spots might be found in both of these but in neither did I feel it duty to travel because the vicinity of Mosilikatse renders it impossible for Makololo or any other tribe to reside there. A change may yet be effected among the Matebele which would change the present aspect of affairs

Believe me, Dear Sir,
Yours affectionately
DAVID LIVINGSTON

LETTER 51

(Original at Scottish National Memorial, Blantyre)

To REV. J. FREDOUX, *Motito*

Town of Sekeletu, Linyanti
28th September 1853.

MY DEAR BROTHER,[1]

I send you the enclosed letter for the Paris Geographical Society which I hope you will be kind enough to address and forward. I do not know the name of the president, not yet having received any letter about the Medal with which they have honoured me. Mr. Thompson informs me it is in his possession but says nothing of a letter. I write to thank them now, because if one delays it may seem to them as if I undervalued their kindness, and whatever may be thought of the gift itself (by those who dont get it) there can be no doubt about the kindness of the motives of those who resolved to bestow it. I ought to thank you too for it, for if you had not sent my letter I should never have been known to them. I shall move a vote of thanks to you when Mary comes. At present I have no one to second it, and it would be a pity to let a good thing fall to the ground for want of a seconder. You do not give me a note though I have been so long without news. . . . I begin to wish that you were north of me that the Newspapers might come to me first. I have not seen a single Advertiser since I left. All

[1] Fredoux (a French missionary) had married a daughter of Robert Moffat and was thus a brother-in-law.

Boasting of slaughter

the Newspapers I received were a few Canadian papers and two or three Frontier Times and two Christian Times, with about a dozen of that valuable production the 'Friend of the Sovreignty' from each of which an industrious person may glean as much as is contained in a little child's picture pocket handkerchief.

We had two slave traders here and a host of Mambari—the former Portuguese—and the latter connected with them in trade or as slaves. One had sixty slaves and will take away from the Bashukulompo villages to which by an intrigue with an underchief who was put to death for it, 100 or 150 more. The Mambari found no market here, and they fled as soon as they heard I had reached the Chobe. One merchant came carried in a hammock slung to a pole. He was probably disappointed in his market for he remained only three days and departed. . . . The Makololo are dreadful savages. Killing is thought nothing of. Indeed it is an every day boast how many men a man has killed. Whatever dispute may arise it immediately degenerates into 'How many men have you killed, you are a coward, you never killed any one &c. &c.' No tribe need the gospel more than they—but the fever is very bad—very fatal even to natives. The devil has it all his own way here as he has had for ages. Four Makololo have been executed in the most cool off-hand manner since I came, and when I remonstrated against shedding human blood they only replied that they 'being still Boers all are not yet taught'. A short path in will be a benefit to this country. I go on horseback. It is reported that a waggon could not pass in consequence of numerous rivers and forests. I have had fever eight times, the last very severe. Never had a touch of it till I came here, though all the people had it on the way. It is not probable that I shall come out to Kuruman again unless I have failed in finding another path. We met Arabs from Zanzibar subjects of the Imaum of Muscat. One of them wrote readily in my note book, from right to left. Portuguese Mambari and Arabs were all intent on the slave trade. It must be profitable.

Article for Vaughan's Review

... Kind regards to Ann. Hope her young ones are thriving —wish I saw mine.

May God bless you and yours is the wish of
Ever affectionately yours,
D. LIVINGSTON

LETTER 52

To REV. Wᴍ THOMPSON, *Cape Town*

11th October 1853. Linyanti.

MY DEAR MAN,

I sent you a few days ago a long letter per a Mr. Francis Thompson who came up as far as the Chobe in company with a trader Mr. Chapman, and since I sent off the packet I find I have had time to transcribe the enclosed paper which I have taken the liberty to believe you will not object to read. It contains the marrow of a much longer one carefully written for the same destination, but it was penned on our way here, and though it contains a much fuller view than this, many points are now out of date and will be much more so before reaching Dr. Vaughan. I had given up the idea of sending it at all, till the idea of an abbreviation struck my mind, and now I fear that the haste evident in its composition and writing will render it unfit for the pages of a Review. However, I send it, and my object in enclosing it to you is to request you to note any passages you may see to be out of date by the time you get it, and signify the same to the Dr. Is this too much to ask? Well! I shall not send you the next, but will just tell you it is much better than this, indeed if it were not my own child I would say it is a very good one, so good I may perhaps keep it to myself altogether. It is on Missions, the privilege of being allowed to engage in them, their future, &c, &c. I wrote it in the weary way across the desert, and if it never does aught else it has comforted my own mind.

The second paper about which I told you, and which Mr. Cameron said would be published, will not trouble you.

Great heat

I meant it to be a continuation of the same subject, believing the one would not be complete without the other. This, it seems, is not admissable in a Review. Much of the Article will be otherwise employed, and as doing good was my object I am quite satisfied. I think I have the same object in the present Article. It is a misfortune to be so far from proofsheets, one could make the composition so much more smooth, and perhaps telling. If I ever send that I have by me at present it will be my last. As I am on the subject of literature I may say you are a very fine Editor—the only letter of any pretensions in your report has 'What is the *result* of these *effects*'? and about ½ a dozen 'admitting's' spanned to one trektow of a sentence like African oxen. You will shelter yourself by saying you promised to give the manuscript to the printer. Ah, very well!

Your friend Anderson has reached the Lake. This will be a useful path for traders to the Lake. But all our Southern coast—viz, of Sebituane's country—is infested by tsetse except one small strip, and a better path than to Walwich Bay must be made. I have lost eight oxen by my people allowing the cattle to wander once. I find the watch given me by the Geo. Soc. an excellent one, and have corrected several errors in Longitude by its means, but send my observations to Mr. Maclear for verification before publishing them. It is probable the Lake is wrong as we never attempted or could attempt, to establish 'its Longitude. We never had watches worth anything. You very kindly say you fear for the result of my going in here alone. I hope I am in the way of duty, my own conviction that such is the case has never wavered. I am doing something for God. . . . The temperature in the shade is about 100° Fahr; during the day, and often 90° at nine o'clock at night. But a merry heart doeth good like a medicine. If I allowed my mind to dwell constantly on the miserable degradation, wickedness, and sad prospects of the people here, I might become melancholy and soon die. But we have a fair world and all the wonderful works of our Father in it, and I believe we ought to allow our minds to dwell on the beautiful

Bechuana labourers killed

more than on the evil. I am never low-spirited. It might be different if I had a crusty companion. I have experience in the matter, and my thoughts never turn with any longing except for my family. I think we are immortal till our work is done, not on the platform only but on the pestilential plains of the glorious Leeambye.

Remember me to Miss Thompson and the young ones. I think this goes by Walwich Bay. If the packet should reach you by this route, a small bag of seeds for the Botanic Gardens accompanies it. They were collected on the way here. I contemplate going to Loanda as soon as the rains begin—they moderate the temperature.—The dry dust with which the winds are now loaded produces fever. Your letters are miserably short.

DAVID LIVINGSTON.

In my other paper I give a hint to Mr. John Pears or Pearson, who wrote a letter in the British Banner, 'A number of Church members proceeding to the funeral of a friend in the vicinity of Cradòck, observed the footprints of 8 Bechuanas who had travelled about 600 miles in search of employment a few years before, and were now returning home with the fruits of their honest industry. After the funeral these Christians armed themselves and in the belief that these Bechuanas were Caffres, followed their trail, found them sitting quietly behind some bushes and shot down seven of them unchallenged and unresisting. The eighth was taken prisoner, and it was then found they were peaceable labourers. This bloody affair was published in the paper and no more notice was taken of it. These Boers passed uncensured to the Table of the Lord. They eat and wipe their mouths and say we have done no wickedness. Can the Rev. John Pears give us any further information on this subject?' We suppose these people were Bakwains, many of them having gone to work in that direction and never returned. Their wives are still waiting for them. This would have been out of date now.

No road due west

I have left a page for your remarks in Dr. Vaughan's note. Although intended for Colonists I cannot permit its publication in the Colony, it is utterly useless to speak to them except through the press of Europe. The gentleman who takes this, Mr. Chapman, goes by Walwich Bay and will deliver the letters to you without the expense of postage through the Colony. He has not been successful in trade, various causes prevented. The seeds will be delivered either to you or to the Botanic Gardens.

This is the 17th October, rain made an attempt to begin last night. Will you send Hoffmeyer's letter to my old lodgings.

LETTER 53

To REV^D DR TIDMAN

Linyanti 8th November 1853

DEAR SIR

By a letter dated September last I informed you of my intention to proceed Westward in order to open up a way to the coast. I was then waiting for rains and as these have now commenced I leave this on the 10th currt. I have altered my mind with respect to the route which I intend to try. We sent men to the Westward in order to examine if there is any strip of country free of tsetse in that direction.—their report was unfavourable. I then resolved to go on the trail of the Mambari but the slave merchant signalized his departure by seizing two men and a woman as slaves—the Makololo assembled immediately and compelled him to unchain the captives This affair made me alter my resolution again, for if I followed his footsteps the different tribes through which we have to pass would naturally believe me to be of the same clan. Indeed knowing what my precursors had done, I should not feel very respectable to myself. I therefore intend going up the river Leeambye to the point at which we turned in August and then ascend the

Riding oxen to be used

Leeba to the people called Balonda and proceed westward by land. The chief has lent me his own canoe and as I was unable to take a horse to the Borotse country on account of the tsetse at this season biting by night as well as by day Sekeletu placed four riding oxen at my service, These are now in that country so I hope to get on. I go in the canoe from this down to Chobe to its confluence, then up the Leeambye and Leeba till we reach the falls reported to exist on that river. The canoe will be sent back and we must do the best we can beyond. I leave in company with Borotse people alone. the people we brought from Kuruman have been rendered useless by fever, so I send them back. I am again through God's mercy and kindness quite recovered from the effects of that disease. I think I am getting rid of intermittent too, and if spared will impart some knowledge of Christ to many who never before heard his blessed name There are many and very large tribes in the direction in which we go. All are sitting in darkness and the shadow of death. I hope God will in mercy permit me to establish the gospel somewhere in this region, and that I may live to see the double influence of the spirit of commerce and Christianity employed to stay the bitter fountain of African misery

In the sketch enclosed in my last I neglected to mention that the ridges noted therein only shew the commencement of lands not usually inundated There are very large tracts of country beyond these which are annually flooded either wholly or partially. The Leeambye is not the only source of the waters of inundation The reports of intelligent natives lead me to believe that the Bashukulompo or Maninché river—The Loeti—the Kabompo The Makoma and Leeambye, are all branches, (of one river), leaving and returning to the parent stream in a remarkably level country . . .

My letter of September contained three enclosures for Mrs Livingston. It contained full information respecting the visit to the Barotse. This opportunity of transmitting letters was unexpected but though I had written fully before, I thought it

Water waist deep

well to let you know of the alteration of my plans, and that I am on the point of starting

I am

Affectionately Yours

DAVID LIVINGSTON

P.S. As Sesheké is only about 7 days on foot from the Maninché and the falls of Mosisatunya may be avoided by sailing down that river into the Zambesi. This may be a good path down to the East Coast. I mention this in case of my being cut off.

D. L.

LETTER 54

To REVD. W. THOMPSON, *Cape Town*

Calimba, 14th May, 1854.

MY DEAR SIR,

I am not far from Loanda and as I shall have very little time in writing there because my purse is light and followers numerous and hungry, I give you a few particulars now. We have had a most tedious journey from the land of the Leeambye. We went up the Leeba 40 or 50 miles, then left the canoes and went forward on ox back to the first Chief of the Balonda called Kabompo or Shinté. He highly approved our object in opening up a way for commerce into his country and showed his sincerity by giving us guides and sending orders to all his people on the route to supply us with food. This kindness hindered our progress for every village must have time to prepare a meal, &c, for us, but the rains hindered us much more.

Never did I endure such drenchings, and all the streams being swollen we had to ford many, the water flowing on the rustic bridges waist deep. Others we crossed by sticking to the oxen the best we could, and a few we made a regular swim of. My Barotse, for with them alone I travelled, did not know I could swim, and the first broad stream we came to excited their fears on my account. 'Now hold on fast by the tail' Don't let go', I intended to follow the injunctions, but tail and all went so deep I thought it better to strike out alone for the bank, and

A Mahommetan Paradise

just as I reached it I was greatly gratified to see a universal rush had been made for my rescue. Their clothes were all floating down the stream, and two of them reached me breathless with the exertion they had made. If we could march I got on very well. I don't care much for fatigue, but when compelled to stand still by pouring rains then fever laid hold with his strong fangs on my inner man. And lying in a little gipsy tent with everything damp or wet, was sore against the grain. Frequent and most severe attacks of intermittent, made me miserably weak, but I never lay by for that, and we managed to make occasional progress through a population and country to which I can offer you no comparison in the South. We came to a village every few miles, sometimes passed 10 in a day. These were civil, how could they be otherwise, the fellows were living in a Mahommetan Paradise. We often entered a village and when sitting on ox back could only see the tops of the huts in a wilderness of weeds. By-and-bye the villagers emerged from their lairs, men and women each smoking a long pipe and followed by crowds of children. Very little exertion is required to procure the staff of life which in these parts is the Manioc. A part of the forest is cleared of brushwood and fires made round the larger trees leave them standing dead. Cuttings of the Manioc are inserted in the ground and the earth drawn up around them. Maize beans, earth nuts, &c, are planted between, and here we have a supply of food for years. The climate is so good they are either planting or reaping the whole year round. All the different grains, roots, &c, may be seen at one time in every stage of growth. Indeed the country generally is fertile in the extreme. And very beautiful. It is flat but lies in ridges or waves, the ridge of each wave is covered with dense dark forest, and the trough a pleasant valley containing either a bog or stream in its centre. The Boerish Eden Magaliesberg will bear no comparison to this land for fertility and beauty. The forest trees shoot up to an enormous height as straight as arrows, and all being covered with white moss shew the humidity of the climate would require no irrigation for

Waters of Lobale

English wheat. Through some of these forests we could scarcely move on ox back. Swinging, climbing plants of from an inch to 3 or 4 in diameter abound, and when drizzling rain makes the darkness of the forest darker we were often caught (*more Absalom*) The ox when you attempt to stop him rushes on the faster and down comes the rider on the crown of his head. Mine a most perverse beast, often went out of the way or narrow winding path on purpose and always tried to administer an effective kick to show how he would act if he had the upper hand. The country to the West of that which we travelled through is called Lobale, and was impassable, the water standing on its plains waist deep. We had sometimes to make a divergence from our path in order to avoid such, and two or three times passed over plains 12 or 15 miles broad about 6 inches deep. Other plains presented the appearance of large rivers flowing fast towards the rivers, and must be the sources of the annual inundations of the Barotse, &c. The water is always clear because the rains fall on a dense mat of grass only. The Southern part of the Lobale is well peopled, but the plains being at other than the rainy season destitute of streams have but a small population. The East is all densely populated and passes by the name Balonda. They are idolaters, near every village an Idol is seen, a block of wood with a rough human head carved on it, or a lion made of clay and two shells for eyes standing in a little shed. The people when unsuccessful in any enterprise, or sick, beat a drum before them all night, and they are otherwise very superstitious. They would not eat with us, nor in our sight, though they took meat from us and ate it at home. When I saw their numbers and thought of the vast multitudes there are in this land all living without God and without hope I often sat down with feelings of despair. When will they be supplied with the Gospel of Christ?

As we approached the Portuguese settlements the people became worse and worse and at last instead of gifts of food we were offered knocks on the head. The Chiboque, for instance, are most outrageous blackguards. We came to them as quiet

Chiboque fierceness

as Quakers, and were spending Sunday on Peace Society principles, when a whole tribe surrounded us fully armed with guns, arrows, spears, and short swords. They were all vociferating and brandishing their weapons simultaneously. I sat down and asked the chief to do the same and then demanding silence requested to know what was the matter. Our crime consisted in one of our men, when spitting, allowing a small drop of the saliva to fall on one of them. I replied if the chief could seriously say such was a crime I was willing to pay a fine. (On such frivolous pretexts we had often to pay enormous fines). He accepted one, but his warriors rejected it and demanded one thing after another until by demanding one of our number to be sold as a slave, we saw their intention was regular plunder, and armed ourselves for the worst. They feared my arms alone, indeed we were as a company unprepared for fighting, but armed as we were, not a man of chief or counsellors would have escaped the first onset. We determined to let them shed the first drop of blood and sat looking at them in all their heathenish shouting. This resolute bearing made them more reasonable, so they accepted an ox and gave us two or three pounds of the flesh to shew they were of a generous disposition after all. We were often so treated, and at last no passage allowed past a town or village without paying for it. I paid away nearly all I had. Oxen for provisions, and riding clothes, razors, spoons, &c. Then we all got angry, chafed in mind, and hungry, and replied angrily to their demands. Sometimes I was furious and would have fought, but my companions were more pacific stripping themselves of their ornaments and paying for passage. At other times they were on the bloody key and I was quakerish and we rose up by night and passed our enemies expecting an assault in every thicket and glen we came to. And after all I thank God sincerely in that he prevented us from shedding human blood.

When we reached the Quango I had made up my mind to part with my bedding for a passage but we were prevented by a small tribe from approaching the ferry. I could not pay both

Help from Portuguese Sergeant

tribe and ferry with what I had remaining, and there they laughed at us with their teeth filed to a point and hair elaborately plaited and ornamented. 'You must just go back the way you came,' 'if you cannot pay us you will see what we can do,' &c. Ah! you Caffres have been spoiled by missionaries I suppose. The Read's have been among you exciting you to rebellion, that they have. Here a young Portuguese Sergeant appeared and enabled us to get over the Quango without more trouble. Our difficulties were ended. All we have met in the Portuguese territory have been civil and Sergt. Cypriano de Abreu began the hospitality which we have everywhere received from the Portuguese. We arrived at Cassange, naked and famished, there they clothed us and fed us. May God reward them! At Ambaca I found the commandant an enlightened friend of Africa. One who has written, spoken, and suffered in her behalf, and his sentiments are in unison with those of many in the upper ranks in Portugal. I have on the whole been agreeably disappointed in the Portuguese. They are extremely polite and hospitable, and all lament the state of supineness into which their nation has sunk.

I have since found out he is so only in profession, one cannot rely on the most plausible speeches of even Governors. They are excessively corrupt. D.L.

Loanda, 14th August.

I reached this city on the 31st of May[1] and was glad to tumble into bed as soon as I arrived, knocked up and no mistake, by fever and Diarrhoea. The first house I called at was that of Edmund Gabriel Esqr. Her Majesty's Commissioner for the suppression of the slave trade, and a most disinterested generous friend he has proved himself to be. He is the only Englishman in this city, and it contains a population of 11,000 souls. I recovered partially, then had a relapse and nearly marched off from the land of the living. I have now however,

[1] This completed the first great journey of Livingstone: Linyanti to Loanda, 1,500 miles in six months. See Campbell, chap. vii.

Edmund Gabriel a good friend

by God's mercy, got round again, and will start on my return on the 20th currt. The officers of our cruizers have been very kind, and the Portuguese authorities too. . . . There are no Bibles here. The prosperity of the city depended on the slave trade, and as that is virtually suppressed they have no hope of gaining filthy lucre except by the revolution of the English or such other blessing as the devil might bestow. The province is fruitful in the extreme and of rare beauty. Two crops of all sorts of fruits per year; coffee, the best I ever tasted, grows and yields in 3 years if they would only stick the plants in the soil; sugar, pine apples, everything in fact, but the Portuguese actually buy all their flour and bread from the Yankees instead of growing wheat themselves. The coffee trees were chiefly planted by the old missionaries,[1] and their churches are all in ruins. But most of the Portuguese of mixed blood can both read and write. They teach each other. How I long for a few Bibles but it is questionable whether I shall return this way. I intend going down the Zambesi to Quilimane rather than this way. So many rivers and thickets prevent me attempting this way with the waggon. They have no roads here and to-morrow is a grand festival in commemoration of having driven the Dutch out of the country. The Dutch began to make a canal to lead water to the city. It has never been completed and all drinkable water has to be carried from the Bengo 8 or 9 miles distant. The Harbour, once a splendid one, is now filling up. Indeed ships cannot now anchor within a mile of the city, and all look on and take the world easy. The trade is in the hands of the Yankees; no English house has established itself. This arose from Loanda getting a bad name some years ago.

George I left at the town of Sekeletu. I wished him to leave as soon as possible after I left. He leans on me. This won't do at all. The Portuguese give ten times as much for ivory as English traders. Kind salutations to your sister and all the family. I have not got a single line from anyone though I

[1] The Jesuits, who were expelled from all Portuguese territory in 1759 by the Portuguese Government.

Coffee growing

wrote you all by a trader called Chapman who was accompanied by one Thompson from Natal.

Ever affectionately yours,
DAVID LIVINGSTON.

LETTER 55
(*Original at Scottish National Memorial, Blantyre*)
To REV. CHARLES LIVINGSTON   (*Then in America.*)

Golungo Alto—
8th Novr. 1854.

MY DEAR CHARLES,

Its a weary time since I heard from any of my former correspondents, and I have but slender hopes of seeing any epistle from you while I am in Western Africa. The ship of the Commodore called the 'Scourge' has gone up to Fernando-Po for the mails. She is much beyond her time and we cannot guess the cause of her detention. But when she comes, my last hopes of hearing from friends will have to expire. I go away into the region where there are no mails to cheer the weary wanderer.

I would have been further away before this, but bad health and good hope kept me a month longer than was absolutely necessary at Loanda. Then when I came up into the Coffee Country, as I had written some papers in a newspaper recommending agriculture instead of slave trading, it was expected I would show some interest in the efforts of a few who are making laudable efforts to establish themselves as coffee growers. The trees are ready planted for them, and all that the best coffee in the world requires is to have the ground partially cleared and the fruit dried and sorted. They showed extraordinary kindness and I had to refuse gifts of coffee, rice etc. I encouraged them to persevere, and among other things I learned that the views of your Professor of Political Economy are nonsense. I shall return to this subject again. In the meantime, I may relate that after spending some three or four days as above I came back to this, the residence of the chief of the District called Golungo Alto, and when on the point of starting

Nurse to a slave owner

he was seized with one of the deadly fevers of this land. I of course could not leave one who had showed me a great deal of kindness when bending under disease. I entered his dwelling on my way down to Loanda. I have been treating him for eight days past. His head became affected, and as he has none but slaves about him, I have to see everything done by night and by day. Pity the poor mortal who falls sick among his slaves. This is a most kind and considerate master, yet he says to me 'if you had not been here I think they would have knocked me on the head'. They run riot among the eatables. As I do not venture to scold in Portuguese, I can only be amused in silence at the affection developed by the domestic institution. They kill the goats and fowls, and then tell me with faces of the most innocent wonderment 'the thing is dead'. When I tell them to throw them away there follows only a comfortable roasting. When the sweetmeats are devoured then one comes and tells me with a countenance of horror 'these slaves are robbing master of everything' and this very one I have come accidentally upon in the act of eating Pine Apples rolled in a large plate of sugar. I can scarcely get the washer woman to put my clothes in order, although I pay her for it. Let who will go for slavery. I vote for the freeman. I have seen a good deal of it now, and from the unstudied words and actions of respectable masters, I very much doubt if there is the least truth in the averment that any masters treat their slaves with kindness. Living in the practice of habitual injustice to them, it is extremely questionable whether the better sort even can claim by a few driblets of civility the appellation of kind masters. It is fortunate that this country contains but few slaves in comparison with free men. In some districts of the Province, the statistics drawn up by those who have no apparent motive for mis-stating the facts show the proportion of slaves in the entire population is 6·79 per cent.

But let us look at the subject of armed force putting down the slave trade. The view entertained by your Professor that such means would only have the effect of increasing the horrors of

Angola slavery

the treatment of those who would be sent notwithstanding, to supply the demand. That no means would be effective for the suppression of this species of commerce, so long as the profits were so large. And then if I recollect rightly in true Yankee style he jerked himself a little beyond the full length of his tether by the windy climax that Great Britain would have consulted the interests of the slaves had she instead of cruizers, fitted out convenient, well ventilated, well found ships to convey the negroes to the Brazils. Bating the wind-bag tacked on to the tail of them, I considered his sentiments just, and would have been pleased had our squadron been withdrawn. But since I came into the country I found that the oft repeated tales of the increased horrors and increased numbers are nothing else than concoction of the slave traders feeling the pressure from without. Angola sent some thousands of slaves annually down to the coast for exportation. The trade was carried on thus—A trader went to the interior to purchase wax, ivory etc., and slaves, and he always purchased as many as would carry his merchandise down to the coast. He was sure of a market. Indeed in 1837 or just before the Treaty for slave trade suppression with Portugal came into operation Mr. Gabriel counted 39 ships in Loanda Harbour all waiting for cargoes of slaves. At present no ship dare appear on the coast with slave fittings except to make a dash into some one or two harbours, load hastily by night and put to sea next morning. But to return to the slaves of the time when there were no British cruizers on the coast, all that came down were sold and exported, and as they cannot now export them neither can they buy them, and therefore a new system of carrying merchandise became necessary. The new system is called 'Carregadores' or carriers, and the native chiefs living under the Portuguese are obliged to furnish these carriers to do the work formerly done by slaves going to be exported. This district supplies 400 monthly, and other districts in proportion. I have met a thousand of them in one day either going or returning and every man of them was a proof of the effectiveness of the English cruizers in

Effects of British interventions

repressing the slave trade, for up to the time when the ships were placed on the coast all this work of carrying was performed by those who had no hope of return.

Again before the English squadron began its operations the prices of the good young slaves throughout the country near the coast or say within 200 miles of the coast line varied from 70 to 80 dollars per head (as they say) Now the very best may be had for from 10 to 20. If the reason is asked it invariably is 'because we cannot now export them'. 'But' say some slave trade abettors 'if they can only get one cargo in four safe into the transatlantic ports they realise handsome profits.' I shall give you my reasons for doubting this. At present the thing seems to cut two ways. Slaves are very cheap now in Angola and that is clearly the intervention of the armed force. They are said to be dear in proportion in Cuba and Brazil. As soon as a trader gets his ten dollars per head, cargo clear off the African coast, does he value them at that or at the 150 or 200 dollars he expects to get in Cuba. Clearly, to my mind his live stock has become very precious in the beast's own estimation, and unless some exception . . . can be proved as existing in his case the most powerful motive he knows comes into play to make him lessen the horrors of 'the middle passage'. Though he regards them as beasts, it is well known all over the world that the most brutal being alive will be more likely to treat well a horse worth £200 than if it were worth £10 only.

My reasons for doubting the plea of handsome profits being realised by the few slave traders who manage to get clear off with an occasional cargo, are the following. I have made many enquiries and have not been able to discover more than two or three who have hold of riches got in the slave trade. But again and again have individuals been pointed out to me as having been once very rich and having lost their all in it. But setting aside particular cases, let us look at the capital of Angola, the city of Loanda. It may be said to be in ruins and if the cause of the decay be enquired into, it is the inability to carry on the slave trade as in, what they term, the Palmy days of the city.

Jesuit introductions

They have an expressive way of indicating the pressure from without. We refrain say they 'pala forca da necessidade' (by the power of necessity) The public gardens on the walls of which stood the inscription written with all the successful slave holders pride, 'Let this serve as an example to posterity', are now in ruins and so unrecognizable a gentleman of the Navy asked me when near it 'where are the gardens spoken of in the accounts of Loanda?'. Many now turn their attention to agriculture who if the tales of antisquadronites were true would much prefer the handsome profits of every fourth voyage. . . .

I earnestly pray I may be permitted to do something for the spread of the knowledge of Christ. Physically it is one of the finest countries in the world, but one would not think so at the coast. In here the luxuriance of the vegetation is wonderful and beautiful. The Missionaries introduced many fine fruit trees from South America. One called Fruita da londa is like cream in taste. A wild one called Masubiri has a large fruit and resembles in appearance the bread fruit. I wish I could send you seeds. Eden's fruits have all been allowed to degenerate except the vine. In the millenium I suppose they will be recultivated and as much improved as the apple is above the crab.

My love to your spouse and sma' family. I shall leave this as soon as my patient is better. I have found an invaluable friend in Loanda, West coast of Africa, in Her Majesty's Commissioner Edmund Gabriel Esq. Any letter sent to him will be forwarded to England by him if I am there. I have written John by same mail. A Yankee vessel will take both to the States.

D. LIVINGSTON

LETTER 56

To REV. DR. TIDMAN

Cassange, Angola, West Africa
Jany 14th 1855.

DEAR SIR

As soon as I was sufficiently recovered from the severe indisposition which kept me prostrate for a long time after my

Balonda insecurity

arrival at Loanda, I wrote you a full account of the journey concerning which you have probably received information from other sources. I regretted you had not received the earliest intelligence directly from my own hand and that regret was increased on learning a few days ago at Pungo Andongo that all my letters and maps had been lost in the wreck of the 'Forerunner' off Madeira.

Having left the River Zambesi or Leeambye in Lat. $14°. 11'$ South and Long. $23°. 40'$ East we ascended the Leeba until we had the country of Lobale on our left, and Londa on our right. We then left the canoes and travelled N.N.W. on oxback till we reached the latitude of this place viz. $9° 37'$. Thence proceeding westwards we at last reached Loanda.

In passing through a part of Londa we found the people exceedingly kind and generally anxious that we should succeed in opening up a new road to the Coast. They belong to the negro race and are more superstitious than any of the Southern Tribes. . . . The Balonda invariably go armed with short broadswords, large bows and arrows and guns, and seem to possess but little sense of security in their own country. Cases of kidnapping of children occurred while we were passing and these with persons who flee from one Chieftain to another are generally sold to half-blood Portuguese who visit the country as slave dealers. The country appeared to contain a large population and it abounds in the necessaries of life. The soil is fertile and the climate admits of the crops appearing in all the different stages all the year round. The time of our visit was unfortunately the season of the heavy rains which appear to follow the course of the sun in his progress North, our experiences can scarcely be considered a fair criterion of what may occur during the rest of the year. Perpetual drenchings—a hot sun, (the temperature never under $84°$ in the shade) quickly drying our clothing, and frequently sleeping in damp beds, prevented me forming a reliable idea of the salubrity of the climate. My companions, all native Zambesians had nearly as much sickness as myself—intermittent fever being the com-

The joy of a bed

plaint from which we all suffered most. The country however, is elevated, and abounding in flowing streams is moreover of great fertility and beauty. The time spent in the way was also longer than may be required at other seasons, because we had to halt early in the afternoons in order to allow the men to build little huts for shelter during the night. The dense tangled forests however presented an insurmountable obstacle to travelling in waggons, but the plains on our West may not be similarly obstructed.

When we came into the vicinity of the Portuguese settlements, the tribes treated us rather scurvily—some levied heavy fines on the most frivolous pretences—others demanded payment for leave to pass at all. I parted with everything I could dispense with, and my men gave all their ornaments and most of their clothes either for food, fines, or ferries. But when we explained that we had nothing we could part with besides, it did not in the least appease the violence of the mobs which surrounded us. We must pay either a man, an ox, or a gun, and were looked upon as interlopers wishing to cheat them out of their dues. At last on reaching the River Quango by the generous assistance of a young Portuguese sergeant of militia we entered the territory of Portugal and received the kindest treatment from all classes all the way to Loanda.

In that city I arrived nearly knocked up and suffering from fever and dysentery. Edmund Gabriel Esq. Her Majesty's Commissioner for the suppression of the slave trade and the only Englishman I know in the city, most generously received me and my 27 companions into his house. I shall never forget the delicious pleasure of tumbling into his bed after sleeping six months on the ground, nor the unwearied attention and kindness through a long sickness which Mr G. invariably shewed. May God reward him. My companions were struck with awe at the sight of a city and more especially when taken on board H.M. Ships of war. The kindness of the officers of the cruizers removed the last vestige of fear from their minds, for finding them to be all my countrymen they saw the fallacy of the

Traffic with Angola?

declarations of the negroes of every village we came to west of Cassange, 'that the white man was taking them to the sea, and would sell them all to be taken on board ship, fattened and eaten'. They were afterwards engaged in discharging coals from a ship for wages, and will marvel till the end of their lives at the prodigious quantity of 'stones that burn' one ship could contain. They previously imagined their own little canoes on the Zambesi the best vessels, and themselves the most expert sailors in the world.

His Excellency the (R.C.) Bishop of Angola, then the Acting Governor of the Province received my companions with great kindness and assured them of his protection and friendship, as well as desire to promote commercial intercourse with the country of Sekeletu. He also sent a present of a horse and handsome dress for that Chief, and shewed very great attention to myself in my sickness. The merchants too, of Loanda took the opportunity of our return to send presents to Sekeletu and as they give much more for the produce of his country than can be, or is done by merchants from the Cape Colony, it is to be hoped that intercourse with either Cassange or Loanda will promote the civilization of the Interior.

I return, because I feel that the work to which I set myself is only half accomplished.[1] The way out to the Eastern Coast may be less difficult that I have found that to the West. If I succeed we shall at least have a choice. I intend, God helping me, to go down the Zambesi or Leeambye to Quilimane. I may, in order to avoid the Falls of Mosioatunya and the rapid and rocky river above that part—go across from Sesheke to the Maninche-Loenge or river of the Bashukulompo and then descend it to the Zambesi. If I cannot succeed I shall return to Loanda, and thence embark for England. I expected letters at Loanda and feel much disappointed at receiving none.

---

[1] He had not yet determined the new centre of work he was seeking nor the best road to it, but another reason also moved him: there were his twenty-seven men to take back to Sekeletu. Probably they could not cope with the difficulties of the return journey without him.

Presents for Makololo

I asked my friends to write to that place, and now suppose they believed I should never reach it. I shall feel obliged if you send a letter to Quilimane. I know not whether I shall reach it. I mean to try. Enclosed in this is a letter for my family.

My companions, decidedly the best I ever travelled with, were given by Sekeletu for my assistance without any idea of remuneration. As wages are a most effectual means of breaking up the feudal system and that form of domestic slavery which prevails throughout Africa, I resolved to give each of them a small payment in goods. For this purpose I drew on you for £50. by a bill in favour of Mr Gabriel dated 19th June 1854. It was sent to his Agents—Messrs Woodhead & Co.—No 1 James St. London. Finding subsequently the balance of that sum insufficient for the supply of goods necessary for the return journey, viz. to purchase food, reward our friends who shewed kindness and conciliate our enemies who verily were 'no better than they should be', I afterwards drew £25 in the same way. The Bill was dated 16th Aug. 1854. This second bill may have gone down in the 'Forerunner'. I hope the above may meet your approbation. . . .

I visited several of the 'extinct convents' or as we should say, deserted missionary stations. The Churches are standing in some instances, and would require but little to put them into good repair. South American fruit trees grow in the neat gardens which the missionaries laid out. The bedsteads stand in the dormitories as they left them, and the big chests in which the brethren stowed their grub, but there were no books nor any inscriptions on the graves which would enable one to learn something of the dust which sleeps beneath. But turning to the people we soon recognize their memorials in the great numbers who can both read and write. There are very few of the people of Ambaca who cannot use the pen and the sight is not uncommon in that district of a black man sitting in the evening with a fire stick in one hand and a pen in the other, writing in a beautiful hand a petition to a commandant. I looked upon

A black canon

these relicts of former times with peculiar interest, because if the labours of the Jesuit missionaries who were expelled by the Marquis of Pombal have so much permanence, surely those of Protestants who leave the living word behind them, will be no less abiding. I was informed by a Canon of the church whom I lately met in Pungo Andongo, and who had recently returned from a visit to Portugal as Conductor of the Prince of Congo—that in the Congoese territory there are no fewer than twelve churches and not a single priest. This gentleman was a wooly headed black—yet a dignitary of the Church, universally respected for his virtues and has had an order conferred on him by the King of Portugal. We English feel very complacent with ourselves when we compare our way of treating people of colour with that of the Americans, but the Portuguese would stare as much as I did to see (as in the case of Botha) a judge treating with levity a case of life and death, and a brandy bottle on the bench beside him in full view of the Court.

The insalubrity of the country is the cause why there are so few priests in Angola. Intermittent fever is excessively prevalent and it usually produces enlargement of the spleen which sooner or later ends fatally.

Among the benefits conferred on the country by the missionaries may be mentioned Coffee. A few Mocha seeds were planted and it has now extended itself over the whole country. The Portuguese are now in a state of transition from illicit commerce to licit commerce, the former being effectually repressed by our cruizers—they turn enthusiastically to coffee plantations, which were daily discovered in the forests, and only require to be cleaned to yield as good quality of fruit as can be found in the world. A few months ago it was discovered near Cassange, 300 miles inland. I cannot send you a map, and this is not so full an account as I wished to send

I am

Affectionately yours

DAVID LIVINGSTON.

Three years without rews

LETTER 57

To REV. W. THOMPSON, *Cape Town*

Linyanti, 13th Sept: 1855.

MY DEAR MR. THOMPSON

We have had an unexpected opportunity of sending letters back to Angola but the time offered has been so short I have sent a few notes only. This will follow the Arab who left this morning, and I hope will reach you some time or other and let you know I am not unmindful of my friends though separated from them by a precious big bump of this which the philosophers call 'our little planet'! I have scarcely had time to peruse my letters which we found had lain on an island in the Leeambye close to Falls of Mosioatunya a whole year. Such a rush of thoughts and trembling sensations when I opened letters from my family you may imagine if you can, taking it into consideration that I have been without information for nearly three years. Thank God I had no reason to sorrow. I requested my friends to write to Loanda, but though detained there for many months by sickness I never got a line, and I suppose their respectful silence may be translated into a rebuke for imagining that I should ever reach that part. 'You think more highly of yourself than you ought to think.' Well! I must try and be thankful even for that.

I commence the descent of the river for Quilimaine at the beginning of October. The path we have already opened up has many advantages. The Portuguese post comes 3 times a month to Cassange 300 miles inland, and goods are considerably cheaper than in the Cape Colony. I mean, such as missionaries require, coffee, tea, sugar, clothes, &c. Labour is extremely cheap in Angola, and anything manufactured by the natives is got for a trifle. I bought a pair of Wellington boots at Pungo Andongo more than 100 miles from the sea, for five shillings and eightpence English money, and that was exactly the price given to natives by a merchant of the place for one pound of ivory. This is more than the slimmest Boer would get in Cape Town. The difference in prices was explained

Relations of black and white in Angola

by the Americans giving larger prices than the English. They have all the Loanda trade in their hands. The advantage to the natives is, out of sight, greater than in the Colony. Take Cassange and any spot 300 miles inland from the Southern coasts of S. Africa, a native will get from five to seven times more in the North than in the South for his ivory. The trade of the Portuguese might have been pushed much farther, but as I saw the other day in a history of Angola, a law was made prohibiting white traders from going into the interior because in almost every case in which war was necessary to punish the natives for the murder of white men investigation shewed that the white and not the black man was the aggressor. Black men 'naõ calçada' might be sent with goods but no white may go himself under a severe penalty. And this law continued in force during successive governments. I think it is still in force for when I was coming through Cassange lately the Commandant sent an order to all the traders (about 40) along the River Quango and other places in the vicinity, to return to the village, and on their refusal the matter was remitted to the Governor of Loanda. There is no restriction on trade except what is implied in the above. It goes on briskly from both coasts, Arabs and Portuguese are met with everywhere. The latter are like our Griquas, namely, half blood, and it is curious they have been found in the course of a few generations, to become black again. The Portuguese marry black women, there being very few white ladies in the country, and never disown their children. . . . The black races in the vicinity of the Portuguese settlements are immeasurably worse than the Southern Tribes among which I have had experience. From the Casai to the Orange River I should say to every traveller or trader, 'Behave like a gentleman and you will be treated as such; play the monkey, be impudent, and try to cheat and you will get "monkey's allowance".' the greater wickedness of the tribes North of the Casai admits of easy explanation, but you must be content with my assertion only, for the present. When I can find time I shall let you into it. Rest assured it has not been

Wagon left at Linyanti

caused by the ruffian zendelings of the Independent's Society. I was the first missionary they ever saw, and we were attacked four times by them. Plunder was their object, once we beat them off by simply sitting and looking at them after telling them they must strike the first blow. They were well supplied with guns and sometimes presented them at us. Another tribe began by plundering the goods carried by those of our party in the rear, firing and shouting ensued when we went back to them, and the chief being busy leading unexpectedly found a revolver within a foot of his stomach, and hostilities were quickly brought to a close without any one being hurt on either side. On several other occasions we were considerably bothered and it appeared as if we must fire, but in addition to a strong aversion to shedding human blood I had the school-boy feeling of 'strike your match' wonderfully strong. . . . At present I firmly believe that we might go back without a tithe of the molestation we experienced, and two or three harmless visits would render the path as safe as a colonial one. It is not likely I shall ever go South again except by sea. My waggon stands as safe here as it would do on Mr. Hoffmeyer's garden. Nothing was touched during our two years absence. It is simply useless except as a house. Canoes are the means of conveyance. The Leeambye and Chobe rose unusually high this year and people went in canoes in nearly a straight line from Linyanti and Sesheke—about 130 miles. I don't know where we shall settle except that it must be to the North of this. The country is finer there. We never carried water but passed two or three good streams each day all the way to Loanda. The natives are all armed with guns and swords, and they have finished the game. The only fault of the new path is it admits of conveyance by human labour alone. The forests and boggy rivers present insurmountable obstacles to waggons. There is another path to the East coast which crosses at a certain point a Lake (Tanganyenka) 3 days broad. From the information I possess it would be easier to go that than the way down the Zambesi, but like the path we have already opened it does not admit of waggons. Clearly then, the path of duty is, that I leave the discovery of another Lake to somebody else, and try to get water carriage to the coast by going down the Leeambye. . . .

My companions, all Zambesians, behaved remarkably well. The Governor sent a present of a general's dress finely ornamented with gold lace, a sash, cocked hat and sword—(A horse which died) and the merchants, two bales of different kinds of cloth—beads, &c, &c, and two donkies: they are not affected by the bite of tsetse. . . . The Arabs pray in the mornings. They say Jesus was a very good prophet but Mahomet was far greater and better. They strike up great friendships with me whenever we meet, calling me father, &c., and telling the people how much we hate the slave trade in which they are engaged. I am very well pleased to see you have lifted up your voice against certain iniquities, though I have not yet read the pamphlets. Onward my man. There are lots of good men and true in the Colony who sympathize with what is righteous and just. It is unfortunate that they have been often spoken of as one and the same with the worst portion of the Transvaal body. The sentiments and conduct are as different as those of the English settlers in Australia are to the Ticket-of-leave gentry. With kind salutations to Captain Holmes and your family,

I am very affectionately yours,
DAVID LIVINGSTON.

LETTER 58

To REV. W. THOMPSON

Linyanti, 27th September, 1855.

MY DEAR MR. THOMPSON,

I have just learned that my Arabian post-office man is detained at Sesheke by the sickness of one of his party so I am glad of the opportunity to write a little appendix to that hurried note of the 13th. I particularly wish to express my sympathy in the bereavement you have been called on to suffer in the departure of your most excellent father-in-law.[1]

[1] Rev. Ralph Wardlaw, D.D., of Glasgow.

Trading v. plunder

I hear of it only now, and as I have always, since my attendance on his theological lectures and ministry, regarded him with very great affection, I think of his removal with unfeigned sorrow. May God grant us grace to follow in his footsteps. Unquestionably he served God in his day and generation with rare abilities and unswerving devotion through good and through bad report. When such are removed we feel somewhat nearer to the grave. There seems to be nothing now between it and us. May we live to Christ and for the prosperity of His great cause and receive the welcome 'Well done' as we have every reason to believe our much lamented friend has. I shall always revere his memory.

I believe I did not refer very pointedly to what may be called missionary prospects in this region. And the reason is I feel perplexed on one point, viz, the insalubrity of the climate. It is no obstacle to myself personally. I think no London Society's 'zendeling' worth his salt would bolt at that. . . . And my better half would go as readily as any one. But I am not clear on exposing my little ones without their own intelligent self-dedication. As far as opportunity goes there is no lack. There are tribes and villages without number to the North and East of this, and all would be proud of the presence of a white man. I know of no hindrance to missionary operations in any part of the country North of the Zambesi and towards the centre of the Continent. And every day we hear of commerce extending its ramifications in all directions. Only think of the way this letter goes. By an Arab from Zanzibar who takes charge of a party of Makololo with ivory for Loanda. When they return my late companions will be ready to start again. So one relay will always be abroad on business. Before my trip the Makololo never visited another tribe except to plunder. They have not given this trade up yet, for two forays were made during my absence. . . . But the remedy for that and every evil is being applied. The blessed Word of the Living God has been preached, though in much weakness; and the prayers of God's people are ascending as incense before the throne of the Hope of Israel.

Goodwill of the Bakwains

The time is coming, the set time, when all nations shall call Him blessed.

I have been guilty of some innocent wonderment in seeing it stated in terms lugubrious enough that the Bakwains, Bakhatla and Bahurutse, &c, were not a whit better for all our labours, nay much worse. I followed the rule invariably of making no enquiries respecting the labours or conduct of other missionaries among natives, and therefore can say nothing about Bahurutse or Bakhatla. But about the Bakwains the verdict would I most sincerely think, require reconsideration. During the whole of our sojourn there we strove so to conduct ourselves as that there should be no cause of offence except concerning the law of our God. I feel humbly and heartily thankful to our Heavenly Father for enabling us to effect this. This is a point of vital importance in estimating what has been done among a people. So when we left we had not one single enemy in the whole Tribe, and if it were necessary for me to seek a 'character' I would confidently refer to the Bakwains for it. And even when the waggon was inspanned on our departure for Sebituane's country Sechele and his principal men tried to persuade me to remove to the (afterwards) scene of the massacre of his people; offering to build a house and church free of expense. I need not refer to my reasons for refusing (I am perfectly satisfied as to their validity) except that the principal one was determined hostility to the requirements of the Gospel, unmixed with any hostility to ourselves. Some may think this hostility to the Gospel evidence of deterioration from their state of heathenism. I believe it to be a most important step in advance from that state, for though they refuse to bow in humility to the Divine law, the truths they have imbibed exert a most salutary influence on their morals. (Sechele asked the Boers on commando not to fight on Sunday.) . . . I know this to be a fact, a plain palpable fact, and if any one doubts it, as he cannot compare what the Bakwains were with what they are, let a comparison be made between the Makololo and Bakwains. Why in coming from Makololo and meeting with

Alleged supply of 'cannon'

them and some of the people near Kuruman, who still hate the Gospel as much as the Bakwains, I used to feel I had entered civilized life. I don't wonder at it. The Word of the Living God has been brought in contact with their hearts and minds. This Word has life and power. Few human hearts can withstand its force, and no hatred, however deep, can quench its power. I bless God from the bottom of my heart for allowing me to sow the good seed among the Bakwains. Their present posture is a terrible one if they continue so to the end, but though they do so, it is God's will the offer should be made, though thousands both white and black, make a bad use of it. You will probably live longer than I shall. Remember seed was sown among the people of Sechele.

I thank you for publishing the 'Pot' defence.[1] I have not seen the remarks of Scholz, or whoever it was that wrote in a defamatory way against me. . . . I think it is not usual for Editors of newspapers to publish defamatory remarks against persons whom they know cannot, for months, or as in my case, years, have an opportunity of answering them. They would not in England publish the like against officers in an Arctic expedition. Would they? But you have got a new constitution now and Mr. Buchanan has crept under the wing of a likelier hen. Requiescat in pace!

I have got only one scrap from you but it accompanied the celestial map and pamphlets. Go on and fear nothing my friend. O! oh! what a shame to spring on the poor bishop, the first bishop and only bishop, and box his ears so unmercifully.

Believe me very affectionately yours,
DAVID LIVINGSTONE.

I get no letters from my wife, cannot account for it. Hope she has not come to the Cape. But you will take care of her no doubt.

---

[1] Livingstone wrote a letter showing how the loan of a cooking-pot to Sechele was magnified into the supplying of a cannon. He sent it to Thompson, who caused it to be published in the *Cape Town Mail* of April 26, 1853.

Survey of the region

May I beg you to give the Directors notice of my welfare at this date. I cannot write them now.

Excuse this nasty Yankee paper I have nought else.

LETTER 59

To THE REV. DR. TIDMAN

Linyanti on the River Chobe,
12th October 1855.

DEAR SIR,

The excessive heat and dust which prevail previous to the commencement of the rainy season, have prevented my departure from the town of Sekeletu, as I intended at the beginning of this month, in order to descend the Leeambye or Zambesi. And though often seized with sore longing for the end of this pilgrimage, the certainty that the present weather would soon lay me up with fever at a distance from friends, almost reconciles the mind to the delay. As I now possess considerable knowledge of the region to which I have devoted some years of toil, I will employ my present comparative leizure in penning a sort of report which may enable you to form a clear idea of inter-tropical Africa as a missionary field.

It may be advantageous to take a glance at the physical features of the country first, in order to be able to appreciate the nature of the obstacles which will (have to) be surmounted by those whom God may honour to introduce Christianity into this large section of the heathen world. The remarks made for this purpose must be understood as applying exclusively to the country between 18° and 10° South Latitude, and situated towards the centre of the Continent. The region thus indicated may be described as an extensive plain, intersected in every direction by large rivers, with their departing and re-entering branches. They bear on their bosoms volumes of water, such as are totally unknown in the South, and never dry up as the Orange and most (other) African rivers do. They appear as possessing two beds, one of inundations and another cut out

Unusually wet year

exactly like the Clyde above Bothwell Bridge. They overflow annually during the rainy season in the North, and then the beds of inundation—the haughs or holms, are all flooded, though, as in the Barotse Valley, they may be more than 20 miles broad. The main body of the water still flows in the now very deep low water bed, but the rivers look more like chains of lakes than streams. The country between this and Sesheke was, during the present year, nearly all under water, the parts which remained dry are only a few feet above the general level and canoes went regularly from Linyanti to Sesheke, the distance being in a straight line more than 120 miles. It was an unusually wet year, and the plains are not yet free from large patches of stagnant, foul-smelling water, though we expect the rains of another season to begin during the present month. The inundation, if I may judge from my own observation, is by no means partial. The exceptions are where outcropping rocks form high banks, and then we have rapids and cataracts, which impede navigation and have probably always been the barriers to inland trade. When the supply of water from the North diminishes, the rivers are confined to the low water channels, and even at their lowest are deep enough to prevent invasion by enemies who cannot swim or manage canoes. Numerous Lakes of considerable size are left on the lately flooded meadows by the retiring rivers, and these are either fringed with reeds or covered with mat rushes, Papyrus plants—the Egyptian Arum—the Lotus and other water-loving plants. They are always drying up but never dry ere the next wet season begins.

The country over which the rivers never rise is nearly 200 feet higher than the holms. More frequently it is under 100 feet. In many parts there are plains so level that the rain water stands for months together 6 or 8 inches deep. We waded across some, upwards of twenty miles broad, and fish, otters and water tortoises appeared in numbers and quite at home among the grass, bushes and trees. These peculiarities result in a great measure from the form of that part of the Continent

Trend of the rivers

to which our attention is directed. It appears to be of a basin or trough form; the hollow is much more elevated certainly than the sea, but it is considerably depressed in reference to two longitudinal ridges or fringes on the Eastern and Western sides. I was led to the recognition of this fact by contemplating the Lotembua running in two and nearly opposite directions. Parting at the Lake Dilolo, the Northern portion is discharged into the Casai and thence into the Atlantic by the Congo. The Southern half disembogues into the Leeba and thence into the Indian Ocean by the Zambesi. The boiling point of water shewed this takes place at the highest part of the basin—it is a sort of partition in it, and both North and South of it all the feeders of the great draining rivers flow from both Eastern and Western ridges towards the centre of the Continent. The general direction of the ranges of hills and the stratification of the rocks dipping down towards a central basin, now much filled up by eruptive rocks I had noticed many years ago: and information received from Arabs of two large shallow lakes within the Eastern ridge, make me wonder I did not recognize what seems so self-evident now. I advance the view to you now with the less diffidence inasmuch as I have just ascertained by the perusal of a speech of Sir R. Murchison before the Royal Geographical Society, that he promulgated the same idea so long ago as 1852. I cannot imagine how he received that information, but from his eminent scientific attainments it is certain to be from a reliable source. And as I reached the conclusion from independent but very jogtrot observation, the view of that gentleman is surely correct.

I may have dwelt too long on the foregoing topic, but you will at once perceive it has a most important bearing on our prospects. The great humidity produced by quick evaporation from such a vast expanse of water and marsh—the exuberant vegetation caused by fervid heat, and a perfect flood of light in a rich moist soil, and the prodigious amount of decaying vegetable matter annually exposed, after the inundations to the fervid rays of the torrid sun, with a flat surface often covered

An imperishable race

with forest, and little wind except at one season of the year, all combine to render the climate far from salubrious for any portion of the human family. I really do not desire to deepen those dark colours in which the climate of certain parts of Africa have been portrayed, but in dealing even prospectively with that sacred thing, human life, it is necessary to be conscientiously explicit. Take the experience of the Makololo who are composed of Basutos, Bakwains and the Bamamgwato, they came from a dry climate than which there are few more salubrious in the world, they have not been twenty years in this quarter, but so great has been the mortality among the men of the tribe, that it presents all the appearance of being destined at no distant day to extinction. I have heard Sebituane (Sebitane his own people call him) and many others complain of the numbers of children who have been cut off by fever, the women are less fruitful than formerly and ascribe the difference to the excessive operation of a natural phenomenon (menstruation) produced by the climate. This may explain why they are generally less subject to fever than the men—the Barotse, Batoka, Bashubea, etc., who belong to the true negro race now constitute the body of the Tribe. Those who can boast of being pure Makololo are considered the aristocracy and are a mere handful. The negroes differ from the Bechuana in being very prolific. Every village we entered in the North swarmed with children. This perhaps explains why notwithstanding all their wars, kidnapping, slave selling, and mortality by fever they are such an imperishable race. I supposed the mortality to be considerable among them because many with whom we formed acquaintanceship on going North were in their graves when we returned. But we saw many aged men, too. Having given the dark side of the picture first the impression may have been produced that it can have no other. Before deciding let me try and give the brighter phase as fairly. No one seeing the country around Linyanti or Sesheke could form an idea of what it becomes further North—the Southern portion is the least desirable of the whole. For when we go beyond the Barotse the land

Luxuriance and Miasma

gradually becomes more lovely untill in Londa (Lunda) we reach an exceedingly well watered fruitful country. It is flat, but the luxuriant loveliness of many a spot will remain in my imagination for ever. As for the interior, Angola, if Eden sent up so quickly such a rush of rank vegetation our progenitor must have found sufficient occupation in dressing it. The very thing to be dreaded, you think. The great moisture does not appear so undesirable after one has been pining as we did, under a sky of brass untill we almost believed the Prince of the Power of the air had too much of his own way there. The miasmata from such luxuriance must be terrible—it rises from the decay of a hundred thousand organisms, every one of which is beautiful. But the London Directors surely have not been such unprofitable hearers of sanitary sermons as to forget that they inhale perennially effluvia, miasmata & poison from many things, almost everyone of which is too horrible to name.

The fever is certainly the great bugbear of this field, but it must ever be borne in mind that it is the only one, there are few other diseases. No consumption, nor scrofula, nor madness. Measles and smallpox paid a passing visit some twenty years ago (singularly enough inoculation was employed in the latter disease). I have seen but one well marked case of Hydrocephalus, three of epilepsy, but none of cholera, cancer or hydrophobia or delireum tremens, and many other diseases common in England. Three cases of mania, one of puerpural insanity & one of senile dementia in 15 years do not require notice in a general statement. 'Silent friends' et id genus omne, would here have light purses. The paucity of complaints renders people less gullible than with you. A person is very rarely suspected of malingering, and though all have the most implicit faith in medicine homeopathy never alters, nor alleviates a single symptom. Indeed Odyle, table turning, popular mesmerism are all the accomplishments of high civilization. The only exception is where a state of ecstacy allied to hypnotism is produced by violent action of the voluntary muscles, the individual pretending to the prophetic afflatus. The

Fever from exposure

application, or even threatened application of that which is recommended for the backs of children and fools, produces instantaneous return to propriety. The most common diseases are inflammations of different organs, but neither these nor fever should form a barrier to the missionary enterprise. I imagine they will not, for those minded to engage therein have never stipulated for a field in which death has absolutely no darts in his quiver. I hope I am not estimating the prospect of subjection to frequent attacks of fever too lightly, for should missionaries who are educated and sent out at great expense be cut off as soon as they enter on their labours, by causes which might have been foreseen and avoided, great losses would be sustained by the Church and world. But can any unfavourable inference be drawn from my personal experience in respect of fever? I believe decidedly not. It is true I suffered severe attacks of the disease no fewer than twenty-seven times in the space of $2\frac{1}{2}$ years, but it will readily be confessed that sleeping month after month with only a little grass, and a horsecloth between me and the ground emitting so much moisture, dew is deposited so quickly on the glass roof of the artificial horizon, if placed on a box, and within it if placed on the trough on the ground, it is extremely difficult to observe the stars. Exposure in comparative inaction to the hot sun by day in a temperature generally upwards of 90° in the shade (My poor ox Sinbad would never allow 'the old man of the sea' to hold an umbrella) drenching showers often making me deposit the watch in the arm pit—the lower extremities wetted regularly two or three times every day by crossing marshy streams, and food in the half journey North and half passage South, purely native (with the exception of fine Angola sugarless coffee) and that is composed of that article which is sold in England as the lesser bird-seed—Manioc roots and meal—all of which contain so very much starch, the eyes become affected, as in the case of animals fed on pure gluten or amylaceous matter only. No ulcer was actually formed, but this I attribute to being occasionally able to procure a fowl and some maize—

Fever and latitude

these constitute a rather pitiful hygiene, and few who follow will have to endure the like. These privations I beg you to observe are not mentioned, as if I considered them in the light of sacrifices. I think the word ought never to be mentioned in reference to anything we can do for Him Who though He was rich yet for our sakes became poor. But I supposed you could not well appreciate my experience at its true, or rather no value, unless I stated the drawbacks to fair treatment of the animal economy I came into collision with. No unfavourable opinion surely can be formed from mine as to what the experience of one less exposed to the vicissitudes of the weather and change of diet might be. I beg that in the event of publication the parts marked by a line on the margin may be suppressed. Unless I mentioned privately the foregoing circumstances it might be supposed I was speaking too lightly of a disease which has inspired so much terror.

The fever may be said to commence at the latitude of Lake Ngami (20° South) and extends to the Equator, or beyond it. But from 8° South Lat. it generally assumes the intermittent or least fatal form. (I would speak in a different tone if I believed this to be the West African Remittent. That terrible disease seems to baffle all remedial means. I believe it occasionally becomes Epidemic in the country mentioned. I have seen a few mild cases, yet in the intervals we have a more salubrious field than the Church, Baptist, American and United Presbyterian missionaries.) The sequelae of this are enlargement of the spleen and great emaciation, which after a considerable period end fatally. Abundant warning is always given to seek cure by change of climate, and we have not far to go, for a few degrees of Southing introduces into the dry, pure air of the desert, and every step in that direction is made in the very remarkably healthy tract termed the interior of Southern Africa. I have had the complaint in its severest forms, and when checked by exposure during the course, vomiting of large quantities of blood ensued, yet I am aware of no organic affection as the result. Indeed I am as well now as ever I was in my life. The

Cure of the fever

greatest inconvenience I was subjected to was being less energetic, or quite useless for long periods as a missionary.

One cause of the great mortality which prevails at certain times, and particularly at the period of drying up of the inundations, is the want of prompt, though not heroic treatment. Neither doctors nor patients hurry themselves. Though his services may not have been asked till danger appears, the medical man must throw his dice first and spend hours of talking over that, then if it is late in the afternoon he will go and dig the roots tomorrow, and even then stirs not till the sun is well up. The treatment, when once fairly in operation, is undoubtedly the best adapted to overcome the disease, for they set themselves assiduously to induce profuse and long continued action of the skin. By a combination of this, with simultaneous but gentle stimulation of the internal organs, which as well as the skin have ceased excretion, I have found no difficulty in relieving and ultimately curing every case submitted to my care. My company of 27 persons were often attacked (two of them being jaundiced, appeared as if affected by something of the West African remittent) but all were brought home in good health. With an equal number of Europeans it might have been otherwise. But I apprehend no great mortality among missionaries—men of education and prudence, who can, if they will, adopt proper hygienic precautions. Excuse me if I remind you this is more than the natives of London can effect, though liable to three, if not four forms of fever, their bread will never be whitened by bone dust, alum or sulphate of copper. The detestable adulterations of which you are the victims are here unknown. . . .

We have enlarged considerably the boundaries of British commerce, and have conveyed an impression to thousands of Africans of British justice and honour. Witness Sechele's faith in the character of Queen Victoria, on the strength of which he travelled from the vicinity of the Tropic to Cape Town (more than a thousand miles) certain that if he could only get near enough to tell her, his case would be attended to. And

Sechele and the Queen

certainly it would have been, for hundreds of his children reduced to hopeless slavery in direct violation of the Treaty is nowhere else looked upon by British statesmen with indifference. At Kuruman I dissuaded him, from the attempt to go to London. 'Will the Queen not listen to my story?' I could not say, Nay. Well, English officers just returning from fighting with Basutos, his own family and friends, with that love of fair play which distinguishes them, generously contributed upwards of £60 to defray his expenses to England. Let our rulers be entreated by all that is good to forbear allowing such noble minded men being employed (as the Russians against Magyers) in crushing men who have for years shewn a devotion to their Chiefs only equalled, not surpassed, by that of the Scottish Highlander to the Pretender. A Caffre war presents no elements of honour, and it is impossible for anyone who loves the English soldier not to view with alarm the persevering efforts to get up another Natal. Some members of a Commission sitting there lately, unblushingly advocate compulsory labour, others removal of 100,000 Caffres by 6,000 whites. And this too though the Recorder of the district declares that history does not present an instance in which so great security for life and property has been enjoyed. The killing modesty of the Colony bravadoes becomes evident when you see the men who say, 'I would drive the 100,000 over the border by force.' 'I would make a law to compel them to give their young men to us to labour'—described by another of the examined as 'generally men who come to the country in search of employment for themselves.' They cannot now dig, but to beg for enrichment by a Caffre war they are not ashamed.

In regard to the people inhabiting this large and populous territory, it is difficult in the absence of all numerical data to present a very precise idea. The tribes are large, but divided into a great number of villages. So thickly were these dotted over the country that in travelling in a straight line, in which we could rarely see more than a mile on each side, we often passed ten or twelve hamlets in a single day. Occasionally,

Security for Missionaries

however, we marched ten miles without seeing any. In no part of the South I have visited is such a population seen. Angola contains 600,000 souls, and Londa seemed more populous and of larger extent than it. The Cape Colony, with 200,000 souls, possesses some hundreds of missionaries and other Christian instructors and schoolmasters, but it will bear no comparison with Londa as a missionary field. The Makololo territory has several tribes of Batoka, Barotse, Bashubea, Banyeti, Matlotlora, etc, and there is no impediment to immediate occupation by missionaries, and to such as aspire to the honour of being messengers of mercy to the actual heathen, there is no more inviting field in South Africa. I am not to be understood as meaning that these people are anxious for the Gospel, they are quite unlike the intelligent, enquiring race in the Punjaub, or the vivacious Islanders of the Pacific. But there is not such callous indifference to religious truth as I have seen, nor yet that opposition which betokens progress in knowledge. But there is a large population, and we are sure if the Word of Life is faithfully preached, in process of time many will believe. I repeat again that I know of no impediment to immediate efforts for their instruction. Every headman and Chieftain in the country would be proud òf a visit or residence of a white man. There is security generally for life and property. I left by mistake a pontoon in a village of Londa, and found it safe months afterwards. Some parcels sent by Mr. Moffat, by means of Matabele, lay a whole year on an Island in the Zambesi near Mosioatunya. It is true it was believed that they contained medicine, which might bewitch, but regular rogues are seldom scared by such preservatives. The Balonda are a friendly industrious race, and thousands of the Batobale find an asylum among them from the slave dealing propensities of their Chiefs. They seem to possess a more vivid conviction of their relation to the Unseen world than any of the Southern tribes. In the deep dark forests near their villages we always met with idols and places of prayer. The latter are spots about four feet broad and forty long, kept carefully clear of vegetation and fallen

Methods of Slavers

leaves. They resemble garden walks, branching off from the common footpaths, and have two or three partitions across them of split sticks or grass, and generally terminate at a tree. Here in the still darkness of the forest night, the worshipper— either male or female—comes alone and prays to the gods (Barimo) or spirits of departed relatives, and when an answer to the petition seems granted, meal or other food is sprinkled on the spot as a thankoffering. The Balonda extend to 7o South Lat. and their paramount Chief is always named Matiamvo. There are many subordinate chiefs, all nearly independent. The Balobale possess the same character but are more warlike, yet no prudent white man would be in the least danger among them.

It seems proper to refer to the Chiboque, Bashinje and Bangala, who treated us more scurvily than any I had previously met with in Africa, and in estimating their action it will be but fair to conceive ourselves as placed in their circumstances. They have often been visited by slave dealers of colour, and the nature of the country precluding the use of vehicles the merchants are always obliged to hire 40 or 50 carriers, whose clannish feelings are all on the side of the tribes mentioned. In any difficulty they are ready to save themselves by abandoning their employer. On arriving at any village they tell how much he has been mulcted at those already passed. The Chief sees he has but one man and a few personal slaves with whom to deal and regulates his demands accordingly, and the merchant feeling his awkward position as well as being desirous to curry favour, in order to induce him to part with his people, his sole source of importance, generally accedes to every demand. Real Portuguese would not submit to the imposition, but the men of colour they employ always do, and justify the squandering of their employer's property, on the ground that resistance would place in jeopardy the whole in going and a great part in returning, for nothing is easier in a densely wooded country than to abstract chainful after chainful of slaves, or kidnap straggling carriers in the rear. The tribes have by this process imbibed

Leaving a good name

the idea that they have as undoubted a right to these fines as our good bishops have to theirs. Could it therefore be otherwise than utterly disgusting to get the impudent answer from 28 chartists 'who had only five guns', 'We won't pay for treading on the earth of God our common father.' They were indignant to behold an unblushing attempt to defraud the revenue, and uttered shouts of most patriotic disgust. Could we have done less? Sometimes they levelled their guns at us, and it seemed as if we must fight to prevent entire plunder and reduction to slavery. A quiet arrangement by which Chief and Councillors were just within range of the spearmen, and our assertion that we were neither slave-dealers nor soldiers, and would fight only after they had struck the first blow. It would have been dangerous to fire without killing, for one being defenceless till the piece is reloaded. The enemy is encouraged by seeing a good chance before this can be effected. These were trying times, the more especially as I had no predilection towards ending my career as a 'soger.' But it cannot be said they acted unreasonably, indeed considering their circumstances and entire ignorance of our previous good conduct, unreasonableness cannot be said to be a more obstinate hereditary complaint in Africa than in Ireland. I thank God we did them no harm, and no one need fear vengeance on our account. A few more visits on the same principle would render them as safe as all other tribes, concerning which it may confidently be stated that if one behaves as a gentleman he will invariably be treated as such. Contrary conduct will give rise to remarks and treatment of scorn.

Reference has been made to the Barotse, Batoka, etc., as of the true negro race, which occupies the interior of the Continent. By their subjection to the Makololo they have acquired considerable knowledge of the Sechuana language. We have thus a very important field open in a tongue into which the whole of the sacred Scriptures will, it is hoped, soon be translated. And the time necessary for learning and reducing the negro language may not be so barren as is usually the case.—The

Language facilities

Barotse, Batoka, Balonda, and Ambonda dialects (or language spoken by the Angolese) with those spoken in Luba and beyond, as also those of people on the East coast, are all undoubtedly cognate with the Bechuana tongue and Caffre. The very considerable number of words exactly alike, or only slightly varied in their inflexions, can only be explained on that hypothesis, for there has been no intercourse between these tribes at least for centuries past. Each of the negro tribes readily learns the language of the others. The Bechuanas, however, often fail to acquire that of the negroes though living among them. Yet my companions acquire it in Angola as readily as I could a smattering of Portuguese, and failed entirely in the latter. Fever prevented my learning more of the Balonda than the interpreter of a late Cape Governor had of Sechuana, when he told his employer that a language into which the Pentateuch is fully and idiomatically expressed in a very great number fewer words than it is in the Septuagint, Greek or verbose English, was not capable of certain remarks made by a Basuta Chief. The influence of the sacred Scriptures in the three negro languages will be immense. If we call the actual amount of conversions the direct result of Missions, and the wide diffusion of better principles the indirect, I have no hesitation in asserting that the latter are of infinite more importance than the former. I do not undervalue the importance of the conversion and salvation of the most abject creature that breathes, it is of overwhelming worth to him personally, but viewing our work of wide sowing of the good seed relatively to the harvest which will be reaped when all our heads are low, there can, I think, be no comparison. It seems necessary in pointing out a large new field and counselling its immediate occupation, that I should advert to this subject, for we have been amused once and again of late with the discovery that concentration of missionary agency is what is needed and not that sowing beside all waters, which led you to send Morison and Milne to be lost among 300,000,000 idolators, and the Church Missionary Society to look to the Antipodes and Patagonia and East Africa, with the full know-

Direct and indirect results

ledge that charity begins at home. The question involves various elements which I have not the means of solving, therefore speak with diffidence, though any report within my reach during the last ten or twelve years seemed to say, 'The more concentration the less success.' i.e. If you increase missionaries so that they bear a proportion of more than one to 2000 or 3000 of the population, in ten years, the proportion of communicants will be very much less per man employed than if the proportion had been one to 20,000 of the people. I refer to Africa alone, and as it has been held forth as an example of the good effects of concentration, it is singular if you glance at the numbers of communicants and numbers of missionaries, the one is in inverse ratio to the other, though it is believed that there is not much difference in the standards of admission. Time is more essential than concentration. Let the seed be sown and there is no more doubt of its vitality and germination than there is of the general spring and harvest in the course of nature. Although I have not the most distant hope that we shall ever approach to anything like converting or 'conversions to order' the subject merits attention inasmuch as it may be elicited that there has been a great deal more done, both directly and indirectly in India than men believe. Will it be out of place to recommend the subject to our friend Mr. Mullens of Calcutta?

It might be premature to contemplate the probability of any results from the circulation of the edition of the Testament which was furnished to Park. But the circumstances are somewhat similar seeing all the Arabs I have met with are able to read and write. We may accomplish that which he was not permitted to do. It will at all events be working in the right direction. Schemers though we may be there is this difference between us and the worldly wise, while they seem annoyed with our fanaticism we are really glad to see their schemes, whether of prison or sanitary reform, Niger expeditions or soup kitchens, and wish they would make another attempt at the commercial aspect of this field. The Africans are all deeply imbued with the spirit of trade. We found great difficulty in getting past

Africans and trade

many villages: every artifice was employed to detain us that we might purchase our suppers from them, and having finished all the game they are entirely dependent on English calico for clothing—it is retailed to them by inches—a small piece will purchase a slave. If they had the opportunity of a market they could raise in their rich soil abundance of cotton and Zinyolia beans for oil. I cannot say they were lazy though they did seem to take the world easy. Their hair was elaborately curled, many of their villages are models of neatness and so were their gardens and huts. Many were inveterate musicians and made one remember how much of our Anglo-Saxon energy is expended in dress and in the howling of pianos. The men who went with me to Loanda did so in order to open up a path for commerce, and without any hope of payment from me. Though compelled to part with their hard won earnings in that city for food on our way home, I never heard a murmur. The report they gave of the expedition, both in public and private, and very kind expression towards myself, was sufficiently flattering. A fresh party was dispatched with ivory, under the guidance of an Arab from Zanzibar, and two days only given for preparation. And when they return, or even sooner, my companions are to start again. That their private opinions are in accordance with their public professions I have evidence in the number of volunteers who offer themselves to go to the East with me, knowing I have not wherewith to purchase food even. And they are not an enthusiastic race either. There is not the least probability of any mere adventurer attaining much influence among them. If the movement now begun is not checked by some untoward event the slave trade will certainly come to a natural termination in this quarter. Our cruisers have rendered slaves of so little value now on the coast, the Mambari purchase for domestic use alone, and they can still buy in some of the Batoka tribes, only on account of the very high value put upon small pieces of clothing they could not come for slaves alone, but the Makololo, feeling the value of the ivory which enables the Mambari to make the trip, have

Arrival at Tette

resolved to purchase it all. Commerce has the effect of speedily letting the tribes see their mutual dependence. It breaks up the sullen isolations of heathenism. It is so far good, but Christianity alone reaches the very centre of the wants of Africa and of the world. The Arabs, or Moors, are great in commerce, but few will say they are as amiable as the uncivilized negroes in consequence. You will see I appreciate the effects of commerce much, but those of Christianity much more. Theoretically I would pronounce the country about the forks of the Leeba and Leeambye, or Kabompo and rivers of the Bashukulompo, as a most desirable central point for the spread of civilization and Christianity. And unfortunately I must mar my report by saying I feel a difficulty as to taking my children there, without their own intelligent self-dedication. I can speak for my wife and myself, we will go whoever remains behind.

Affectionately yours,
DAVID LIVINGSTONE.

LETTER 60

To REVD. WM. THOMPSON.

Tette or Nyungwe on River Zambesi. East Africa,
2nd March 1856.

MY DEAR SIR,

Reached this the farthest inland station at present occupied by the Portuguese early this morning, and though I feel pretty well tired out from marching through a rough, stoney, bushey country without path for the last week or so; It gives me much pleasure to be again able to address those whom I left some years ago in the world. When we came to the Zambesi below the Falls, or rather near its confluence with the Kafue or Bashukulompo River, we found ourselves among tsetse, which soon settled all the oxen. The usual mode of travelling is by canoe, and the thick jungle and hills all along on both banks of the river make travelling on foot very tedious. Had I been a little

Portuguese conduct

richer and had purchased a canoe I should have been here six weeks ago. But I am in perfect health (and when rested will probably be ready to forgive my ancestors for always acting on the principle of 'Man wants but little here below, nor wants that little long.') The Portuguese are as kind here as they were in Angola, and that is saying a great deal. Somehow or other I had imbibed a sort of prejudice against them, probably from their obstinate persistence in the slave trade. But actual intercourse has fully convinced me that we are liable to form a very wrong opinion of the majority from the contumaceous acts of the few. I believe I am a good deal indebted to Mr. Duprat for his kind recommendations. I have not met with a single instance of incivility among them, and many of them are men of intelligence, with whom it is refreshing to pass an hour. . . .

I cannot give you any very precise information in this note. I believe our prospects are pretty fair, though there will always be enough of danger in the enterprise in these parts to make none but men of pluck engage in it. I think we have water carriage all the way by this fine River to within 1° or 2° of the Makololo. Near the coast the fever prevails more than it does inland, until you get into the great Valley. Then here and below this there is danger of being robbed. But on the whole I am not disposed to think our prospects dark. Having once been robbed by a congregation of Christian marauders, one is not so timorous of the heathen.

After resting a few days I intend going down the River to Quilimane.

> Believe me,
> Ever yours affectionately,
> DAVID LIVINGSTON.

I enclose the Directors' letter[1] to you. It would be a mercy to them to have it copied. It was so hot the ink would not stick, yet some of it is for them only.

---

[1] This was Letter 59 (Linyante, Oct. 12, 1855), addressed to Tidman as Secretary of the Society.

The new route

LETTER 61

To REV^d Dr TIDMAN

Tette or Nyungwe on the River Zambesi, Africa.
2^d March 1856.

MY DEAR SIR,

Having by the mercy of God reached the farthest inland station of the Portuguese this morning I gladly avail myself of an opportunity via Quillimane to advise you (and Mrs L. by the enclosed note) that I am thus far on my way down the river. It will be gratifying for you to hear that I have been able to follow up without swerving my original plan of opening a way to the sea on either the East or West coast from a healthy locality in the Interior of the continent. Not untill two months ago, was I aware of the existence of any salubrious point though I now recollect a reference made thereto by Sebituane, (but I followed out the other points with the persuasion I was doing good if only by leading commerce towards breaking up the old sullen isolation of heathenism). And now I can announce not only a shorter path for our use but if not egregiously mistaken a decidedly healthy locality. By this fine river flowing through a fine fertile country we have water conveyance to within 1° or 2° of the Makololo. The only impediments I know of being one or two rapids (not cataracts) and the people in some parts who are robbers. I have come thus far with but little loss (and as we are trying to civilize those whom the worldly wise would call by no better name and be content to pay well for getting them shot we may risk a little without fear of bankruptcy.) The Portuguese have been amazingly kind. Here they are no less so than in Angola, and much of it is owing I believe to my public spirited friend Alfredo Duprat Esquire, at Cape Town, and to the Right Reverend Bishop of Angola. [The kind interest which many of my countrymen have shewn in my work makes me feel deeply grateful and somewhat ashamed withal at having done so little to deserve it. Many would have done much more than I could effect and done it better. This is true on the one hand, but one may take the comfort of believing that there is a pretty large sprinkling of clever people who would not have done so much. I am not so elated in having performed what has not to my knowledge been done before in traversing the continent, because the end of the geographical feat is but the beginning of the missionary enterprise. May God grant me life to do some more good to this poor Africa

I have a report[1] written for you but it requires copying. I rest a few days here because I have been on foot through a very rough stoney country. Oxen all dead by tsetse and too poor to buy a canoe. With one I could have been here a month ago. In excellent health, no fever all the way from Linyanti.

          Affectionately yours,
            DAVID LIVINGSTONE.

LETTER 62

To REV. W. THOMPSON, *Cape Town*

         At Sea. H.M. Brig *Frolic*.
           8th August 1856.

MY DEAR FRIEND,

I could not have been more surprised by your own personal appearance at Quilimane than I was by that of George Fleming, on the 10th ult. and when I witnessed all the kind preparations you had made for my comfort in travel it appeared like a scene we see in dreaming. I had begun to fancy my letters contained an order forthwith to return whence I had come. On perusal however, I found that I am somewhat to blame in not stating explicitly my intention to go from Tette to Quilimane soon after the despatch of my letters, and thence proceed to England. I had mentioned my plans so often I unfortunately took it for granted that all my friends knew them perfectly. And when

---

[1] The report was Letter 59, dated Linyanti, 12th October 1855, and sent to William Thompson at Cape Town to be copied. Livingstone received at Quilimane—after his exhausting march of 4,300 miles (Linyanti–Loanda–Quilimane)—a letter from Tidman which contained a few prudent official phrases as well as congratulations. But the prudent phrases, probably written from force of habit, outweighed the rest in their effect upon Livingstone, as will be seen from the following letters.

true on the one hand, but one may take the comfort of believing that there is a pretty large sprinkling of eleven people who would not have done so much. I am not so elated in having performed what has not been done before in traversing the continent, because the end of the geographical feat is but the beginning of the missionary enterprise. May God grant me life to do some more good to this poor Africa

Part of a letter to Dr. Tidman, dated March 2nd, 1856
(See letter No. 61)

The Directors' hesitancy

the Tette packet left I intended to proceed down the river in a few days afterwards. Indeed I fully expected to overtake it at Quilimane, but my good friend Major T. A. d.' A Sicard, the commandant of Tette, generously advised me to remain untill the beginning of the healthy season in the Delta, viz, April. I was not without need of rest, for our cattle having been all killed by tsetse I had a severe spell of trudging on foot and had become tired and thin enough. My men got food from the worthy Major, and employment in carrying wood, and in canoe work also. About 16 came down with me to Senna, eight returned thence to Tette, and eight came to Quilimane, but were glad to go back too for there was a famine in the land which cut off thousands. My head man, named Sekwebu, I have taken with me—a sensible worthy heathen, but for whose tact and knowledge of the Zambesi language I might not have been here today. The rest, about 110, are to remain at Tette till I return to take them to their own land again. Such was my plan; but a short time before the arrival of the *Frolic* I got a letter from the Directors by way of Mosambique, in which I am told that 'they are restricted in their power of aiding plans connected only remotely with the spread of the Gospel,' and they add, that even though certain obstacles (fever, tsetse, &c) should prove surmountable 'the financial circumstances of the Society are not such as to afford any ground of hope that it would be in a position within any definite period to undertake untried remote and difficult fields of labour'. I had imagined in my simplicity that both my preaching, conversation, and travel, were as nearly connected with the spread of the Gospel as the Boers would allow them to be. The plan of opening up a path from either the East or West coast for the teeming population of the interior, was submitted to their judgement and secured their formal approbation. I have been seven times in peril of my life from savage men, while laboriously and without swerving, pursuing that plan, and never doubted but that I was in the path of duty. Indeed so clearly did I perceive that I was performing good service to the cause of Christ I wrote my

Money matters

brother that I would perish rather than fail in my enterprise. I shall not boast of what I have done, but the wonderful mercies I have received will constrain me to follow out the work in spite of the veto of the Board. If it is according to the Will of God means will be provided from other quarters.

I received all the articles sent in charge of Captain Peyton and George Fleming, as noted in the lists which accompanied them. Some, as the clothing for myself, bedding, stockings, &c, were most welcome, and did not come certainly before they were needed. Some woolen articles, and others which would spoil by keeping, I directed to be sold, and others, as the desk and workbox, I left at Quilimane for future use. The money, viz, fifty sovreigns and 500 Spanish dollars, I took with me. I have some debts against me up the river for clothing, &c, of which, though my kind friends there refused to give a formal account, I consider myself bound to repay by bringing articles which I know they require. As I could not settle my affairs at once I leave it for a future time. About 18 tusks belonging to Sekeletu are left also in charge of Colonel Galdino José Nunes, in whose house I lived at Quilimane with orders to sell them in case of my death and remit the proceeds to Sekeletu. The money from you I reserve for oceanic use. The dollars are said to be worth 4/2 or 4/1 only, at the Mauritius though, you gave, I hear, 4/6 for them. Rather than part with them at such a loss I shall, if not needed as passage money, keep them for the Zambesi again. I suppose all goes down to my account with the Society. I prefer the overland passage to that by the Cape because I have a chance of a free passage from one of the companies, P.O.O. I believe, and none from the common vessels which pass your way. I wish to come back without any delay in England.

I was happy to see Ralph's[1] name among those who received

---

[1] In the records of the Society he is found as Rev. Ralph Wardlaw Thompson, B.A., D.D., 1881–1914. He became Foreign Secretary, in the time of Tidman; South African affairs received, as was natural, the most understanding and efficient attention during his term of office.

Visit to Mauritius

prizes at the College. Hope he will profit largely by the mental discipline he now enjoys and become fit to serve our great Creator in his day and generation. How are the two other little Hottentots, Jessie and Willie? . . .

12th August.

We came into Port Louis, Mauritius, this afternoon, a lovely island it seems, but not nearly so fertile looking as the banks of the Zambesi (inland). I cannot, of course, give any notice of my future, but may tomorrow. I intend to live on board *Frolic* till I sail homewards, for I had a little touch of my African fever yesterday, and the purer the air the better. I shall visit Mr. Lebrun when I can, and see his Malagassi. At St. Augustine's Bay we saw many of them, they resemble closely the better classes of Makololo and many words in their tongue shew them to be true negroes. The French are causing them to emigrate to Bourbon by promise of wages and facilities for returning. It seems all fair and above board work for they had an official of the French Govt. aboard to see that none but free men were taken.

Respecting George Fleming I suppose it will be best to settle with him in Cape Town, for besides not having more money than I may need, supposing I get not a free passage, the agreement does not specify what was to be given supposing he was required to do no more than has happened. Here he has able seaman's pay as Captain's servant. (He serves me too.) He came to Quilimane with another man of colour who left us at St. Augustine's Bay. He would have found no difficulty in going to Tette as it is all fair sailing though against the stream. Whatever you think proper to give please put it to my account. I have full confidence in your discretion. I only feel sorry that my not noticing my plans in the Tette packet should have caused you so much anxiety and perplexity.

I send letters for the Kuruman along with this. Sekwebu's mind seems affected by the marvels he sees. The steamer which took us into the Port was a terrible apparition to him. All are very kind to him. One who went to Loanda became insane also but recovered in a few days, as I hope Sekwebu will.[1] Remember me kindly to Captain Holmes and thank him for a letter of recommendation he kindly sent for Mr. Azevedo—that gentleman was not at Quilimane but I met him three days beyond, near his estate, and with his well-known benevolence he lent me a covered boat, which was extremely acceptable to me, suffering from a raging fever. . . .

Ever affectionately yours,
DAVID LIVINGSTONE.

LETTER 63

To REV. W. THOMPSON, *Cape Town*

Claremont Mauritius,
17th Sept. 1856.

MY DEAR MR. THOMPSON,

I have, as you will see by the date, remained here considerably longer that I intended, but having arrived with a severe affection of the spleen, a consequence of the Fever in the Quilimane Delta, and finding that this climate was proving curative, I have delayed my departure till the present time. I have been most kindly and hospitably entertained by Major General Hay, and as his house is situated about five miles from Port Luis, and on an elevated spot with a cool climate it has answered the end of completely curing me. I had but two returns of tertian and the pain in the spleen is gone. I am ready to go back to Africa again, thanks to the Author of all our mercies, not forgetting the good kind-hearted man with whom I am living.

I have had another object in view besides health, viz, a wish to see the Commodore and thank him for his kindness. I wished also to talk to him about Africa; as I intend to work still in that poor trodden down country even without the aid of our Society, if I can only get back again. I got a letter at Quilimane, the only one since I saw you last, and I am informed that 'the

---

[1] Sekwebu's insanity ended in suicide. He threw himself overboard. See *Travels*, p. 683.

Signs of severance from Society

Directors are restricted in their power of aiding plans connected only remotely with the spread of the Gospel,' and also that even 'though certain obstacles (as fever, tsetse, &c) should prove surmountable, the financial circumstances of the Society are not such as to warrant the hope that it would be in a position within any definite period to undertake untried remote and difficult fields of labour'. As these statements are embalmed in some flattering sentences of approbation respecting my late efforts in opening up the Continent to the sympathies of the friends of Christianity, I suppose that it is intended to send me to some of the tried, near, and easy fields where I may wax fat and kick like Jeshuruh. As the proposition to leave the untried, remote, and difficult fields of labour as they have been ever since our Saviour died for the poor sinners who inhabit them involves my certain severance from the L.M.S. and the attempt to support myself and return in the best way I can, I have given a certificate to George Fleming for the money, viz, 500 Spanish dollars and fifty sovereigns which you sent and which I told you in another letter I meant to retain for the homeward voyage. I go 'overland' because I have a hope of a free passage part of the way. If I am not successful in obtaining that then there will be but little over.

I have a waggon and about 18 oxen at Linyanti, another at Cape Town, which does not seem to have been repaired according to promise, and will not sell for much. I managed to get through all my clothing, &c, &c before I got to Quilimane, but have a sextant chronometer watch and double barrelled gun, and about £50 of debts of honour to black men, so am not exactly in the position of the prodigal returning to his father, but am poorer considerably than when I landed in Africa some sixteen years ago. Yet I shall leave you without abuse of any sort. The Directors have always treated me well and I shall remember you all with affection. . . .

I am sorry too that my statements respecting going to England were not more specific, thereby causing you much anxiety on my account. I thank you most heartily and sincerely for all the trouble you put yourself to and pray that God may abundantly reward you.

Affectionately yours,
DAVID LIVINGSTON.

LETTER 64

To REV. W. THOMPSON

On Board S.S. *England*.
31st October, 1856.

DEAR MR. THOMPSON,

Having left the Mauritius on the 22nd we now find ourselves within two days of Galle, and as we may find the steamer for Aden about to leave as we enter that Port I prepare a note to let you know of my progress thus far. I believe I let you know by a letter per George Fleming that I had by my sojourn at Mauritius got completely over an affection of the spleen, entailed on me by frequent attacks of fever. This happy result was owing, by God's blessing, to the salubrity of Claremont, the residence of Major General Hay, who-se hospitality I shall ever remember with gratitude. I saw but little of Mr. Le Brun,[1] but hear he has been very useful in Mauritius, and is deservedly respected. I saw less of his sons. One lately went to Seyschelles with his wife who is consumptive. The Bishop has gone thither also, in the *Frolic*, but for religious purposes. As I was five miles from the town I did not form many acquaintances, and have for a long time been longing most ardently for reunion with my family. As for the future I can say nothing. I shall let you know how I shall act when I have seen my way clear myself. If you are writing to Kuruman I shall feel obliged by your mentioning that I am so far well and on my way home. Also if George Fleming is near, say, (as he cannot write or read what is written) that he must look after ten shillings which he directed a man of the *Frolic* called Muno, or some such name, to receive and pay to Mrs. Wright for my washing. Muno re-

[1] Rev. John Le Brun, a Swiss, was missionary in Mauritius from 1814 to 1833, and again from 1841. His two sons John J. and Peter also served.

Sextant broken

ceived the money as directed, but told Mrs. W. that George owed it to him, and I had to pay Mrs. W. another ten shillings instead. Muno is a coloured man and George will know him by this if I have mistaken the name. My peacoat which you sent from the Cape, is gone, and a new blanket is substituted by an old one, which served me all the way from Loanda and was given to the poor fellow who drowned himself. Another is taken away which I prized as that thrown over me by Sekeletu during a terrible storm. I don't know whether these things have been stolen or not in the *Frolic*. The parcel does not seem to have been touched. But about the money there can be no doubt, and George can manage that when the *Frolic* comes to the Cape.

Believe me affectionately yours,
DAVID LIVINGSTON.

Misfortunes don't come alone—my sextant got smashed by George putting it to the tiller below, he had packed it without knowing. Tell Mr. Maclear my misfortune. . . .

3rd November.

Found the *Nubia* ready to sail for Suez at Galle yesterday. Will sail today at 4 o'clock.

¶ Between September 1856 and October 1858 (the date of the next letter here printed) many things happened.

The young man who went out quietly in the barque *George* in 1840 returned sixteen years later to find himself the most famous man of the year. Few men have achieved so much in so little time.

Shrewd Mrs. Moffat wrote to her daughter: 'He is certainly the wonder of his age, and with a little prudence as regards his health, the stores of information he now possesses might be turned to a mighty account for poor wretched Africa.'

In time they were, but for two years he was hurried from one function to another receiving degrees, diplomas, and applause.

The first coal found

He laid the foundations of the Nyasa Mission and the Universities Mission to Central Africa by his appeals in Edinburgh, Oxford, and Cambridge.

He spoke to the British Association, was received by Queen Victoria, and, hardest of all, he wrote a book. His *Missionary Travels and Researches in South Africa* first appeared in 1857, and John Murray, the publisher, proved in many ways a good friend to the author.

The events of these two years are vividly set forth in Blaikie's *Life of Livingstone* and Campbell's *Livingstone*.

The next letter in the present series is dated 'River Kongone 4th October, 1858'. He had been taken there in H.M.S. *Pearl* from Liverpool, having as his companions Dr. Kirk, Commander Bedingfield, Charles Livingstone (his brother), R. Thornton, T. Baines, and G. Rae. He had the rank of Consul for Inner Africa and his expedition was to attempt the opening up of the Zambesi to the world. To his old friend Thompson he writes a letter which sounds as though it had been written on the day following his previous letter. He is back again in his own place and drops naturally into the scene.

LETTER 65

To REV. W. THOMPSON

River Kongone,
4th October, 1858.

MY DEAR MR. THOMPSON,

I could not possibly write you by last opportunity from the Zambesi, but there was so little to communicate you were no loser. We have now had more time to look about us, and I think we have ascertained the point that entering these Rivers at the time we did is really quite safe if no delay takes place among the Mangrove swamps. We have been favoured with fair health, and had ailments more like common colds than fever. Two of the party are now at Tete, and the others hope to join them shortly. We got a ton and a half of coals there, the first ever taken out of the earth in that country, and as the

Value of Kongone River

Portuguese have shewn a great deal of public spirit we are almost certain of a larger supply when we return. My poor fellows received me with great joy. They had often been taunted by the Tete people that their Englishman would never return, but they hoped on and have amassed quantities of beads to take back to their own country. Thirty of them died of smallpox and six were killed by a rebel chief at the confluence of the Luenya. The confidential servant of Sekwebu is with me now on board the Launch. This thing is so small we could not bring more of them down, though they were anxious to come on service.

We found the country in a state of war, and the Portuguese were too busy with that to help us with canoes. It is finished now and my old friend Major Sicard at once helped us with the luggage—but it has quite depopulated the lands adjacent to the river. We see the river in this month at its very lowest and as it spreads out into from one to three miles in width the broad parts are very difficult. When we get to Lupata our difficulties vanish, for above that point it is in one or two channels of about 1000 or 1,200 yds broad. I admire its size more than ever. When I came down in a canoe it was full and I saw but one channel where now we see two or three. If the Portuguese would bear the expense of a few piles driven in to effect what snags sometimes do now—deep channels might be secured for the whole year.—They are going to build a fort and custom house at this on the Luabo.

Your things left at Kilimane did not go off by sale, so I have directed my friend there to send them back to the Cape at my expense, and possibly they may realize the sum which the Directors, I think most unjustly, saddled upon you. I promised to pay it all, but wished to think it over, and now I consider that the publication of the same document in England ought to have been defrayed by the Secretaries if they thought you were liable too.

With kind regards to Mrs. T. I am &c,
DAVID LIVINGSTONE.

Views on Pacifism

I hear the new missionaries[1] have come. I hope they will all reach their destinations in safety.

If the articles do not bring the whole sum I shall make it up.

LETTER 66

To JOSEPH W. STURGE[2]

Tette, 11 Decr 1858.

MY DEAR MR STURGE

You were kind enough to write when I was in England in commendation of the views you hold respecting war and the taking away of human life. I am sorry that I could not give that due attention to the subject as put forward by you as it deserved, and the letter having been mislaid I think I cannot do better than try to enlighten you by way of answer. The loss of the letter having left me in such a state of darkness that will procure pardon for my presumption.

I love peace as much as any mortal man. In fact I go quite beyond you for I love it so much I would fight for it. You who in a land abounding in police and soldiery ready to catch every ruffian who would dare to disturb your pretty dwelling may think this language too strong, but your principles to be good must abide the test of stretching. Fancy yourself here— a man whom I cured of fever at Quilimane when on my way to England in 1856 no sooner heard of Luis Napoleon's emigration scheme than he purchased a quantity of gunpowder— armed his slaves and made a foray into the Licunga country— & brought back some hundreds of captives. Had you been one of the Licunga you would have been knocked on the head as too old, and your wife and children would have lost that liberty for which our fathers fought and bled. Ah, but I would not have used any defensive arms say you; I would have been

---

[1] The new men were John Mackenzie and Roger Price for the Makololo country, William Sykes and Thomas M. Thomas for Matebeleland.

[2] Jos. Sturge, an eminent member of the Society of Friends, had been influential in improving the lot of the West Indian slaves during the apprenticeship stage and hastening the date of complete emancipation (see Blaikie, p. 225).

Retaliation expected

safe. Well six of my Makololo men—very fine young elephant hunters all of them—went down from this about thirty miles *totally unarmed*. They had been in the habit of visiting different chiefs in the vicinity and were usually invited to shew the dances of their country. After doing this they generally were rewarded with a handsome present of food. In this instance the chief named Bonga requested them to dance. They did so. He then ordered them to be taken to a certain hut where there were provisions on pretence of giving some, and killed the whole six. He was perfectly aware of their being my men but he wanted certain parts of their bodies as medicine and killed two of them very cruelly. Had they been armed with revolvers their lives would have been safe. I think so, though it is the most earnest wish and prayer of my heart that I may never be placed in those circumstances in which it may be necessary to take away the life of a fellow man. I have done nothing but speak to his nephew about it, and send a message to the murderer—the only excuse he urges is a false one—not knowing they were my men. Well the moral effect of doing nothing is this. Wishing to be on friendly terms with another chief North of this I sent him a handsome present, and a message explanatory of our objects, our wishes to put an end to their wars &c. &c. He received it in a very cordial manner and sent two men to see me. He presented two elephant tusks also. I would rather not have received them but it was said a refusal would be considered an insult. I treated the two men as well as I could but they thought that I ought to have given more. I offered the tusks but they went off in high dudgeon roaring out the threat that they would kill any of my men they met and taunting me with—'though Bonga killed six of your men YOU DID NOTHING to him'! The people near to the Portuguese are much worse than those farther inland but this is the place where your principles ought to be tested not where the people are friendly or where the policeman keeps the peace. I have in no way been mixed up with country affairs. We went from side to side during the actual war—bought what we needed from each—

cut wood on the rebels bank one day and wooded on the Portuguese bank the other. I am widely known as a man of peace. I could quote this were I disposed to accept evidence all on one side, but I know the other side of the question too, and I can never cease wondering why the Friends who sincerely believe in the power of peace principles dont test them by going forth to the heathen as missionaries of the cross. I for one would heartily welcome them from the belief that their conduct would have a good influence though it would never secure their safety.

D. LIVINGSTONE.

LETTER 67

To REVD. DR. TIDMAN.

Chicova, Zambesi,
10th November 1860.

MY DEAR SIR,

On reaching this country of the Makololo in August last, I learned, to my very great sorrow that our much esteemed and most worthy friends the Helmores had been cut off by fever after a very short residence at Linyanti. Having been unexpectedly detained in the lower part of this river until May last, my much longed for opportunity of visiting the upper portion was effected only by performing a march on foot of more than six hundred miles, and then I was too late to render that aid which I had fondly hoped to afford. The poignancy of my unavailing regret is not diminished by remembering that at the very time when the friends were helplessly perishing we were at a lower and much more unhealthy part of the river, and curing the complaint so quickly that in very severe cases the patient was able to resume his march on foot a day or so after the operation of the remedy. It was first found effectual in the cases of my own children and an English party at Lake Ngami in 1850, and has been successful in every case of African fever met with since, without causing loss of strength to the patient. Aware how readily one may deceive himself as to the

A likely country

effect of particular remedies, I said little about it more than is stated towards the end of the 'Missionary Travels.' The ample experience of this expedition seems to warrant speaking of its value more positively. The medicines employed are common ones, but used in a way which many believe ought not to be attempted without certain preliminary measures. I take the liberty of enclosing the prescription.

From all I could learn the Makololo took most cordially to Mr. Helmore—they wished to become acquainted with him—a very natural desire—before removing to the Highlands, and hence the delay which ended so fatally. Had his life been spared a little longer there is no doubt but a promising Mission would have been established. He told the people subsequently to the death of his wife, that nothing would prevent him from going and doing his duty whither he had been sent, whoever did, he would never turn back from his work. This I have learned from my present Makololo companions, and I hope that the same spirit may animate the members of the Society that sent him.

Our course for part of the way lay along the North bank of the Zambesi above the Kafue. The country on both banks literally teems with people. There at a month's distance from Mosilikatze we heard the message of the missionaries to that Chief to abstain from deeds of blood. All were anxious to know if Sekeletu would give heed to similar words of peace. Turning Westwards and ascending some 2000 feet to near the base of a mountain called Tabacheu, we breathed the clear cold air of the Highlands. In that magnificent country where we actually saw hoarfrost and a little ice, we had hoped that a Mission might have been formed and those influences put in operation which alone can produce peace on the earth. There being no more communication between Tette and Linyanti than between London and Timbuctu we had till then anticipated the pleasure of meeting with our friends, and had no foreboding that we should stand by their graves at Linyanti instead. The Makololo are quite ready to remove, they are

Cure of fever

perishing themselves and should they not depart from these Lowlands soon they will break up as a tribe. . . .

We examined the whole river below the falls by dropping down from Senamanes in canoes, and have no doubt but an ordinary steamer could ascend while the river is in flood. While in the lower part of the River we had no news to communicate about the country in which you are specially interested, hence the silence of yours

Affectionately,

DAVID LIVINGSTONE.

Fever Powder

Take of Resin of Jalap and Calomel of each eight grains Quinine & Rhubarba of each four grains. Mix well together, and when needed, make into pills with spirit of Cardamoms Dose from (10) ten to (20) twenty grains. The mixture keeps best in powder.

If the violent symptoms are not relieved in from four to six hours by the operation of the pills a dessert spoonful of Epsom salts may be taken. Then quinine in four or six grain doses completes the cure. It is usually given till the ears ring or deafness is produced.

DAVID LIVINGSTONE

Tette 26th Nov^r
1860

LETTER 68

To REV. W. THOMPSON

South Central Africa, November 1872.

MY DEAR MR. THOMPSON,

Your note and pamphlets kindly sent in July 1866 came to hand in Unyanyembe in August 1872. Postal arrangements are scarcely perfect all over the world yet, but I was thankful to get anything at all. I was plundered of large amounts of goods, four several times, through my money being handed over without any precautions that I know of, to an oily tongued Banian, and by the connivance of the Governor of Unyanyembe the stores were nearly all plundered by members of a slave trading ring or coterie, and every effort made by the destruction of my letters to prevent information of the losses going to

Arab slavery

the coast. They were pretty successful, for the Banian Ludha Damji, who really was at the bottom of all the villainy, alone had the ear of my friend, and on the strength of a note from his agent Shereef, who sold off all my goods at Ujiji for slaves and ivory, which stated that he was about to send off slaves with all I needed, the half truth was uttered 'that all Dr. L's wants had been supplied' and it was repeated in the house of Lords. The little sent was so little and so inferior, it was intended to force me back—the slaves solemnly swore that they were instructed by the highest authority to force me back, and they persisted in this all over the country, in fact quite overacted their part. All expected me to die, and deprived of nearly all European comforts for two years, it is a wonder that their expectations did not come true. The Arabs outside the ring were all extremely kind, but Banian money carried on all the slaving in Manyuema and I gave great umbrage by going into their mart. They work it quietly and well, for the Manyuema women are very pretty and are usually sold off for very large prices as soon as captured, or at least long before they reach the coast. No gang in chains is ever sent down, but these wretched British Indian subjects who would not hurt a flea are by their money, arms, ammunition, and goods, in the hands of the Arab agents really the worst cannibals in all Africa. If my disclosures lead to the suppression of the wickedness I shall not grudge the pain and toil I have endured. Captain Holmes' countrymen H. M. Stanley, and James Gordon Bennett, of the New York Herald, acted nobly, and both deserve and have my lasting gratitude for the relief sent to me, and for Stanley's truly noble braving of death and danger to serve me as a son might have done. Thanks for the notices of your family. I can recollect them only as children and would pass them on the street unwittingly. Ralph was a lithe blithe boy—Jessie had smiles and tears in perfect command—the banker I cannot recal. My blessing on them. Ralph's ordination was well calculated to elicit all the pith and unction in you, and you were very happy in your charge. Your friends paid a graceful tribute to you in franking

Africanders' diamonds

you home and back again, and conferred honour on themselves. May they long flourish in doing similar deeds. Glad to hear that the Africanders have got diamonds. They first set the example of plundering me at Kolobeng—if they heard of the Arab and Banian deeds in the same line they would make amends by sending me lots of diamonds in expiation, half a muid[1] will do to ease my ghost from haunting them, as I am not greedy.

Remember me to Saul Solomon, and Rutherfoord.

DAVID LIVINGSTONE.

[1] Muid : a measure of capacity. Half a muid equals a bushel and a half.

INDEX

Abercrombie, Dr., 183.
Abreu, Sergeant Cypriano de, 221.
Abyssinia, 31.
Addressees, *see* List of Letters, p. xxi.
Aden, 264.
Africanders, 274.
Aldersgate Street, 4.
Algoa Bay, 7, 10, 19, 20, 22, 27, 28, 55, 57, 108, 109, 127, 128, 167.
Alheit, Mr., 172, 173, 174.
Ambaca, 221, 231.
Ambonda, 252.
American Missions, 208, 246.
Americans, 234.
Amhurst College, U.S.A., 195.
Anderson, Mr., 213.
Andover, U.S.A., 139.
Angola, xi, 225, 226, 227, 232, 233, 234, 244, 245, 249, 252, 256, 257.
Angola, Bishop of, 230, 257.
Apothecaries Hall, 9.
Arabs, 211, 234, 236, 237, 242, 254, 255, 274.
Arkwright, Lieut., 137.
Arnot, Mr. David, 144.
Arrowsmith, Mr., 147, 148.
Arundel, Rev. John, 85.
Ashton, Rev. William, 103, 162, 163, 172, 199.
Azevedo, Mr., 262.

Bagalaka, 99, 100.
Bahurutse, 107, 146, 148, 180, 238.
Bain, Mr. A. H., 78.
Baines, Mr. T., 266.
Bakaa, 34, 36, 37, 48, 52, 53, 54, 129.
Bakalihari, 32, 46, 47, 48, 52, 55, 144, 162.
Bakhatla, 32, 41, 45, 51, 52, 60, 61, 62, 64, 65, 67, 69, 70, 71, 79, 80, 81, 88, 98, 107, 146, 180, 186, 187, 238.
Bakoba, 138, 147, 157.
Bakwain, 32, 33, 45, 50, 52, 54, 70, 80, 83, 88, 97, 98, 99, 107, 109, 111, 112, 121, 122, 124, 125, 134, 142, 145, 146, 153, 158, 160, 161, 162, 172, 176, 178, 180, 188, 196, 197, 200, 203, 214, 238, 239, 243.
Balala, 134.
Balobale, 250.
Balojazé, 157.
Balonda, 215, 217, 219, 228, 249, 250, 252.
Bamaeris, 135.

Bamangwato, 34, 35, 36, 47, 48, 49, 52, 53, 158, 162, 163, 243.
Bamaponda, 157.
Bamosetla, 99.
Banajoa, 149.
Bangala, 250.
Bangwaketse, 146.
Bangweolo, Lake, xi.
Banigenko, 157.
Banyeti, 205, 209, 249.
Baobab Tree, 195.
Baptist Missions, 246.
Baralongs, 135, 195.
Barghash, Sultan, xviii, xix.
Barigelong, 133, 134, 199.
Barker, Rev. George, 170, 171.
Barotse, 151, 157, 159, 165, 190, 201, 204, 205, 207, 209, 216, 217, 219, 243, 249, 251, 252.
Barotse Valley, 241.
Bashinje, 250.
Bashubea, 157, 243, 249.
Bashukulompo, River, 151, 209, 211, 216, 230, 255.
Basuto, French Mission, 126.
Basutos, 243, 248.
Batlapi, 50, 70, 75, 79, 88, 99, 133, 134.
Batlaros, 99.
Batobale, 249.
Batoka, 157, 209, 243, 249, 251, 252, 254.
Bay of Biscay, 11.
Bechuanaland, xi, xvi, xix, 7, 9, 26.
Bechuanas, 5, 26, 28, 30, 31, 32, 35, 37, 38, 41, 58, 67, 69, 71, 73, 75, 80, 85, 87, 95, 101, 114, 133, 135, 157, 173, 186, 195, 214, 243, 252.
Bedingfield, Commander, 266.
Belgian Congo, xvii.
Bengo, 222.
Benguela, 206.
Bennett, Rev. James, D.D., 86.
Bennett, James Gordon, 273.
Bennett, Dr. Risdon, 4, 28, 49, 83, 110.
Bethelsdorp, 28, 168.
Bibliotheca Sacra, 193.
Birt, Rev. Richard, 63.
Blackmore, 9.
Blaikie's *Life of Livingstone*, xiii, xvi, 4, 23, 139, 266, 268.
Blantyre, 2, 4.
Blantyre (Scottish National Memorial), v, 28, 40, 74, 83, 90, 94, 192, 210, 223.
Blantyre Works, 1.

275

Index

Bloemfontein, 137.
Boatlanama, 144, 149.
Boers, 21, 23, 48, 61, 62, 109, 110, 126, 136, 145, 161, 171, 172, 173, 174, 176, 177, 178, 179, 182, 183, 187, 188, 189, 195, 196, 200, 207, 208, 209, 211, 214, 233, 238, 259.
Bonga, Chief, 269.
Botha, Andries, 176, 177, 179, 232.
Bothwell Bridge, 241.
Brazil, 139, 225, 226.
Bredencamp, 174.
Bridges, Rev. Charles, M.A., 8, 87.
British and Foreign Bible Society, 6, 18.
British and Foreign School of Medicine, 3.
British Banner, The, 164, 214.
British Navy, The, xvii.
British Quarterly, The, 183, 190, 196.
Bubi, Chief, 32, 34, 45, 88, 89.
Buchanan, Mr., 239
Bunyan, John, 195.
Bushmen, 30, 31, 32, 138, 149, 162, 197, 200.
Buys, Conrad, son of, 47, 101.

Caffirs, 21, 75, 90, 109, 117, 176, 177, 183, 189, 190, 214, 221, 248, 252.
Calderwood, Rev. H., 175.
Calimba, 217.
Cambridge, 266.
Cameron, Mr., 212.
Campbell, Rev. John, 27, 41, 44, 50, 78, 87, 118, 187.
Campbell, Dr. R. J., 266.
Cape Colony, 230, 234, 249.
Cape Town, xi, xiv, xvi, 20, 139, 164, 165, 166, 168, 170, 171, 180, 187, 189, 191, 198, 199, 212, 217, 233, 247, 257, 258, 262, 263.
Cape Town Mail, The, 239.
Carr's Lane, Birmingham, 128.
Casai, River, 234, 242.
Cassange, Angola, 221, 227, 230, 232, 233, 234.
Cathcart, Sir George Gilbert, 189, 190.
Cecil, Rev. Richard, 2, 8, 9, 23, 108.
Chalmers, Dr., 57, 135, 193.
Chapman, Mr., 212, 215, 223.
Charing Cross Hospital, 4.
Chase, Mr., U.S. Consul, 140.
Chiboque, 219, 250.
Chicova, 270.
Chobe, River, xiii, 149, 158, 200, 201, 209, 211, 216, 235, 240.
Chonuane, xii, 83, 88, 89, 90, 94, 97, 99, 106, 110, 111, 126, 127.

Christie, Mr., 168.
Church Missionary Society, 23, 246, 252.
Clyde, River, 241.
Colesberg, 27, 68, 107, 109, 144, 167, 168.
Congo, River, xi, 242.
Congregational Unions of England and Scotland, 42.
Coupland, Professor R., xv, xix.
Cradock, 214.
Cromwell, Oliver, 4.
Cuba, 226.
Cumnock, 9.

Darling, Lieutenant-Governor, 177, 178.
Delagoa Bay, 52, 99.
Dick, Dr. Thos., 1.
Dickson, Rev. H., 5.
Dickson, Mrs., 6.
Dilolo, Lake, 242.
Drummond, Rev. George, 7, 19, 40, 74.
Drummond, H., Esq., 24, 59, 118, 128, 147.
Drummond, Mrs., 10.
Duprat, Mr. Alfredo, 256, 257.

Eardley, Sir Culling Eardley, 164.
East India Company, 85.
Edinburgh, 266.
Edwards, Mr. R., 23, 25, 28, 33, 38, 43, 56, 65, 66, 71, 77, 82, 106, 176, 180, 186, 187.
England, S.S., 264.

Fairbairn, Mr., 189.
Fairbrother, William, 74.
Falcon Square (Silver Street Chapel), 4.
Fernando-Po, 223.
Fever Powder, Receipt for, 272.
Fever, West African Remittent, 246, 247.
Finney, *Revivals of Religion*, 20.
Fison, Mr., 10, 11, 64.
Fleming, George, 171, 173, 175, 181, 196, 197, 222, 258, 260, 261, 263, 264, 265.
Forerunner, S.S., 228, 231.
Frédoux, Rev. J., 210.
Freeman, Rev. J. J., 32, 37, 133, 141, 145, 147, 164, 199.
Frere, Sir Bartle, xviii.
Friends, Society of, 270.
Frolic, H.M. Brig, 258, 259, 261, 264, 265.

Gaboon American Mission, 208.

Index

Gabriel, Mr. Edmund, 221, 225, 227, 229, 231.
Gaika, 175, 189.
Galle, 264, 265.
George, Barque, 20, 265.
Gibson, Mr., 37.
Gill, Mr., 109.
Glasgow, 104.
Golungo Alto, 223.
Goodwin, Dean, 120.
Graaf Reinet, 24, 27, 108, 109.
Grahamstown, 127, 155, 168, 183.
Grant, Dr., 17.
Gravesend, 11.
Griqua, 105, 148, 149, 153, 154, 184, 234.
Griqua Town, 24, 26, 27, 28, 41, 104, 134, 171,

Hamilton, vi, 38, 65.
Hamilton, Dr., of Leeds, 113.
Hankey, 84, 198.
Harris, Rev. J. C., 138, 163.
Hay, John, 40.
Hay, Major-General, 262, 264.
Helmore, Mr., 127, 134, 270, 271.
History of the London Missionary Society, 147.
Hoffmeyer, Mr., 215, 235.
Holmes, Captain, 192, 202, 236, 262, 273.
Holt, Mr., 191.
Hottentots, 23, 41, 57, 84, 109, 165, 175, 179, 189.
How I found Livingstone (Stanley), vi.
Howe, John, 4.
Hughs, Mr. Isaac, 27, 127, 171, 174.

Independents, 235.
Indian Ocean, xiii, xv, 242.
Inglis, Rev. Walter, 40, 66, 106, 107, 179, 186.
Islesteps, Dumfries, 104.

Jesuits, 222, 232.

Kabompo, 216, 217, 255.
Kafue, River, 255, 271.
Kalahari Desert, xii, xiii, 194.
Kat River Mission, 104.
Katima-molelo, 205.
Khake, Chief, 88, 89, 90.
Kiria, Hill, 148.
Kirk, Sir John, xviii, 266.
Kirk on the Zambesi, xv.
Kolobeng, xii, xv, 110, 111, 113, 115, 118, 123, 124, 129, 133, 136, 138, 139, 142, 144, 145, 146, 147, 150, 153, 161, 163, 169, 172, 177, 178, 182, 186, 187, 274.

Kongone, River, 266.
Kruger, Memoirs of Paul, 178.
Kuakoe, 111.
Kumadow, Lake, 148.
Kunyeri, River, 148.
Kurrechane, 71, 78.
Kuruman, xii, 7, 20, 22, 24, 27, 28, 32, 33, 36, 37, 42, 49, 59, 63, 64, 66, 71, 75, 76, 77, 83, 86, 90, 91, 94, 96, 110, 123, 124, 127, 129, 130, 133, 134, 141, 143, 152, 156, 160, 161, 162, 165, 168, 170, 172, 173, 174, 175, 178, 181, 184, 187, 189, 192, 193, 195, 197, 199, 200, 202, 203, 211, 216, 239, 248, 261, 264.

Lakeville, New York, 139, 140.
Lanark, West Canada, 139.
Langa, 135.
Last Journals, vi.
Lattakoo, see Kuruman, 21, 62, 64, 70, 83, 84, 86, 133, 149, 150, 154, 190.
Le Brun, Rev. John, 261, 264.
Lechulatebe, Batauna Chief, 137.
Leeamby, River, 201, 202, 205, 206, 209, 214, 215, 216, 217, 228, 230, 233, 234, 236, 240, 255.
Leeba, River, 206, 207, 215, 216, 217, 228, 242, 255.
Lekatlong, 133, 134.
Lemue, Mr., 135.
Licunga, 268.
Limaoe, 146.
Limpopo, River, 98, 99.
Lingopeng, 133, 135.
Linyanti, xiii, xiv, xv, 202, 206, 210, 212, 215, 221, 233, 235, 236, 240, 241, 243, 256, 258, 263, 270, 271.
Livingston, Neil, vi.
Livingston, Phillip, vi.
Livingston, Robert, 132, 154.
Livingston, Thomas, 154, 165.
Livingston, Thomas (Viscount Teviot), vii.
Livingston, Thomas Steele, 131, 132.
Livingstone, Agnes, 132, 154 166.
Livingstone, Anna Mary, v.
Livingstone, Charles, 94, 129, 139, 140, 192, 223, 266.
Livingstone, David, v, vi, vii.
Livingstone, Mrs. Mary, vi, xv, 92, 100, 111, 113, 118, 123, 126, 129, 131, 132, 136, 138, 141, 159, 160, 164, 168, 169, 170, 178, 184, 185, 189, 199, 208, 210, 216, 239, 257.
Livingstone, Oswell, 154.
Livingstone (Campbell's), 266.
Livingstons of Callandar, vi.

Index

Llanbrynmair, 78.
Loanda, Saint Paul de, xiii, 163, 207, 208, 214, 217, 221, 222, 224, 225, 226, 227, 228, 229, 230, 233, 234, 235, 237, 254, 258, 261, 265.
Lobale, 200, 219.
Lobale, River, 157, 228.
Loenge, River, 230.
Loeti, River, 201, 216.
Londa, River, 201, 202, 206, 207, 228, 244, 249.
London Missionary Society, v, 1, 39, 42, 108, 165, 167, 237, 263.
Lotembua, River, 242.
Luabo, River, 267.
Luba, 252.
Ludorf, 184.
Luenya, River, 267.
Lupata, 267.

Mababi, River, 149.
Mabalwe (Mebaloe), 67, 71, 77, 92, 93, 98, 99, 100, 104, 111, 113, 134, 138, 178, 180, 182, 192.
Mabotsa, xii, 62, 68, 72, 74, 76, 78, 79, 82, 87, 88, 97, 106, 107, 115, 127, 128, 135, 176, 186, 187.
Macabe, Mr., 194.
Mac-an-Leighs, vii.
Macgibbon, Mr., 191.
Mackenzie, Bishop, Memoirs of, 120.
Mackenzie, Rev. John, 268.
Maclear, Mr., 145, 213, 265.
McRobert, Mr. and Mrs., 104.
Madeira, 11.
Madras, Governor of, 65.
Magaliesberg, 218.
Mahura, Chief, 50, 75, 88, 133, 135, 180.
Mainaloe, 107.
Makabba, Chief, 50, 87, 146, 154.
Makablea, 150.
Makalaka, 34, 36, 37, 48, 52, 53, 162, 201.
Makololo, xiii, 155, 159, 188, 192, 201, 203, 205, 208, 209, 210, 211, 215, 237, 238, 243, 249, 251, 254, 256, 257, 261, 268, 269, 270, 271.
Makoma, River, 216.
Makone, 71.
Malagassi, 261.
Malatsi, 174.
Mambari, 151, 152, 209, 211, 215, 254.
Mamochisane (*see* Sebitoane), 154, 158, 190.
Mamogale, Chief, 99.
Mampoore, Lake, 87.
Mamusa, 133.
Maniché, River, 216, 217, 230.

Mañkopane, 99, 101.
Mantatees, 87, 149, 154.
Manyema, 273.
Marikoe, River, 97.
Marshall, Miss, 9.
Mashona, 34.
Masoma, 157.
Matabele, 44, 45, 46, 53, 75, 87, 99, 150, 158, 210, 249.
Matiamvo, 250.
Matlomaganyana, 193.
Matlotlora, 249.
Mauritius, 260, 261, 262, 264.
Mebaloe, 71, 77, 92, 93.
Melechoe, Chief, 101.
Milne, Mr., 252.
Misericordia Hospital, 15.
Missionary Labours and Scenes in S. Africa (Moffat), 133, 154.
Missionary Travels and Researches in S. Africa, 266.
Mochuara, 135.
Moenge, 157.
Moffat, Mary, xiv, 74, 76.
Moffat, Robert, xii, 18, 25, 28, 39, 40, 41, 42, 49, 52, 63, 64, 65, 68, 72, 74, 76, 98, 111, 120, 127, 133, 142, 143, 146, 154, 167, 173, 176, 177, 178, 180, 184, 185, 186, 194, 195, 199, 249, 265.
Moffat, Robert, jr., 110.
Mokhatla, Chief, 97, 98, 99, 126.
Mokhoro, Lake, 51.
Mokwain, 196, 197.
Molehane, David, *see* Mabalwe.
Molehane, Paul, 97, 98, 99, 104, 107, 111, 112, 126, 134, 180, 182.
Molopo, River, 78.
Moloso, 136.
Moore, Mr., 40.
Morison, Mr., 252.
Morukanelo, 113.
Moshesh, Chief, 192.
Mosiatunya, Falls of (*see* Victoria Falls), 151, 209, 217, 230, 233, 249.
Mosielele, 135.
Mosiga, 48.
Mosilikatse, 41, 46, 48, 49, 50, 52, 67, 97, 98, 99, 110, 158, 159, 162, 185, 210, 271.
Motchuana, 57.
Motheebe, 133, 134.
Motito (Moteeto), 32, 66, 184, 210.
Motlabani, 133.
Moyle, Mr., 182.
Mozambique, xi, 259.
Mullens, Mr., 253.
Murchison, Sir R., 242.

Index

Murray, Rev. Andrew, 24, 27.
Murray, Mr., 191.
Murray, Mr. John, 266.

Nariele, 205, 206, 207.
Nasmith, Mr., 60.
Natal, 223, 248.
Navigator's Islands, 5, 74.
'Nchokotsa, 149.
New Englander, The, 193.
New South Wales, 139.
New York, vi.
New York Herald, 273.
Ngami, Lake, xiii, xiv, 138, 142, 148, 246, 270.
'Ntwétwé, 149.
Nubia, 265.
Nunes, Colonel Galdino José, 260.
Nyampi, Supreme Being, 158.
Nyasa, Lake, xi.
Nyasa, Mission, 266.

Oberlin, Ohio, 117, 139.
Ongar, 2, 3, 4, 5, 6, 8, 23, 108, 109, 141.
Orange, River, 174, 175, 177, 200, 234, 240.
Oswell, William Cotton, 136, 140, 147, 148, 149, 150, 159, 166, 168, 170, 189, 191.
Ourie or Limpopo, River, 98, 99.
Owen, Mr. (C.M.S.), 23.
Oxford, 266.

Paarl, 170.
Paris Geographical Society, 199, 210.
Passmore, Mr., 108.
Peace Society, 14, 220.
Pearl, H.M.S., 266.
Pears or Pearson, Mr. John, 214.
Peecho, 66, 172.
Peyton, Captain, 260.
Philip, Dr. John and Mrs., 19, 20, 22, 23, 27, 76, 104, 108, 127, 139.
Philipolis, 27, 148, 153.
Philosophy of a Future State (Dick), 1.
Pilanie, Chief, 98.
Pilgrim's Progress, The, 195.
Plympton, Mass., 192.
Pococke, Mr., 192.
Pombal, Marquis of, 232.
Port Natal, 21.
Portuguese, xvi, 152, 156, 206, 207, 209, 211, 219, 221, 222, 224, 225, 228, 229, 232, 233, 234, 250, 255, 256, 257, 267, 269, 270.
Potgeiter, Hendrick, 171, 172.
Prentice, Mr. Thomas, 6, 7, 9, 10, 16, 22, 40, 62.

Pretorious, 136.
Priestcar, 174.
Price, Rev. Roger, 268.
Pungo-Andongo, 228, 232, 233.
Pyne, Mr. Benjamin, 141, 147.

Quango, River, 220, 229, 234.
Quilimane, xiii, xiv, 222, 230, 231, 233, 256, 257, 258, 259, 260, 261, 262, 263, 267, 268.

Rae, G., 266.
Religious Tract Society, 6.
Revivals of Religion (Finney), 20.
Rhodes-Livingstone Institute (N. Rhodesia), v, 10, 12, 16, 22, 62, 115.
Rider, Alfred (Ryder), 137.
Ridley, Miss, 6, 10, 12.
Ridley, Mr., 63.
Rio de Janeiro, 12, 13, 15, 17, 18, 20.
Robertson, Captain D., 169.
Robertson, Dr., 177, 178.
Robson, Rev. Adam, 167.
Ross, William, 20, 42, 63, 65, 66, 75, 106, 135.
Royal Geographical Society, 142, 144, 147, 148, 153, 163, 213, 242.
Rutherfoord, Mr., 128, 140, 171, 180, 274.
Ryder, Alfred, 137.

Samogoe, Chief, 99.
Sandillah, 177, 178.
Sansureh, River, 200.
Scholtz, Chief Commandant, 178, 239.
School of Medicine, British and Foreign, 3.
Scourge, S.S., 223.
Sebeque, Sebbewe, 44, 45, 50, 51, 52, 87, 88.
Sebitoane, Sebituane, 137, 138, 142, 145, 146, 149, 151, 152, 153, 154, 155, 157, 158, 161, 165, 166, 171, 193, 194, 196, 198, 201, 202, 206, 213, 238, 243, 257.
Sebube, Sebubi, 134, 180, 186.
Sechele, Chief, 45, 83, 88, 89, 94, 97, 105, 110, 111, 116, 121, 122, 124, 125, 128, 129, 136, 137, 144, 176, 178, 179, 180, 181, 182, 186, 187, 188, 192, 195, 196, 198, 201, 204, 238, 239, 247.
Sechuana, 194, 195, 251.
Sehele, 46.
Sekeletu, Chief, 163, 198, 202, 204, 209, 210, 216, 222, 230, 231, 240, 260, 265, 271.
Sekhosi, 205.
Sekomi, Chief (Sekhome), 34, 35, 36, 163, 191, 193.

Index

Sekwebu, 259, 261, 262, 267.
Senamanes, 272.
Senna, 259.
Sentuje, 136.
Sesheke, 151, 154, 156, 157, 163, 171, 217, 230, 235, 236, 241, 243.
Seunturu, 157.
Sewell, Mrs., 4, 5, 6, 7, 9, 140.
Shereef, 273.
Shinté, Chief, 217.
Shobo, Chief, 159, 162.
Sicard, Major A. T. d'A., 259, 267.
Sicuana Grammar, 112, 183.
Silver Street Chapel, Falcon Square, 4.
Simon's Bay, 19.
Sitchuana Dictionary, 157, 163, 185.
Sitchuana Testament, 17, 26.
Skeit Fontein, 171, 172, 174.
Slave Trade, xvi, xvii, xviii, 248, 249.
Smith, Sidney, 136.
Snow, Mr., Bookseller, 137, 164.
Solomon, Rev. Edward, 104.
Solomon, Saul, 274.
Somerset, 168.
Sonta, River, 158.
South African Missions, 108.
South Seas, 4.
Southampton, 104.
Spaulding, Rev. Justin, 17, 18.
Stanley, H. M., vi, xiv, xv., 273.
Steele, Captain (Coldstream Guards), 65, 144, 145, 153, 163.
Stowmarket, 10, 40.
Sturge, Mr. Joseph, 268.
Sultan Barghash, xviii, xix.
Sultan of Zanzibar, xviii, 206, 211.
Sykes, Rev. William, 268.

Tabacheu, Mount, 271.
Tahiti, Papaoa, 7, 19, 21,
Tamunakle, River, 159, 160.
Tanganyika, Lake, xi, 235.
Taong, 133.
Taylor, Isaac, 132.
Teogé or Teophé, River, 148, 194.
Tette, 156, 255, 257, 258, 259, 261, 266, 267, 268, 271, 272.
Teviot, Viscount, vii.
Thomas, Rev. Thomas M., 268.
Thompson, Mr. Francis, 212, 223.
Thompson, Rev. Ralph Wardlaw, D.D., 260.
Thompson, Rev. William, 129, 133, 139, 140, 147, 170, 171, 174, 178, 181, 189, 190, 198, 210, 212, 217, 233, 236, 239, 255, 258, 262, 264, 266, 272.
Thornton, R., 266.

Tidman, Rev. A., D.D., 42, 64, 68, 76, 78, 87, 96, 123, 136, 138, 139, 144, 148, 153, 163, 164, 168, 170, 184, 202, 215, 227, 240, 256, 257, 258, 270.
Tlaganyane, 133, 135.
Trafalgar, R.M.S., 168.
Tsetse Fly, 138, 149, 150, 151, 158, 159, 166, 194, 200, 202, 205, 213, 215, 216, 236, 255, 258, 259.
Tylor's Green, 9.

Uitenhage, 27, 108, 109, 168.
Ujiji, 273.
United Presbyterian Mission, 246.
Universities' Mission to Central Africa, 266.
Unyanyembe, 272.

Vaal, River, 127.
Vanderkemp, Dr., 59.
Van Lingen, Rev. Albert, 109.
Vaughan, Dr., 212, 215.
Victoria Falls (*see* Mosiatunya), 151.
Victoria, Queen, 247, 248, 266.

Waller, Horace, vi.
Walwich Bay, 213, 214, 215.
Wanketzes, 7, 107, 134, 150, 180, 186, 187.
Wardlaw, Rev. Ralph, D.D., 236.
Waterboer, Chief, 24, 89.
Watt, Rev. D. G., 115, 143, 149.
Webb and Codrington, donors of pontoon, 200.
Wesleyan Missionary Society, 167.
Westminster, 61.
Westminster Abbey, vii.
Whish, Mr. Charles, 90.
Williams, Dr., 28.
Williams, John, 6.
Williams, Rev. W., 55, 78, 84.
Wilson, Mr. (Trader), 137, 191.
Woodhead & Co., Messrs., 231.
Wright, Mr. and Mrs., 9, 41, 134.

Zambesi, River, xi, xiii, xv, xvi, xviii, 151, 152, 153, 156, 159, 164, 217, 222, 228, 230, 235, 237, 240, 242, 249, 255, 257, 260, 261, 266, 270, 271.
Zanzibar, xvii, xviii, 206, 211, 237, 254.
Zanzibar, Arab Sultan of, xviii, 206, 211.
Zouga, River, xvi, 138, 144, 148, 149, 153, 155, 156, 165.